Japanese Targeting

Successes, Failures, Lessons

Jon Woronoff
Correspondent
Asian Business

W0235426

Palgrave Macmillan

ISBN 978-1-349-12563-0   ISBN 978-1-349-12561-6 (eBook)
DOI 10.1007/978-1-349-12561-6
© Jon Woronoff 1992
Softcover reprint of the hardcover 1st edition 1992
All rights reserved. For information, write:
Scholarly and Reference Division,
St. Martin's Press, Inc., 175 Fifth Avenue,
New York, N.Y. 10010

First published in the United States of America in 1992

ISBN 978-0-312-07188-2

Library of Congress Cataloging-in-Publication Data
Woronoff, Jon.
Japanese targeting : successes, failures, lessons / Jon Woronoff.
p.   cm.
Includes bibliographical references (p.   ) and index.
ISBN 978-0-312-07188-2
1. Industrial and state—Japan.   2. Japan—Commercial policy.
3. Competition, International.   4. Japan—Industries.   I. Title.
HD3616.J33W67   1992
338.0952—dc20   91–35974
                                                      CIP

JAPANESE TARGETING

Also by Jon Woronoff

ASIA'S 'MIRACLE' ECONOMIES
HONG KONG: CAPITALIST PARADISE
INSIDE JAPAN, INC.
JAPAN AS –*ANYTHING BUT* – NUMBER ONE
JAPAN: THE COMING ECONOMIC CRISIS
JAPAN: THE COMING SOCIAL CRISIS
JAPAN'S COMMERCIAL EMPIRE
JAPAN'S MARKET: THE DISTRIBUTION SYSTEM (*with
    Michael R. Czinkota*)
JAPAN'S WASTED WORKERS
THE JAPAN SYNDROME
KOREA'S ECONOMY: MAN-MADE MIRACLE
ORGANIZING AFRICAN UNITY
* POLITICS: THE JAPANESE WAY
UNLOCKING JAPAN'S MARKETS
WEST AFRICAN WAGER: HOUPHOUET VERSUS NKRUMAH
WORLD TRADE WAR

Also from Palgrave Macmillan

Contents

Foreword   ix

Acronyms and Abbreviations   xi

PART I   WHAT, WHO, HOW

1 Background   3
   Definitions   3
   Japanese Style   6
   Historical Origins   9
   Reasons and Rationalisations   15
   The Great Industrial Policy Debate   19

2 Institutions   25
   The Politicians   25
   Mighty MITI   28
   Other Agencies   36
   The Business Community   42
   Bureaucrats v. Businessmen (First Round)   48
   Is There A Japan, Inc.?   53
   The People   57

3 Techniques   60
   Market Manipulation   60
   Financial Support   65
   Technological Advance   71
   The Competitive Urge   76
   Creating the Right Climate   82
   Company Targeting   87

PART II   CASE STUDIES

4 Risen Sectors   97
   Coal, Oil and Petrochemicals (1)   98
   The Steel Industry   100
   Shipbuilding and Transportation (1)   103
   Textiles (1)   107
   Farming   109
   Financial Services   111

5 Rising Sectors – Public   116
   Computers   117
   Semiconductors   123
   Telecommunications   128
   Machine Tools   132
   Pharmaceuticals   138

6 Rising Sectors – Private   141
   Automobiles   142
   Motorcycles   148
   Consumer Electronics   151
   Construction Equipment and Office Automation   156
   Sundry   161

7 Sectors Slated to Rise   165
   New Materials   166
   Robotics   168
   Biotechnology   170
   Nuclear Energy   173
   Aircraft and Engines   179
   Aerospace   185

8 Declining Sectors   192
   Textiles (2)   193
   Coal, Oil and Petrochemicals (2)   198
   Shipbuilding and Transportation (2)   202
   Aluminium (and Steel)   205

PART III   RESULTS AND REACTIONS

9 Rating Success   211
   Faster, Further, More Forcefully   213
   Picking Winners . . . Mostly   215
   Easier Said Than Done   219
   How Rational?   225
   Bureaucrats v. Businessmen (Second Round)   230
   People's Costs and Benefits   234

10 Foreign Repercussions   240
   What Targeting Wrought   241
   The Victims   243
   Mixed Reactions   247
   Was There a Conspiracy?   250

11   What Now?   255
       No End To Targeting   255
       Learning From Japan   260

Notes   267

Bibliography   277

Index   281

Foreword

Few economic topics have aroused as much interest – or been as controversial – in recent years as the Japanese brand of industrial policy which is increasingly known as 'targeting'. It is not only studied in order to find out how it works, or doesn't work, who does it and why, it is highly praised by some and roundly denounced by others. This is an issue which has not only impassioned economists, politicians and academics, it has intrigued the general public as well.

Yet, despite some valiant and laudable efforts, there is not much more understanding now than before. The debate has generated tremendous heat but shed little light. Worse, it has created entrenched camps of supporters and critics. This book is an attempt to provide more light. It will try to do so in the following ways.

First of all, since industrial targeting is an exercise with both economic and political aspects, unlike in many other books, it will be studied here from both angles. We will look into the various economic techniques that have been used as well as the economic results that were achieved. Success will be evaluated in terms of not only whether new industries emerged but what they cost the nation and whether the benefits were adequate. We will even wonder whether other techniques might not have yielded equal or greater results.

Politically, it is necessary (unlike in other books) to consider *all* the players. Of course, MITI still gets pride of place. But it is not the only bureaucracy involved, others have played a significant role which should be mentioned. The other principal actor, the business community, has been overlooked too much elsewhere. We will pay more heed to how companies participate in industrial targeting and also engage in some of their own. We will also examine how the bureaucrats and businessmen interact and which actually run the show.

This is not a book on theory. It adopts a very practical bias, showing not only which techniques are used but how they actually help industries emerge and companies compete. Indeed, this comes fairly close to a 'how to' book for those who want to follow a similar recipe. That is one reason why the language is quite simple and the style rather straightforward. The other is that this subject is sufficiently important that it should be accessible to anyone who is interested and not just to specialists.

The middle sections include case histories, not just one or two but several dozen. Admittedly, none of them dig as deeply as the few excellent industry studies that now exist. But this approach has a definite advantage. It is possible to see how the same or different techniques were used in a whole series of cases. This reveals the parallels and contrasts. It also reduces the temptation of extrapolating too much from a single instance or assuming that what was done in one case must have been done in all.

These many case histories also make it easier to perceive that the degree of success varied. Some exercises ran very smoothly and achieved their goals, others were indifferent and some were outright failures. While the majority were positive and contributed mightily to Japan's economic progress, a look at the failures shows what can go wrong. Moreover, by measuring 'success' with other yardsticks than purely economic ones like growth or competitiveness, it is possible to determine what the advantages and drawbacks were to society as a whole.

Naturally, this book deals largely with the past. It relates what has been achieved in over four decades of industrial targeting (and even looks further back on occasion). But this helps build a foundation for looking toward the future. Contrary to some assertions, the practice has not ceased and Japan is still targeting many new sectors while its companies refine further export products. Meanwhile, other countries must decide how to cope with Japan's resurgence and decide whether or not to adopt some of her techniques to help their own economies.

That is why the author hopes that any light shed will help generate some heat. Industrial targeting has become more important than ever for all of us, those who target and those whose industries are targeted. So, reading this book should be more than just a learning experience. It is nice to know how Japan targets, and why, and what the results are. It is even more essential to reflect on how Japan might temper its policies and how everbody else should react.

JON WORONOFF

Acronyms and Abbreviations

AIST	Agency for Industrial Science and Technology
ANA	All Nippon Airways
BIDEC	Bioindustry Development Centre
BOJ	Bank of Japan
BRA	Bicycle Rehabilitation Association
CTDC	Civil Transport Development Corporation
DA	Defence Agency
EA	Environment Agency
EPA	Economic Planning Agency
EPDC	Electric Power Development Company
ERAAE	Engineering Research Association for Aero-Jet Engines
ERATO	Exploratory Research for Advanced Technology
Ex–Im Bank	Export–Import Bank
FHI	Fuji Heavy Industries
FILP	Fiscal and Investment Loan Program
FTC	Fair Trade Commission
GATT	General Agreement on Tariffs and Trade
HDTV	High-Definition Television
IBJ	Industrial Bank of Japan
IC	Integrated Circuit
ICOT	Institute for New Generation Computer Technology
IHI	Ishikawajima-Harima Heavy Industries
IPA	Information Technology Promotion Agency
ISAS	Institute of Space and Astronautical Science
JAEC	Japan Atomic Energy Commission
JAERI	Japan Atomic Energy Research Institute
JAL	Japan Airlines
JAMA	Japan Automobile Manufacturers Association
JAPCO	Japan Atomic Power Company
JAROL	Japan Robot Leasing Company
JDB	Japan Development Bank
JECC	Japan Electronic Computer Corporation
JETRO	Japan External Trade Organisation

JIRA	Japan Industrial Robot Association
JIS	Japan Industrial Standards
JMTBA	Japan Machine Tool Builders Association
JNR	Japan National Railways
JRDC	Japan Research Development Corporation
JVC	Victor Company of Japan
KDD	Kokusai Denshin Denwa
Keidanren	Japan Federation of Economic Organisations
Keizai Doyukai	Japan Committee for Economic Development
LDP	Liberal Democratic Party
MAFF	Ministry of Agriculture, Forestry and Fisheries
MCI	Ministry of Commerce and Industry
MHI	Mitsubishi Heavy Industries
MHW	Ministry of Health and Welfare
MITI	Ministry of International Trade and Industry
MM	Ministry of Munitions
MOC	Ministry of Construction
MOE	Ministry of Education
MOF	Ministry of Finance
MOT	Ministry of Transport
MPT	Ministry of Post & Telecommunications
NAMCO	Nihon Aeroplane Manufacturing Company
NASA	National Aeronautics & Space Administration
NASDA	National Space Development Agency
NHK	Japan Broadcasting Company
Nissho	Japan Chamber of Commerce and Industry
NTB	Nontariff Barrier
NTT	Nippon Telegraph & Telephone
OECD	Organisation for Economic Cooperation and Development
PNC	Power Reactor and Nuclear Fuel Development Corporation
STA	Science and Technology Agency
STAC	Society of Japanese Aerospace Companies
STC	Science and Technology Council
TDA	Toa Domestic Airways
USITC	United States International Trade Commission
VCR	Video Cassette Recorder

Part I
What, Who, How

1 Background

The beginning is not the worst place to take up the story of industrial policy and targeting. It is admittedly rather tame and not as exciting as letting the reader know right off how absolutely wonderful or excruciatingly vicious these phenomena are, as is increasingly the practice nowadays. But that can always be done at the end, when the reader has more knowledge to decide whether or not such conclusions are correct.

The beginning, as with many subjects, should include a definition of the essential terms. Not everybody, including the supposed 'experts', seems to know just what industrial policy and targeting are. This is not surprising since they have already been overlaid with connotations and images that weigh very heavily. But they are not as strange as all that, and they are also not so new or unique, as a look at the somewhat broader economic scene will show. The Japanese have brought them to higher levels of effectiveness but something similar has been, is being and will continue to be used elsewhere.

Then on to the debate, at least the more rousing and vociferous portions thereof. It is useful to know why quite ordinary economic tools, which would normally receive little notice outside of specialised circles, have suddenly become the focus of attention. It is still too early to come down on one side or the other, but at least the more extreme and improbable views can be discarded at this point.

DEFINITIONS

Although the debate on industrial policy and targeting has been raging for several decades now, it has been difficult to follow because of a regrettable lack of precision. Almost every commentator freely uses words which have become so commonplace that we are tempted to think we know what they mean when, in fact, we do not and when, in fact, each commentator implies something rather different by them.

One would assume that there should be nothing easier than to define industrial policy and targeting in order to know what they are, what they are not, how they differ from one another and from other things they are not supposed to be. Yet, many of the books, reports

3

and papers on the subject give no formal definition whatsoever and those authors who are considerate enough to define terms do so very loosely and ambiguously.

Magaziner and Hout refer to industrial policy as 'the application of government resources and influence to industrial affairs'.[1] Pepper et al. say they apply the term industrial policy more narrowly, namely 'the specific use of policy instruments to foster growth or rationalization in particular sectors, industries or firms'.[2] The United States International Trade Commission is a bit more precise. Industrial targeting means 'coordinated government actions taken to direct productive resources to help domestic producers in selected industries become more competitive'.[3]

Yet, despite such laudable efforts, these definitions often do not fulfil the most elementary function of excluding those things which do not comply and including only those which do. Under them, just about every country in the world is engaged in industrial policy most of the time. The definitions are wide enough to include not only industrial policy and targeting but also planning and even quite ordinary macroeconomic measures adopted in countries whose leaders would shudder to think that they did something so improper or daring as to target.

The following are not intended as rigorous scientific definitions. That would be impossible when describing practices that are constantly evolving and have already gone through several distinct phases and frequently use different techniques to deal with different situations. Still, they may be useful working definitions, the kind you would want in order to explain to an apprentice carpenter what hammers and nails are. They are based on observations of what industrial policy and targeting involve in the Japanese context.

Industrial policy is the adoption by the government of specific measures to strengthen the economic position of private companies. These include ordinary measures such as can be found in many countries, such as adjusting interest rates, regulating monetary growth and shaping taxation. But they extend into more structured action to protect markets, promote exports, increase financing and support research and development. What differs is, first of all, the degree of organisation. These measures are not adopted individually or haphazardly but as part of a definite programme. They are then inserted in an overall framework which may be stated formally or may just reflect a regular pattern. This makes it possible to combine the measures in order to enhance their cumulative effectiveness.

Another difference is intent. The goal is quite specifically to boost the competitiveness of domestic companies. It is not enough merely to produce adequately. Steps are taken to strengthen and expand national champions which can produce goods or services of a higher quality and/or lower price than foreign rivals so as to hold their share of the home market and expand abroad. Finally, there is a time element. Everything is done to accelerate the rise of sectors which would ordinarily appear at a later stage of development or to hasten the decline of those that are no longer viable.

Targeting is the process whereby sectors or specific products are selected for special support. This selection may be based on various criteria which usually assess their significance to the economy as a whole. It is determined whether they play a strategic role, provide essential goods or services or have multiple linkages with other sectors. Subsequently, suitable companies are chosen to forge the sector or make the products. Targeted industries will then be backed with industrial policy. In this sense, the two are clearly connected.

It should be noted in passing that the use of the word 'industrial' does not mean, in practice at least, that this approach can only be adopted to support industry in the restricted sense of manufacturing. Something quite similar can be done to foster agriculture, mining and services. In fact, by extension, one can even target and promote broader goals like improved welfare, better housing or stronger defence. What excludes the latter is that, in general, sectors are targeted to create a competitive edge and usually also to boost commercial gains.

While industrial policy can only be applied to states, which transfer increased assets to private enterprises in targeted sectors, it is possible for companies to engage in something similar. They can also select specific products and shift assets from other divisions to support these new lines. Indeed, in countries where industrial policy is most deeply engrained, companies do not hesitate to do some targeting on their own.

While not very tidy, these definitions do exclude other practices that are quite different. It cannot really be argued that the United States or most of Europe apply industrial policy just because they have macroeconomic policies or subsidise and/or protect certain sectors. The organised framework and intent are basically lacking. Nor could one claim that this resembles the old Soviet command system. That went much further and there was no distinction between public and private sector. It also differs from the somewhat more similar import substitution strategy of developing countries by having an external dimension.

For those who want something neater, more succinct, we might try the following 'nutshell' definitions. Industrial policy is the use, by the state, of broader economic measures to promote specific sectors, whose products are generated by private companies, in order to enhance their competitiveness at home and abroad. Targeting is the selection of these sectors and products, whether by the state or by private companies. Together, they might be called industrial targeting, which includes both promotion and selection.

In the rest of this book, so as not to get hung up on words, industrial policy will be used when it is clearly a question of the support system and targeting when just the selection process is involved. Most often, we will fall back on the catchall phrase industrial targeting, which includes both.

JAPANESE STYLE

Obviously, if that were all there is to it, there would never have been much of a debate on industrial policy and targeting. As defined, they are rather tame and nondescript creatures, more often in the middle than at the extremes of economic doctrine. They would not have aroused much notice in a world with so many bolder, more compelling isms. In addition, most of those who practised the more common industrial policies did quite poorly, so poorly indeed that it was more likely to provoke derision and be brushed aside as unwise or futile.

The only reason the public finally awoke to the potential of industrial policy, and more acutely, targeting, is that they were a success in Japan. Japan's practice went much further than that of others. It was far more dynamic and effective and more worthy of attention. But it was such a success that it became worrisome for others.

By now, the publicity is perhaps too great since it has turned industrial policy and targeting into caricatures in the average person's mind. Many of the comments and descriptions have merely contributed to a folklore or mythology which has to be dissipated to uncover the realities. Unfortunate as that may be, they did at least have the merit of generating substantial interest.

The primary idea is to promote rising industries and the Japanese have been doing that with a vengeance. Over the years, countless sectors have emerged, one after another. Each was on a larger scale or used more sophisticated technologies than the others. There was an amazing progression bringing the economy to the point where it could field companies in virtually every sector. Meanwhile, Japanese products – once seen as cheap and shoddy – became known for the highest quality. So impressive was this that doting observers credited Japan with an uncanny ability to 'pick winners'.

To hear them tell it, having picked the right sectors the Japanese deployed extraordinarily effective measures to hoist them to world levels. These included the judicious use of funds, applied where they would do the most good to produce multiplier effects. There was a notable R&D component to boost technology. While the market had to be closed, the time was at least put to good use. In short order, Japanese factories achieved a scale and productivity that enabled them to compete against all comers.

The Japanese not only picked the right sectors and used the right techniques, they formally proclaimed goals which everyone strove to attain. They were forever presenting brilliant views of the future, some five, ten, even twenty and thirty years down the road. And this was backed up with numerical objectives – so many tons of capacity, so many trillion yen of sales, so many million dollars of exports. These were just forecasts, but they were so spectacular and seemingly accurate that they became 'targets', helping to popularise the expression targeting. Those who made them, let us call them 'targeters', were assumed to be on target most of the time.

No less sensational was the way the government and private sector cooperated, or so they say. Rather than squabble over jurisdictional boundaries and prerogatives, they were able to work together for the good of the nation. The politicians and bureaucrats crafted plans and set goals and then helped businessmen achieve them. The businessmen threw their weight behind the targeting exercises and spared no effort to upgrade production and quality. Meanwhile, the whole population was willing to make necessary sacrifices to boost growth and was, one assumed, well rewarded for those efforts by a benevolent government and caring management. This sort of thing was almost inconceivable to Westerners, accustomed to adversarial relations. So they admired this 'harmony' and 'consensus'.

Not all observers bought the glorified version. They pointed out that all of the sectors picked by the targeters already existed elsewhere. They had been pioneered by other countries and companies and what the Japanese did was nothing more than imitate what others had done. That was not a particularly original or creative approach. Until the Japanese could get beyond mere copying and become true innovators and inventors there was no special reason to praise them unduly.

As for the methods they used to strengthen industries, they were not entirely above board. Indeed, some insisted, industrial policy and targeting were a form of cheating. Many of the special measures adopted broke the accepted rules of the game. The more correct, proper way was to abide by laissez-faire, whether domestically with free enterprise or internationally with free trade.

Market restrictions were not uncommon in a broad array of countries. Their existence had been accepted with few qualms in dozens of developing countries and also in Japan, when it still had a fragile economy. But refusing to liberalise later on was seen as 'unfair'. Even more galling was that, after formally opening the market, the Japanese erected nontariff barriers and other impediments. That could hardly be construed by foreigners as anything but 'dirty tricks'.[4]

Yet, that was not the most bothersome aspect. The bigger threat was that Japanese businessmen used this closed market as a springboard for exports. The government backed this campaign with subsidies and other support. Soon Japanese products were pouring into foreign countries, sold at exceedingly low prices that undercut local producers. Exporting, under these conditions, was also regarded as 'unfair' and 'predatory'.

In this operation, there was not just cooperation between the government and the private sector. It came closer to collusion in which the politicians, bureaucrats and businessmen intrigued to manipulate the economy to their mutual benefit. They formed a common front against the Japanese people as a whole and, even more solidly, against foreigners. Concern was only heightened by the patent secretiveness and imputed deviousness of those running the machinery. This idea has been conveyed by the concept of 'Japan, Inc.'.

No matter how you looked at it, according to these opponents, the Japanese economic system itself was different and probably also wrong. It was clearly not socialist. But it was not really capitalist as generally understood or encountered in other parts of the world. The government intervened too much, private companies cooperated or colluded with it in their own interest, and the two together closed the market to foreign penetration while making massive incursions abroad.

All this inspired a second meaning for targeting, a very different one. It was no longer a question of fostering infant industries and bringing them to maturity. It was no longer positive and constructive. Rather, it implied picking foreign industries, learning them and then trying to wipe out foreign competitors. The fact that the offensive was not over a broad front but instead over very narrow areas led critics to charge that one foreign product after another was being targeted for annihilation.

The most graphic comparison, one that was repeatedly made – in this case by Sir Terence Beckett, Director-General of the Confederation of British Industry – was to a laser beam. The Japanese, according to him, 'adopt a laser beam approach, concentrating on particular targets and virtually obliterating those industries one by one'.[5]

In this way, targeting became something very menacing and evil. Since it was used by a clique of politicians, bureaucrats and businessmen in an economy where things occurred in curious and questionable ways, and no one could really say who was doing what, it is not surprising that there should be talk of a 'conspiracy'.[6] Moreover, since the Japanese competed so aggressively, and showed so little concern about what happened to their victims, it was almost inevitable that there should be talk of a 'Third World War'. Targeting was the secret weapon to win for Japan what it had failed to accomplish before.

Thus, we not only have a peculiar type of industrial policy and targeting that are 'typically' Japanese as opposed to the more general cases, we can choose between two radically different versions of how they are used and to what ends. Targeting is a positive, constructive strategy to raise up an economy, according to the supporters, or a negative, destructive one to crush rivals, according to the critics. Or, as shall be done further on, one can look for something in between.

HISTORICAL ORIGINS

Judging by innumerable comments made about industrial policy and targeting, they are somehow unusual, exceptional, perhaps even an aberration from normal economic policy. They seemingly flout the agreed rules and are played by special rules. They involve considerable government intervention and manipulation as well as excessively close relations between private companies. There is an attempt to evade market forces by promoting specific industries and sheltering domestic companies from outside competition.

While there is definitely a deviation from laissez-faire and economic liberalism, which most of its critics regard as the norm, it is not
enough simply to relegate those who practise industrial targeting to a
deviant category. There are just too many of them. And they have a
pedigree that is almost as long and impressive as that of the liberals.

Industrial policy emerged not so long after the industrial revolution
among countries which were envious of Great Britain's success and
sought to replicate it, but did not know how without involving the
state. A good example was France of Napoleon III, which actually
built on much older precedents going back to Colbert's day. Even
more notable was Bismarkian Germany which targeted heavy and
chemical industries. Frederich List obligingly formed a comprehensive theory of state intervention and assistance. In the United States,
Alexander Hamilton propagated similar ideas.

But that was not the end of it. Many European countries still have
economic systems involving considerable state intervention and by
now rather large state sectors. The Soviet Union and East bloc
countries engaged in comprehensive planning which embodied many
elements of industrial policy, although more stringent and invasive;
and, of course, without a private sector. The majority of developing
nations have opted for industrial targeting as they see it, picking
industries and doing their best to promote them through import
substitution. All in all, it is the practitioners of statism who are in the
majority and not those of liberalism.

That is not surprising. Industrial policy – and even targeting – are a
very tempting choice for latecomers. They apparently offer the best
chance of concentrating resources for a dash toward development.
Japan adopted them for much the same reasons. It was also a late
developer which required special efforts to catch up and thought that
laissez-faire would be too slow or too uncertain. The only way in
which it truly distinguished itself from many others is that it refined
the techniques and was far more successful.

Another misconception is that Japan only introduced these techniques after the last war in order to compensate for its defeat. This
makes them something new and novel. This idea is hardly tenable in
the light of Japanese history. Today's industrial policy and targeting
have been in gestation for well over a century. Naturally, there were
periods when such practices were more or less prominent and they
did not always take the same form. But there has been an amazing
degree of continuity.

Antecedents can already be found in the feudal period, not only for Japan but also for France or Germany. Guilds existed in various trades whereby members could organise and also manipulate production and sales. Merchants controlled many of the commercial channels, zealously blocking new entrants. This was not objected to by rulers, who sought stability and also became dependent on loans in return for which they granted protection and occasionally charters or monopolies. There was minimal concern for workers or consumers who had less to offer. Liberalism then was not only not in vogue, it was downright subversive.

A nascent industrial policy received a notable impulse when Japan was opened to international commerce in the mid-nineteenth century. For the first time local leaders and tradesmen espied the abundance of products and technologies that had emerged in the West. Some of these products were so coveted that industrial enterprises were immediately set up by more enlightened lords and the *shogun*. The projects were not only military, although armaments were the prime concern, but also for shipbuilding, metals and textiles.

When the emperor was restored in 1868, the process was greatly accelerated. The Meiji government launched a policy of *shokusan kogyo* (develop industry and promote enterprise). Under this it created the basic infrastructure for communications and transportation and consolidated banking. It also helped introduce many new industries, whether by aiding private entrepreneurs or on its own. It erected numerous factories, complete with Western machinery, Western technology and even Western managers and technicians. They were to serve as models for others.[7]

Unfortunately, many of the state-run factories were not a commercial success. With the government in a serious financial crisis, they had to be sold off by Finance Minister Matsukata in the 1880s. But that was not the end of the government's role. It merely signaled a switch from hazardous attempts at running its own establishments to more indirect efforts at influencing the economy while leaving the actual founding and management of companies to private initiative.

In the ensuing period, the government provided crucial assistance. It offered cheap loans and outright subsidies, it helped obtain foreign technologies, it sometimes granted monopolies to specific companies. As soon as it was allowed to introduce tariffs, it did so to protect domestic companies from imports. It directed its own purchases toward firms which could replace foreign goods.[8]

The support of business was not haphazard. The state did not back every industry but only those which were regarded as particularly important. Most favoured were those related to military strength, namely arms and munitions. To make them, however, it was necessary to promote steel production, other metals and chemicals. In order to create a fleet, shipbuilding and shipping were aided. Textiles were supported as a producer of goods which could be exported massively in order to pay the import bills. Other industries were added later on, especially machinery and vehicles.

During the early Meiji period, when much of the power lay in the hands of the emperor's closest advisors, they were the ones who picked the companies to be helped. Close relations were established with certain businessmen and it was not only patriotism which determined who would win but more mundane considerations. Government backing was precious because it not only accelerated the replacement of imports by local goods but also gave the producer a vital headstart over domestic rivals.

During the 1890s, the situation evolved gradually without the government ever adopting true laissez-faire. It always showed an interest in specific sectors or, at least, in specific projects of use to a given industry, company, region or politician. The major change was that the bureaucrats now played a more significant role since they possessed greater technical knowledge, could better evaluate the merits of projects and also increasingly controlled the purse strings. During this period, they entered into close relations with the businessmen whom they served and who were now considerably more advanced, more competent and had greater finances and political clout. Indeed, the most dynamic ones founded broad industrial combines called *zaibatsu*.

The move to increased government involvement came in the 1930s when the military clique gained control and there was a gradual drift into foreign adventures and actual wars. The top priority then was to strengthen the army and navy and, to that end, the economy was placed at their service. With time, the militarists imposed their will on the politicians and bureaucrats and sought businessmen they could work with. When the old *zaibatsu* proved recalcitrant, they turned to new ones (*shinko zaibatsu*) that did their bidding and in return enjoyed more government aid.

During this period, the Ministry of Commerce and Industry (MCI) came to play a leading role in the economy. It introduced laws to promote specific industries, set up strong administrative bureaux to monitor the situation and formed consultative councils consisting of government, business and academic leaders to sanction any decisions. Vigorous measures were proposed to support designated industries through loans, subsidies, tax exemptions and import protection.[9]

Under the bureaucrats, and inspired by the militarists, the basic concern was twofold. One side was that strategic industries should be strengthened. These industries were related to military needs: steel, shipbuilding, aircraft, motor vehicles, machinery and, of course, arms and munitions. The other side was that they should be dominated by trusted national companies. Where such companies did not exist, efforts were made to encourage entrepreneurs to enter the sector. Where they already existed, local firms were strongly supported and foreign ones gradually driven out, as was the case for automobiles with the rise of Nissan and withdrawal of Ford and General Motors.

Coordination with the private sector was arranged through countless trade associations which included all major players. They could organise the respective sector, provide enhanced cooperation between companies and report to the government. Going yet further, on occasion, companies were urged to merge or cartels were formed.

This system was made much stricter as the country entered the war. Companies were brought under specific bureaux of MCI, which was ultimately renamed the Ministry of Munitions (MM). Trade unions were disbanded and workers forced to join a national front. Managers increasingly obeyed orders that were issued and stipulated many things that had formerly been left to private judgement. It was determined exactly which industries would expand or shrink, how much of given products would be manufactured, which essential materials would be allocated to which sectors and, more specifically, which companies.

At first blush, the wartime defeat and collapse of the economy signalled a new beginning. There was much talk of free enterprise and the Occupation authorities broke up the *zaibatsu*, disbanded the trade associations, purged many politicians, bureaucrats and businessmen, adopted laws protecting labour and fostered trade unions, etc. But they also had to revive the economy and, to do so, imposed a certain degree of central control, rationing out scarce goods and funds, controlling foreign exchange and thereby trade, and so on. They also decided which industries should be restored first and set up special banks to provide the needed finance.

When the Occupation was over there was a good deal of backsliding. After all, the new liberal economy was unfamiliar to most businessmen. It was actually the older, purged ones who had earlier entrepreneurial experience while younger ones, who now ran the revived companies, were quite ordinary employees who had always followed orders. More fateful, the bureaucrats had on the whole gone unpunished. The same people who ran the prewar MCI and wartime MM were now working for the postwar Ministry of International Trade and Industry (MITI). The same applied to other ministries. Moreover, some of the old bureaucrats reemerged as politicians and were instrumental in defining economic policy, such as Nobusuke Kishi.[10]

On this basis, with so much more experience in a controlled economy, with so many of the people involved attuned either to giving orders or to obeying them, with hardly anyone really aware of how a truly free economy functioned, it was not surprising that the past should cast a heavy shadow over the future. The links were not entirely broken and the old practices were not fully disowned. Indeed, everything was in place for a new phase of government intervention and public–private cooperation to rebuild the economy.

The resort to industrial policy and targeting, however, did not spring from any master plan that had been conceived by Japan's leaders. Like the earlier phases, it was almost spontaneous. Partly, it was a reversion to practices and patterns with which the Japanese felt more comfortable. Partly, it was a response to difficult circumstances. Never, not even in the midst of the war, was there any such thing as a doctrine or code of conduct. People reacted to specific challenges, albeit in rather predictable ways, and what they did was subsequently dubbed industrial policy and targeting. The action preceded the definition and not the other way around. Indeed, had anyone bothered codifying the practice, it would have been altered before the ink was dry.

Japanese policy has always been strongly affected by circumstances and subject to the whims of those personally involved, even in a supposedly scientific process like industrial targeting. It has never followed a precise and minutely prescribed path. That has been noted repeatedly by observers, including Hugh Patrick.

A careful, detailed examination of Japanese industrial policy over the postwar period shows that it has often been ad hoc in nature, not always carefully thought out or focused, usually quite flexible in response to changing analyses and circumstances, and on occasion subject to considerable political pressures. In other words, like much of history it was complex and messy, rather than simple and clear-cut.[11]

REASONS AND RATIONALISATIONS

There was no shortage of justification for resorting to industrial policy and targeting rather than trusting in the workings of market forces. The reasons were political, economic and social and appeared sufficiently convincing to move many governments to adopt the techniques that are described further on. But, and this must also be recalled, some of the causes were more emotional or philosophical and a good number were rationalisations more than actual reasons.

The most popular explanation was based on the 'infant industry' argument. It was espoused by Japan as well and, in so doing, it showed no great originality. The same sort of approach had been adopted decades before by the Germans, citing Frederich List's theories. And they are being put forward today throughout the Third World. This is a standard tack for developing countries – of which Japan was one – when trying to catch up. For, and this should never be forgotten, their concern was the difficulty not only of making a new industry or sector grow but of protecting it from more advanced, predatory companies abroad.

The basic idea was that, to make up for lost time, it was necessary for the government to promote and protect. In the absence of adequate capital, it should offer financial backing. In the absence of technologies, it should help acquire them. Even in the absence of suitable entrepreneurs, it should create them or, if necessary, replace them for a while. Finally, it had to erect barriers to keep national producers from being stunted or smothered by imports.

The goal was to nurture (*ikusei*) new industries. However, in most cases, these industries were only new in the more backward country, having been developed already by others who were busily exporting. Thus, in practice, it was really more a matter of replacing foreign imports with local products. The Japanese have a word for this, *kokusanka*. But it is known more widely as 'import substitution'. Of course, or so say the practitioners, this was not intended as a permanent policy. It was only adopted until the emerging industry had grown strong enough for the support and protection to be removed.

Sometimes this happened; sometimes it did not. That was usually because, in addition to the economic rationale, there were political ones. It was possible to persuade the government that a given industry was truly crucial or strategic and deserved special assistance. Or it was such a pillar of the economy that if it were weakened the whole structure would collapse. Even when such a case could not be made, it was possible to press the concerns of the owners who might lose their capital and the workers who might lose their jobs. With adequate political support, it did not matter much whether the arguments held water.

Once having decided that certain industries should be promoted and protected, it was necessary to determine which ones. This was also approached on a rational and almost scientific basis, at least among the economists and planners. They pointed out that certain sectors were far more decisive than others because they had a much greater impact on overall economic development. They had close linkages with many other sectors so that, by aiding them, one was also helping those which either purchased their products or provided them with inputs. These few should be targeted because that would do the most good.

Stress was therefore placed on selecting 'strategic' industries which could lead the march to economic progress. Although the economists and planners gravely measured things like the effect of dispersion coefficients and drew neat input–output tables, the question was obviously too political to be left to them alone. In addition, one considered the importance of the companies, workers or geographic regions which would benefit. This left plenty of room for lobbies to stress the advantages of their pet projects. There was also a tendency for the whole population, on its own or influenced by publicists, to take a fancy to a given sector because it was supposedly the backbone of the economy, or the wave of the future, or at the cutting edge of technology, etc., etc.

It was relatively easy to argue the merits and demerits of industries which were being promoted on the basis of their comparative advantage under the existing resource endowment. It could be demonstrated whether a country had an abundance of labour, capital or brain-power and should thus enter sectors that were labour-intensive, capital-intensive or knowledge-intensive. And this was done routinely for all sorts of projects. But the results were not always popular. Few politicians (or employers) wished to plug labour-intensive projects because they were not as imposing. Even capital-intensive projects lost their allure when fashion shifted to high tech.

The real difficulties came when passing from the relatively safe phase of current industrial policy to the more audacious and chancy exercise of targeting future growth sectors. This implied 'picking winners' on the basis not of hard evidence about the existing situation but of more or less educated guesses as to how things would be a few years or decades hence. It involved many unproven hypotheses about what might happen and, to fill the gaps, there was more than enough room for wishful thinking or plain fantasising.

To give this process a more scientific aura, the Japanese developed the concept of 'dynamic' comparative advantage as opposed to a 'static' one. The resource endowment would change over the years and one could assume that – at a given point in time – the endowment would be such that more advanced sectors would become appropriate. Thus, rather than leaving things to their own course, if one were to intervene effectively, and artificially change the endowment, say, by providing more capital or by acquiring technologies, it would be possible to skip intermediate stages and leapfrog ahead.

In working out its industrial structure policies, according to Myohei Shinohara, who was a member of the Industrial Structure Council for almost twenty-five years, MITI applied two essential criteria: income elasticity and comparative technical progress. This dynamic element enabled MITI to escape the premises of traditional economic theory, which 'assumes away not only any dynamic intertemporal shift in comparative advantage for the industries but also the selective growth capability of the industries concerned. . . . MITI's industrial policies were expected to foster the industries whose demand growth and technical progress were comparatively high. At the same time they proved successful in strengthening some key industries which took a "backward linkage" position in relation to the processing industries.'[12]

This last justification or rationalisation, depending on one's viewpoint, is extremely important in Japan's case. For the targeters clearly decided to leapfrog as much as possible the simpler, more labour and less capital-intensive industries which would normally have received priority in earlier years. Even Shinohara conceded that there were serious qualms and not everybody agreed.

Whether it was steel, petrochemicals, or other industries, dissenting voices were raised claiming that the development of capital-intensive industries was irrational. The cost of international steel products was then comparatively high, and the industry was highly capital-intensive. In terms of classical comparative cost theory, such industries as textiles, apparel, and shipbuilding were in comparatively advantageous positions during the 1950s.[13]

The concept of *dynamic* comparative advantage sounds fine in theory. In practice, it frequently boiled down to seeing where other countries that preceded Japan had gone. It was assumed that, in a given period, Japan would have roughly the same factor endowment as, say, Great Britain in the 1950s and should therefore get ready to produce the same things. But what was really desired deep down was to catch up with the United States. So, in most cases, targeting was little more than figuring out how to produce the same goods as soon as possible. Pride and an inferiority complex were doubtlessly as much involved as were more objective elements.

These, by the way, were far from being the only subjective influences. The most widespread and pervasive was the idea that the Japanese were living on small and precarious islands, surrounded by a not overly friendly outside world. This 'poor island' mentality affected the propensity to save and willingness to work. It made it easier to band together and cooperate, at least in the face of external threats. Indeed, it almost imposed 'harmony' between the politicians, bureaucrats and businessmen for the greater good of the country.

It also inspired the notion that Japan must become as self-sufficient as possible so that it did not have to depend on outsiders. In a pinch, they could not really be trusted. Thus, domestic industries should belong to and be run by fellow countrymen. If need be, the economy should even aim for relative autarchy. Yet, this did not keep the Japanese from feeling that they must export as much as possible. After all, as a poor island nation, they were dependent on others for natural resources and advanced technology. This imperative was even expressed officially by MITI. Japan faced 'the nightmare choice of either exporting or perishing'.[14]

Finally, there has always been a deep competitive streak. Distrust of foreigners did not entirely preclude suspicion of one another. People regularly formed teams, once based on villages or clans, then regions and now companies, which rivalled one another to produce the best or the most. This naturally extended into international rivalries as well. The Japanese felt that they had to show other nations that they could do certain things not only as well but better. They had to win the respect of others and claim their rightful place in the world.

Chalmers Johnson writes admiringly of the rationality of Japanese policy.[15] James Abegglen claims, 'in the case of Japan, the national policy is explicit, economically rational, and internally consistent'.[16] Careful scrutiny of Japanese industrial targeting will readily prove them wrong. The targeters were clearly swayed by other factors with regard to rising sectors. When it comes to declining sectors, they were as bad as anyone else in calling for urgent measures to defend national producers, rescue vital industries, save jobs and so on. On top of all that, they had to bolster their own reputation as workers of economic 'miracles'.

THE GREAT INDUSTRIAL POLICY DEBATE

In past sections we have been busily defining and describing industrial policy and targeting because, perhaps mistakenly, we think they exist. But that is far from self-evident to judge by the debate which is currently taking place on the subject. Or rather, the second of two debates. While one group of commentators is arguing about whether Japan's peculiar practices are effective or ineffective, good or bad, for them or for others, another group is sparring over whether they even exist.[17]

It does not take long to realise that there is a targeting claque which proclaims industrial policy in general, and targeting in particular, to be among the most extraordinary economic tools yet devised. There is repeated mention of farsighted, almost omniscient targeters picking just the right sectors for Japan. They then entice or push local companies toward producing the goods while the overall economy is pulled this way and that to underpin the effort. The result: a profusion of extraordinary products, exports to all corners of the earth and an industrial juggernaut that rolls steadily ahead crushing everything beneath it.

One of the first to 'discover' the phenomenon was Norman Macrae of *The Economist*, who called the Japanese economy the 'most intelligently *dirigiste* system in the world today'. According to him, 'the ultimate responsibility for industrial planning, for deciding in which directions Japan's burgeoning industrial effort should try to go, and for fostering and protecting business as it moves in those directions, lies with the government'.[18] Gene Gregory, who covered industry for the *Far Eastern Economic Review*, treated readers to an outpouring of articles heralding the success (real or imaginary) of one sector after the other.

As long ago as the mid-1950s, Japan's industrial policymakers targeted the 1980s as the decade when the information age would emerge in full bloom, with electronics as the basic technology that would power the economy into the 21st century. Right on schedule, in 1980 the Japanese electronics industry soared into orbit as the leading growth sector in a distinctly new stage of Japan's industrial revolution.[19]

While commentators on this side of the debate agree that industrial targeting is, indeed, powerful and effective, they disagree sharply on whether it is good. Some praise the Japanese for their ability, diligence and gumption. Others regard them as crafty and devious. They are only interested in winning and do not hesitate to cheat when it is in their interest. Worse, the government and private sector have united in an unholy alliance that is frequently referred to as 'Japan, Inc.' The result is, according to Marvin J. Wolf, 'a plot to dominate industry worldwide'.[20] This view was endorsed by many politicians and labour leaders in countries which were at the receiving end of the targeting exercises.

On the other side of this debate are sceptical (or blinkered) observers who claim that all the fuss is about nothing. There is no conspiracy, there is no special cooperation between government and business, there is no Japan, Inc., there is no industrial policy, there is no targeting. Japan's economy is just like any other, based on free enterprise, and it just happens that its businessmen are smarter and its employees work harder. If there should be something that might be regarded as industrial targeting, then it is just what others do, but done somewhat more efficiently. At most, this is a minor variation on standard themes.

A good example of this school of thought was provided by Philip Trezise of the Brookings Institution, who argued that industrial policy was not the major reason for Japan's success and, to judge by his writings, seemed to think it was quite minor. He insisted that the Japanese government allocated most of its funds to ordinary expenditures and not targeting. 'The amounts directed to specific industrial sectors are quite small, almost trivial. Tax policy aims at a wide range of objectives beyond revenue raising. But most of these objectives are only incidentally related to recognizable industrial policy.'[21]

The Japan-does-not-target case was taken even further by Katsuro Sakoh of the Heritage Foundation. According to his paper, *Industrial Policy: The Super Myth of Japan's Super Success*, 'interference in the economy has been sporadic and slight – including efforts aimed at industrial development'. The government's contribution 'has been based not so much on what it did for the economy but on how much it restrained itself from doing'.[22] The most extreme view came from, of all people, Norman Macrae, who now praised Japan for having the 'lowest level of government interference', and said his earlier comments which were quoted above were 'always balderdash'.[23]

This strange debate was interwoven with an even odder twist in the official Japanese position. In the 1950s, 1960s and 1970s, Japanese spokesmen were extremely proud of their accomplishments. They did not hesitate to lecture the outside world on how useful and successful industrial policy was. That much can be gathered from this statement by MITI Administrative Vice-Minister Yoshihisa Ojimi to the Organisation for Economic Cooperation and Development (OECD).

> The Ministry of International Trade and Industry decided to establish in Japan industries which require extensive employment of capital and technology, industries that in consideration of comparative cost of production should be the most appropriate for Japan, industries such as steel, oil refining, petrochemicals, automobiles, aircraft, industrial machinery of all sorts, and electronics, including electronic computers. From a short-run, static viewpoint, encouragement of such industries would seem to conflict with economic rationalism. But, from a long-range viewpoint, these are precisely the industries where income elasticity of demand is high, technological progress is rapid, and labour productivity rises fast. . . . According to Napoleon and Clausewitz, the secret of a successful strategy is the concentration of fighting power on the main battlegrounds; fortunately Japan has been able to concentrate its scant capital in strategic industries.[24]

As the reference to Napoleon and Clausewitz shows, the Japanese were not ashamed of industrial policy and, to the contrary, they tended to recommend it to others. This was done by Saburo Okita, one of Japan's leading economists who had been Director-General of the Economic Planning Agency and then Foreign Minister.

> Our government and our business people very carefully studied the industrial field, searching for those industries with future potential, those in which we would have comparative advantage in the world

market, and determined the type of support that should be extended to those industries in their formative years. . . . The policy was: carefully select industries, prevent ruinous competition at the infancy stage, nurse them up to a competitive stature, and then expose them to outside competition. This has more or less been the industrial policy of Japan. Western nations frowned upon our methods, but we felt it was the right policy for the late-comer to pursue.[25]

However, by the mid-1970s, the mood was changing abroad. Foreign politicians and union leaders were annoyed by Japan's ability to target industries which gradually overwhelmed their own. They complained that it had still failed to open its home market adequately. And they traced many of their domestic woes to none other than industrial policy. Noticing this, Japanese politicians, bureaucrats and businessmen promptly reversed the story. Instead of exalting industrial policy, they claimed it either did not exist or was rapidly disappearing. What was more, they now insisted that other countries actually engaged in more industrial policy than Japan did.

This new line was defended most energetically by none other than the Ministry of International Trade and Industry. In a special background paper circulated to foreign journalists and opinion leaders, MITI argued that 'criticism of the industrial policy of Japan as "targeting" is meaningless and unproductive'. It was even worse. It was plain wrong.

If 'industrial targeting policy' is taken to mean that the industrial policy is an export industry fostering policy designed to bring about the domination of United States markets and those of the world through the selection of certain industries (notably high-tech industries), through the enactment of protectionist measures for these select industries and through lavishing government subsidies on them, then there is no such policy in Japan.[26]

MITI went further to point out that 'the United States is following an industrial policy of its own'. That is largely through projects of the Department of Defense and NASA. The European countries, of course, also subsidise industries and protect sectors. Compared to them, Japan is abiding by the rules. 'The industrial policy of Japan follows a soft-handed, indirect, and inductive approach. It offers fewer subsidies and imposes milder regulations than that of the Western countries.'[27]

These views were promptly echoed by Western specialists, including some who were frequent apologists of the system. Coming from foreign, non-official sources, these comments seemed to carry more weight. But they were equally hard to substantiate. An extensive study by Gary Saxonhouse, prepared for the US International Trade Commission (USITC), reduced industrial policy to an almost negligible residual. It also supported the view that Japan did less targeting than others. 'Examination of the familiar instruments of industrial policy indicate that Japan gives less formal aid and comfort to its high technology sectors than do the governments of most other advanced and industrialized economies. Targeting is largely reserved for agriculture.'[28]

Bradley Richardson, the other academic who appeared before the USITC, conceded that industrial policy prevailed during the 1950s and 1960s, but claimed that most of the tools were gradually withdrawn and the phenomenon hardly existed by the 1980s aside from the machinery and computer industries. Moreover, since neither of them had much to do with targeting for export purposes, the issue was pretty much closed. In fact, according to him, 'industrial "targeting" of the intensive industry modernization variety has virtually disappeared as a government practice'.[29]

Such comments, whether coming from Japanese officials or foreign friends, make very little sense. First of all, we know that industrial policy and targeting were actively pursued for decades and to deny this is perfectly ludicrous. There are countless government documents which lay down very precisely which industries or products were selected, which measures were adopted to promote them and which agencies were responsible for implementation. There is also comprehensive data on the tax rebates granted, the subsidies offered and the budgetary allocations for research. Last but not least, there are endless statements from Japanese officials and foreign commentators to the effect that industrial targeting not only existed but flourished.[30]

As for industrial targeting being a thing of the past, that is as easily dismissed. As will be seen in the case studies, there are two essential categories which are being actively promoted at present. One consists of high-tech sectors, and not only machinery and computers. There are also new materials, biotechnology, aerospace and nuclear energy.

The other group consists of declining industries, dozens of which are already covered by official government programmes, and many more can be expected to join.

One could safely go even further. Not only have industrial policy and targeting not disappeared, they are unlikely to completely vanish ever. The roots are much too deep. Today's activities have grown out of traditions and practices which have emerged during well over a century now. They express the kind of relations which remain characteristic of Japanese society, close ties between businessmen, bureaucrats and politicians as well as close ties amongst businessmen, including those who are formally competitors. Most of the crucial phenomena are part of the business culture and if they are not expressed in one way, then they will certainly be manifested in another.

2 Institutions

By now most people who have been familiarised with the concept of industrial targeting assume that a study of the institutions involved must focus primarily on the Ministry of International Trade and Industry. Most of those for and against the practice regard it not only as the mainspring but as almost the only source of such activities. An objective view of the situation provides very different insight.

Even assuming that MITI were the only targeter, it would still be necessary to see just who else cooperates in the process. For this, one would have to consider the political leadership, especially the government, which adopts the basic legislation and votes the budgets. It would also be indispensable to look into the other ministries and agencies with which MITI must work to accomplish its ends. Then there is the business community, which we already know must participate fully in these exercises. Last, and in this case least, the population at large contributes to an effort in which it has little say.

In fact, as will be seen more amply in the case studies, MITI is far from being the sole practitioner of industrial targeting. The practice is very widespread and the exercises are amazingly dispersed. They take place in a dozen major bodies, in some of them almost as actively, like the Ministry of Transport (MOT), Ministry of Post and Telecommunications (MPT) or Science and Technology Agency (STA). Moreover, targeting is undertaken not only by the bureaucrats but by the businessmen themselves. Companies are organised in such a way that they can carry out their own exercises.

THE POLITICIANS

In most countries the political leadership is in charge of economic policy. It holds the levers of command and is accountable to the electorate for fulfilling certain goals which should maintain it in power. While the same rule may seem to apply in Japan, on closer scrutiny it most assuredly is not the politicians who decide how the economy should be run.[1]

This appears a bit confusing at first, especially since Japan actually engages in 'planning'. That is relatively unusual for a capitalist economy and would lead one to assume that the political leadership were coordinating and stimulating the economy more than elsewhere. But any such impression quickly dissolves on examining Japanese planning. It is purely indicative, clearly stating that the guidelines are nothing more than that and that private businessmen are perfectly free to follow them or not. In addition, and this is more surprising, the overall plans are just a juxtaposition of sectoral plans, each emanating from the authority concerned, which have never been coordinated.

The idea that planning actually exists in some real sense, and was once quite effective, stems from the 1950s and 1960s when certain plans seemed to give an impulse to the economy. This was the case for Prime Minister Ikeda's famous 'income-doubling' plan. Indeed, most early plans not only attained but exceeded their targets. But this overfulfilment, although welcome, showed that the plan was one thing and the economy another. The contrast became less flattering during the 1970s and 1980s when the plans were much less ambitious and still never reached their objectives.[2]

Even general macroeconomic policy, a more common activity in most economies, does not quite live up to its name. The government almost never adopts comprehensive packages of economic measures which cover most aspects and are balanced against one another so as to be coherent or, at least, not internally contradictory. It may take fiscal steps or launch public works, but it has done little in the way of monetary policy. And, for years, it did not ensure that expenditures were actually covered by tax revenue, which resulted in huge, unwanted budget deficits. The timing was also rather poor, often stimulating or slowing down the economy at just the wrong time.[3]

Here too what passed for macroeconomic policy was merely a juxtaposition of policies emanating from various ministries. But they were not suitably coordinated at the cabinet level by ministers who decided which measures should be implemented when. Nor was there an attempt anywhere in the government to come up with a coherent, long-term economic policy. While this ineffectuality contradicts many views of Japan, it definitely applies at the political level. Indeed, over the past decade or so, there has hardly been any government policy that merited the name.

What the politicians have done, and this is very important, is to mobilise the nation for the struggle for economic development. They have given economic progress the highest priority ever since the war. In fact, during the first few decades it was almost the only programme that enjoyed much support. Only since the 1970s has there been noticeable concern for other issues like better living conditions, environmental protection or enhanced welfare. No matter how popular these were, they remained subordinated to promoting economic growth. In a pinch, if there were not enough resources to go around, it was always economic development which won.

During this whole period, the ruling Liberal Democratic Party (LDP) has been solidly and steadfastly pro-business. Indeed, conservative politicians have essentially been lobbyists for business interests, seeing to it that the government fulfilled as many of their requests as possible. They backed legislation that would support one sector or another, they agreed to any necessary tax breaks or subsidies, and they did what they could to keep other popular concerns related to the quality of life from getting in the way. Since the LDP has been in power virtually since the war, this provided an amazingly stable and supportive platform.

But the politicians did not take the initiative for industrial targeting. The real impulse almost systematically came from the bureaucrats. There are various reasons for this. One is that the politicians simply did not have the knowhow. Rather few politicians were ever in business and almost none bothered studying economics. Even ministers with economic portfolios were not very conversant with the basic issues and, since most of them only stayed one or two years, they did not have the time to learn. They merely served as liaison with the ministry, passing on the views of their subordinates and defending them with as much zeal as possible instead of doing what might normally be expected, namely imposing government views on the bureaucrats.

While there has been some slight attenuation in recent years, throughout the whole postwar period the bureaucrats have run the administration. They have fixed priorities and devised policies pretty much on their own. More significantly, they have supervised the implementation of official policies and even altered them when it suited their purposes. But they have done so largely within the confines of their own ministry which explains why there is so little coherence of overall policy. Indeed, often each bureau within a given ministry adopted its own stand which did not necessarily coincide with those of other bureaux.

It is from this level that industrial policy and targeting emanate. They derive from the work of bureaucrats in the individual ministries, and more particularly bureaux, deciding how to improve the lot of the industries and companies they are responsible for. A feeling for this process can be gained from the comments of a contemporary observer.

> The industrial bureaus of MITI proliferate sectoral targets and plans; they confer, they tinker, they exhort. This is the 'economics by admonition' to a degree inconceivable in Washington or London. Business makes few major decisions without consulting the appropriate governmental authority; the same is true in reverse.[4]

There is no doubt that leaving much of the initiative to lower levels is not only characteristic of Japanese decision-making, it has great advantages. The junior bureaucrats and their business counterparts are more aware of the details of administration and the nitty-gritty of business. They do not waste their time with theory but instead concentrate on practice. But there are also drawbacks. The businessmen act strictly in the interest of their companies and the bureaucrats largely in the interest of their clientele. They too readily lose sight of the big picture and tend to think that what is good for their sector is good for the economy and country as a whole.

This brings us back to the politicians. There is no doubt that there is some merit in leaving the bureaucrats to do what they can do best. They have the knowhow, they have the responsibility and they have the will. But there must always be some higher authority to handle certain things. One is to provide enough coordination so that all the various policies and measures form a whole. Another is to see that there is relative equity, so that sectors or companies do not fare better simply because they are supported by a stronger bureaucracy. There must also be some concern for other aspects, social, ecological, welfare, etc. Finally, there must be a degree of accountability so that the bureaucrats are judged for what they do and how well they do it. Most of this is lacking because the politicians are too weak or indifferent.

MIGHTY MITI

The foremost practitioner of industrial policy and targeting, it is generally agreed, is the Ministry of International Trade and Industry.[5] Although only established formally in 1949, it is the successor of the earlier Ministry of Commerce and Industry and Ministry of Munitions. It has traditionally held a commanding position in all matters relating to economic development and especially industrialisation. Its present competences are still very broad, encompassing not only industrial policy but also trade policy, patents, energy and natural resources policy, regulation of the distribution system, regulation of electric power and gas, environmental protection, aid to small business and regional development.

It is worthwhile pausing to take a closer look at these assorted activities. They show more concretely what MITI actually does when grouped around certain themes which will be studied more carefully later, namely market, finance, technology, competition and 'climate'.

Under its power to regulate trade, MITI has been able to obtain legislation which closed the Japanese market, or at least varying portions of it, during an extensive period after the war. It also managed to regulate officially, and unofficially influence, any foreign investment for almost as long. The enabling acts were the Foreign Exchange and Foreign Trade Control Law of 1949 and the Foreign Capital Law of 1950. But they were supplemented, that is to say tightened up and manipulated, by countless rules and administrative orders and interventions. The result was one of the most impenetrable markets among the industrialised countries.

This is what initially won MITI the nickname of 'Ministry of One-Way Trade'. Yet, while it was applauded for this at home, it increasingly came under criticism abroad. Japan was clearly out of step with the United States and European countries which preached free trade and took dramatic measures to open their markets. It was not until Tokyo fully joined the General Agreement on Tariffs and Trade (GATT) and the OECD in the early 1960s that it was formally committed to liberalisation. But this process was entrusted in MITI which was worried that local industries would be swamped by imports and local companies bought up by foreign capital. It was also afraid that 'liberalisation might eliminate its raison d'etre'.[6] So, MITI bureaucrats delayed any opening as long as possible.

As much as 60 per cent of Japan's imports came under quotas until 1963, after which they were gradually reduced to about two dozen items at present. However, while removing the quotas, tariffs were introduced to impede imports, some being quite prohibitive. The highest tariffs naturally protected articles which had been targeted or were part of the overall move toward industrialisation; low tariffs were for goods of lesser importance or raw materials and machinery needed by Japanese companies. Here too the average level sank until, in the late 1970s, it was lower than that of the United States or the European Community. But there were still peaks sheltering favoured sectors like computers, semiconductors and processed foods. As the tariffs fell, existing nontariff barriers became more visible and bothersome, and new ones sprang up. Even into the 1990s, the existence of numerous NTBs belied Japan's claim to be one of the world's most open markets.

The old foreign exchange law was gradually relaxed as well, although it was not replaced by a new one until 1980. As for investment, that was liberalised considerably from 1966 to 1971. Despite this, it was still difficult to invest or obtain wholly-owned subsidiaries in certain sectors. Not until the mid-1980s was the legislation on investment brought into line with that of other advanced countries. By then, alas, the number of sectors in which it made sense to invest had shrunk and the cost of investment had swollen grotesquely. And it was still hard to acquire Japanese companies.

With regard to finance, MITI had only limited funds of its own, a meagre 1.5 per cent of the national budget or some ¥1 trillion in the early 1980s. Most of these funds were needed to cover its administrative costs. But it could spend modest amounts on such useful tasks as technology promotion, resource and infrastructure development, energy development and programmes for small and medium enterprises. And it had access to other sources. Through its connections, it could direct funds in the general budget toward public-works projects of particular interest to the industries or companies it was fostering. Then came even larger allocations from the Fiscal and Investment Loan Program (FILP). As much as 40 per cent of its kitty or some ¥8 trillion in the early 1980s was channelled into significant infrastructural projects or passed on to other agencies financing industrial development, regional development or small business.

MITI could not actually lend money but it could be extremely helpful in obtaining loans. It exercised most direct control over several bodies lending to smaller firms, especially the Small Business Finance Corporation. Its writ was followed rather closely by the Japan Development Bank (JDB) which many insiders referred to as 'MITI's bank'. It also retained considerable influence over the Long-Term Credit Bank and Industrial Bank of Japan (IBJ). To support exporters, it could count on the Export–Import Bank. Aside from this, in order to help perennially cash-short small companies, it arranged to have their credit bills discounted more expeditiously by the Bank of Japan (BOJ).

Another related institution had a different function, namely the Japan External Trade Organisation. JETRO, created in 1958, could provide overseas market information, assistance with export formalities, organisation of trade shows and exhibits and even contacts with foreign buyers. This was done at reduced cost, or free, and represented a tremendous saving to smaller or novice exporters.

MITI could not grant tax breaks. But, through its connections with the government and pressure on the Ministry of Finance (MOF), it could obtain very favourable treatment of companies in targeted growth industries and later depressed sectors. For the former, there was increased initial depreciation or accelerated depreciation of plant and equipment, especially machinery embodying new technology or used in 'important industries'. Other incentives were provided for research and development. Exporters could maintain tax-free reserves for overseas market development and overseas investment losses and get special write-offs for income from overseas technical services and other activities. The latter could write off excess capacity more generously.

When it comes to technology, MITI could be useful in more ways than one might imagine. By preventing both imports and investment, it left foreign companies with few other ways of profiting from knowhow than licensing technologies or entering joint ventures. MITI controlled both of these procedures, deciding which technologies should be acquired and which investments approved. By withholding approval of licensing agreements, it helped Japanese licensees exert pressure for more lenient conditions and lower royalties. It could similarly convince potential partners to accept a smaller share in a joint venture or contribute their best as opposed to second-best technology.[7]

Through its control over the patent office, MITI was able to slow down the process of approving foreign applications, which left local firms more time to assimilate the contents and come up with other variants.[8] When software became a crucial element in its strategy, MITI proposed loose copyright legislation that would have given limited protection for a shorter duration. This effort was only frustrated by foreign protests and pressure. In like manner, MITI controlled the standardisation machinery resulting in the granting of Japan Industrial Standards (JIS). Since the JIS mark was rarely granted to foreign companies and products, no matter what their quality, and Japanese standards varied notably from international ones, this formed the basis of countless NTBs.

In the more constructive task of promoting research and development, MITI played a notable role. This was not so much due to its research budget, a mere ¥200 billion a year in the early 1980s and about twice that in the early 1990s. But the money was put to very good use. First, it was directed toward areas where it made a difference, namely those being targeted at the time. The projects then focused on crucial technologies needed for local producers to forge ahead. In addition, the benefits were spread more widely by subsidising smaller shares of a larger number of projects. Quite often, projects were not undertaken with just a few companies but many which were organised in research associations or nonprofit organisations.

The responsibility for MITI's own R&D effort was entrusted to the Agency for Industrial Science and Technology (AIST). It oversaw more than a dozen laboratories which covered most essential fields including electrotechnology, chemistry and chemical engineering, fermentation, and polymers and textiles. AIST's work was overwhelmingly related to technologies with direct commercial applications, many of them inserted in major ongoing programmes. Most significant were the Large-Scale National Research and Development Program, launched in 1966, and the Project on Basic Technology for New Industries, initiated in 1981. It was also in charge of the Sunshine Project and Moonlight Project dealing with alternative energies and energy conservation.

The activities referred to thus far are not uncommon in other countries. Where MITI's approach differed significantly was with regard to industrial 'rationalisation' and 'structure'. The basic thrust of the former was to enhance Japan's international competitiveness. The targeters were concerned that excessive competition would result from too many, too small companies and that any shakeout would create undue damage and confusion in the sector. This could be remedied by artificially restricting the number of players.

This was easiest in emerging sectors, many of them cultivated by MITI. While it was not always possible to control the number of entrants, in some sectors it was necessary to receive an authorisation not only to build a factory but even to expand capacity. In the early period, MITI also regulated the acquisition of foreign technologies. Those companies which intruded against MITI's better judgement would not obtain loans from state banks or other assistance. This process worked most effectively in industries where large scale was essential and start-up costs were high, such as steel and petrochemicals.

It was harder to restrain competition in other sectors in which companies could enter easily enough on their own, or in older ones that were already crowded, and increasingly so if they were declining. For this, MITI had to obtain special legislation or use persuasion to tighten the ranks in an orderly manner. In 1952, an Enterprise Rationalisation Promotion Law was adopted and suitable provisions were inserted in other laws devoted to specific industries. However, when MITI tried to generalise and intensify the process under a far-reaching Special Measures Act for the Promotion of Designated Industries (Tokushin Ho), from 1962 to 1964, it was defeated. Business circles feared that MITI was going too far and prevailed on cooperative politicians to block the legislation.[9]

Nonetheless, even more strenuous efforts at rationalisation began about a decade later. This time they were directed at declining industries which sorely needed MITI's help and therefore did not object. This was done under various laws relating to individual sectors facing a recession, especially textiles, and then under much broader legislation covering several dozen sectors. This included the Law for Stabilisation of Specific Depressed Industries (1978) and its successor the Law for Structural Adjustment of Specific Industries (1983). Among other things, they authorised cartels to dispose of excess capacity and encouraged concentration of production and marketing.[10]

This legislation, and other actions that were tolerated if not specifically authorised, permitted MITI, first of all, to stimulate cooperation among companies in a given sector. They could engage in joint purchase of raw materials, joint marketing of products or joint research to combine their efforts rather than compete. If this were not possible, they would be urged to specialise in somewhat different product categories. In certain cases, mergers among comparable companies or absorption of smaller firms by larger ones were proposed. Since MITI provided financial inducements itself or through the banks, such efforts were facilitated, if not always fruitful.

It was only under more severe conditions that MITI resorted to cartels, most of which required a waiver of the antitrust laws and authorisation of the Fair Trade Commission (FTC). Under one law after another, cartels were permitted to prevent excessive fragmentation, overcome recessions, help out depressed industries or simply advance 'rationalisation'. Other cartels were instituted as a result of trade problems, usually in order to keep exports from being sold at prices regarded as too low or in quantities regarded as too large by trading partners. In the mid-1960s, there were over a thousand authorised cartels and as many as five hundred into the mid-1980s.[11]

While the measures related to market, finance and technology provided the foundation, and 'rationalisation' the thrust, of MITI's policy, it was 'structure' which created the focus. Not every sector enjoyed full support. Indeed, if all had, there would not have been much impact because limited resources would have been spread too thin. So, it is necessary to consider the process and machinery of selection, the core of targeting.

Most of MITI's work was not done by the broad-based 'horizontal' bureaux, some of them created more recently, which dealt with general issues like trade, industrial location or environmental protection. Rather, the lead was taken by the older, stronger industrial bureaux covering specific branches of manufacturing and mining. These 'vertical' bureaux (and their divisions) covered sectors like basic industries (steel, nonferrous metals, chemicals, biotechnology, etc.), machinery and information (industrial machinery, electronics and electrical machinery, automobiles, aircraft, aerospace, etc.) and consumer goods (textiles, fibres, paper and pulp, ceramics, construction materials, etc.). In each of these bureaux (and divisions) middle (and lower) level staff were keenly interested in what could be done to help their respective areas. They came up with proposals for protection, promotion, research and so on. These formed rough policy guidelines for quite small, compact branches of industry.[12]

It was the task of the Industrial Policy Bureau (and formerly the Enterprises Bureau) to balance the various proposals, coordinate them and set priorities. What has been done traditionally is, rather than disperse efforts among all the sectors, to select those where a strong push would do the most good. The order is based on 'dynamic' comparative advantage, namely taking those sectors where reasonable external help is needed to overcome a relative disadvantage while leaving alone those that can shift for themselves and holding off on more advanced ones where too much support would be necessary. Ultimately, or so it was argued, each sector would have its turn and all would benefit. But the benefit would be that much greater if the efforts were concentrated on the right sector at the right time.

To obtain broader backing for its position, the Industrial Policy Bureau had its proposals endorsed by an advisory body, the Industrial Structure Council (formerly the Industrial Rationalisation Council). It had numerous committees, each of which examined the situation in the individual sectors while the 'independent' Council coordinated and set priorities. But the final decision usually conformed very closely to MITI's initial position, which was not at all surprising since the background papers and proposals were written by the bureaucrats. Still, the discussion was regarded as useful and agreement supposedly expressed a national consensus.

The results of the various deliberations were conveyed in an endless stream of reports, White Papers and 'visions'. These last captivated foreign public opinion since they took an impressively long and broad view. Some 'visions' were devoted to specific sectors whose time had come. They included steel, synthetic fibres, paper and pulp, clocks and watches, colour television and computers, among others. Other 'visions', the most sensational, peered into the future, covering the 1960s, 1970s and 1980s. In 1980, the Industrial Structure Council issued a 'Basic Plan for an Industrial Society in the 21st Century'. The 'Vision for the 1990s', however, included no mention of industrial policy since it had become a sensitive issue.

In addition to enthusiastic and high-minded pronouncements on future prospects, there were catchphrases which characterised a period, such as 'heavy-and-chemical industrialisation', 'knowledge-intensive industry' or the 'information society'. More spectacular yet, MITI made bold numerical forecasts of crucial figures like the growth rate or share of GNP of different sectors. For rising industries, it predicted the anticipated production, demand and sales on the domestic and world markets and calculated the cost of attaining this growth in terms of funding and facilities. These were the much touted 'targets'.

It was still necessary to have legislation enacted, so MITI's bureaucrats drew up bills which were perfunctorily considered by the ruling party and submitted to the Diet. After more superficial debate, and with hardly any modifications, they were approved. Such laws were adopted for numerous industries and, by checking the date, it was easy enough to keep track of what was being targeted when. Those of particular importance, in order of presentation, dealt with textiles, steel, petrochemicals, machinery, automobiles, electronics, computers and so on.

Some of these laws were still relatively general, covering rather broad sectors and thus more related to industrial policy. Where targeting arose more specifically was when such legislation empowered MITI to draft 'elevation plans' in consultation with the advisory bodies. These plans focused on specific products, machine tools, metal machinery, computers, semiconductors and dozens more. They included more precise capacity and production goals, technology acquisition and funding requirements and methods of increasing standardisation and specialisation. To all intents and purposes, this authorised an all-out crash programme for Japan to get ahead.

Naturally, laws could not foresee all eventualities and there was need for considerable flexibility and periodic adjustments. MITI also wished to retain a fair degree of discretion in wielding any tools. Thus, ample room was left for interpretation and additions which were handed down abundantly by MITI's bureaucrats in the form of 'administrative guidance' (*gyosei shido*). This consisted of directives, requests, suggestions, encouragements and warnings but not strictly speaking orders since they were not legally binding or enforceable.[13]

Thus, in various ways, formal and informal, the Ministry of International Trade and Industry provided most of the elements needed to help industries succeed and it integrated them, to some extent at least, in its industrial targeting. This was quite an accomplishment. There was no other ministry or agency that engaged in as many comprehensive exercises. For this, it certainly deserves credit. But not for more than it actually did.

OTHER AGENCIES

Although MITI was a trailblazer and source of much industrial targeting, it would be a mistake to assume that it was the only agent. It simply was not. First of all, much of what it did depended on the backing of other ministries, agencies and lesser bodies. More importantly, some of them engaged in their own exercises. If they were to be overlooked, then not even half of the total phenomenon would be embraced and industrial targeting would look much more circumscribed than it actually was.

Industrial policy and targeting took place in roughly the same way in other institutions. They also consisted of bureaux which worked very closely with specific branches, in not only the secondary but the primary and tertiary sectors as well. They sometimes had a staff that was considerably larger than MITI's and could do more on its own. Some also had much bigger budgets. In addition, they had access to external resources. Thus, they could arrange tax relief, obtain special loans and provide grants for R&D or carry it out alone. Finally, they could arrange formal trade protection and, when that was not enough, create administrative complications and nontariff barriers. What they did was not incidental or sporadic but part of organised programmes for which plans and 'visions' were issued, replete with numerical forecasts and targets.

The most important player in this context has been the Ministry of Finance. It has very broad competences relating to taxation, budget allocation and general financial policy. It also exerts substantial influence on the state banks and Bank of Japan. Only some pertinent aspects of its operations need be mentioned here.

It was MOF which, at the suggestion of other ministries or influential politicians, could grant a whole range of fiscal incentives to those entering designated sectors or exporting. Likewise, it could provide tax breaks to sectors in difficulty. More generally, however, it was the only major agency arguing for fiscal responsibility and lower government spending, which kept the overall tax rates down. In apportioning taxes, it has been sensitive to the needs of business and, although the formal level of corporate taxes was high, in practice companies paid much less, because of lenient monitoring of tax returns and a surprising tolerance of tax evasion.

The Ministry of Finance was the key player in allocating the national budget among the various government bodies and fields of activity. In so doing, it went along with the prevailing economic bias. With regard to the Fiscal Investment and Loan Program, its role was even greater since FILP was administered by its Finance Bureau. Through allocations to the Japan Development Bank, Export–Import Bank, small-business and regional development institutions, it influenced funding of many crucial projects. But its most decisive contribution was more pervasive. With the Bank of Japan, it determined interest rates for savings and, by keeping them low, allowed both commercial and state banks to lend more cheaply to the business community.

Admittedly, MOF was more active in financing development during the first three decades when public funds were readily available, although it always had to restrain MITI and other ministries which wanted ever more money. Since the mid-1970s, however, it has had to be more restrictive because of recurring budget deficits and mounting national debt.

Aside from these general activities, MOF engaged in certain targeting exercises of its own. Since it regulated entry and controlled the operations of banks, securities houses, insurance companies and other financial intermediaries, it was in a position to help. One way was by keeping foreign competitors out. Another was to avoid excessive crowding and unruly competition which might prove harmful.

Finally, since it influenced interest rates, brokerage commissions, insurance premiums and so on it could set them at levels which almost guaranteed a decent profit to the intermediaries.

To some, the Bank of Japan was even more instrumental in promoting the economy. As noted, it followed a policy of keeping interest rates down so that companies could borrow more easily and cheaply. To help exporters, it almost routinely manipulated the exchange rate so that imports were more costly and exports less so. The difference between the correct rate and the artificial one was substantial on occasion, to judge by the sharp appreciation of the yen in 1971, 1978 and 1985–86.

The BOJ's most significant function was as a bank of last resort or rather, as Henderson quipped, 'first resort'.[14] To permit commercial banks to lend as much as possible, it allowed them to keep quite minimal reserves and issue loans which greatly exceeded their capital base. This was known as 'overloaning'. Since the commercial banks were not worried, as they were solidly backed by the Bank of Japan, they did lend much more extensively. Private companies, which received the funds, then expanded their operations considerably and felt safe with leverages that far exceeded those abroad. This system made it possible for a relatively modest monetary base to generate extraordinary investments. It so impressed James Abegglen that he put BOJ at the centre of Japan's industrialisation in even more glowing terms than Johnson used for MITI.

> The Bank of Japan is the financial center, and with the bank's help each rapidly growing industry can incur more debt than it could on its own; the borrowing power of the entire portfolio – Japan itself – is available to each industry. Hence the economy as a whole funds new enterprises, holds prices down, competes successfully in the world market and earns large profits.[15]

The Ministry of Transport is one of the government agencies which engaged most actively in industrial policy. It launched a programme to restore and expand the shipbuilding industry shortly after the war. This was a huge operation as regards the size of the facilities, amount of financing and extraordinary promotion and protection. At the same time, it reinforced shipping lines and regulated transportation. Two of the public corporations under its supervision also did some targeting. The Japan National Railways (JNR) did its best to create domestic suppliers for its rolling stock. Japan Airlines (JAL) had to buy domestic material . . . when available. More recently, JNR and JAL have tried to perfect linear motor cars.

The Ministry of Post and Telecommunications also played a notable role. It was in charge of telecommunications and, since the rise of computers, has also been interested in data processing. Most of its industrial activities, however, were entrusted in the then public corporation Nippon Telegraph and Telephone (NTT). The fuzziness of the demarcation lines between what MPT could do to provide the best possible service and what MITI could do to promote the related industries was a continual source of rivalry. In a rare joint effort, the Japan Key Technology Center was established by MPT and MITI, in cooperation with the private sector, to promote basic research on advanced communications.

While MPT did not engage in much industrial policy directly, Nippon Telegraph & Telephone most emphatically did. It formed a group of suppliers known as the 'NTT family' and encouraged them to produce virtually everything it needed, from quite ordinary equipment to the most sophisticated. In cases where the technology was not available domestically, it urged them to license the knowhow or develop their own. To help, it ran a huge R&D programme in its own specialised laboratories. It also provided the market since NTT was closed to outside suppliers until 1981 and only bought grudgingly thereafter. With annual procurement of more than ¥550 trillion in the early 1980s, it could engage in a tremendous amount of targeting.[16] The enormous costs were paid by the users, in the final analysis, because MPT saw to it that the rates were high enough to subsidise NTT's operations. This system was definitely attenuated, but not completely ended, when NTT went private in 1985.

The Ministry of Health and Welfare (MHW) has done much more than look after hospitals, clinics and like institutions. It actively fostered the pharmaceutical industry by impeding imports and inducing domestic production. Now it is encouraging the makers of medical equipment and promoting the rise of biotechnology. The Ministry of Construction (MOC) helped producers of cement, building materials and construction equipment as well as prefabricated housing. The Ministry of Agriculture, Forestry and Fisheries (MAFF), along with concern over food production, has had time to promote manufacturers of farm implements, tractors and fertilisers.

Other ministries and agencies which seemed even less likely to nurture industries have also played a remarkable role. The Ministry of Education (MOE) has a research budget four times as big as

MITI's. While many of its projects are more abstract, it does support work on medicine, nuclear energy and rockets. The Defence Agency (DA), although it could have equipped its forces with imported weapons, has preferred that Japanese companies supply not only ordinary armaments but also tanks, ships and aircraft.

Given the growing importance of technology, the Science and Technology Agency, created in 1956, deserves special mention. Its broadest competence is to fashion a national policy which it does in cooperation with advisory bodies like the Science and Technology Council (STC). In the early period, however, it was supposed to harness science and technology to economic growth. Even now that slogans about 'welfare' and the like have been added, it takes a rather practical tack. This is most visible in the areas of nuclear energy and aerospace, where it works through the Power Reactor and Nuclear Fuel Development Corporation (PNC) and National Space Development Agency (NASDA). It is also noticeable in the work of a number of specialised laboratories including the Institute of Physical and Chemical Research, National Institute for Research in Inorganic Metals, National Research Institute for Metals, National Aerospace Laboratory and others.

Although STA deals with more advanced, frontier technologies than the other ministries and agencies, its activities have definite commercial spinoffs. The laboratories undertake useful projects relating to nuclear energy, new materials, laser technology, metallurgy, aerospace and so on. Since it had an annual budget of ¥400 billion in the early 1980s, also doubled a decade later, it disposed of three times more than MITI's AIST and could accomplish quite a lot. To make certain that any results were properly used, it established the Japan Research Development Corporation (JRDC) which sponsored and financed private efforts to commercialise new technologies. Part of this was done under a programme known as Exploratory Research for Advanced Technology (ERATO) which has launched 16 major projects since 1981.

In addition to such administrative agencies, there are a number of significant financial institutions. Foremost is the Japan Development Bank. JDB was established in 1951 as a successor to the Reconstruction Finance Bank. Its primary task was to promote industrial development and most of its loans were directed toward key sectors of mining, manufacturing, transportation and power. The total revolved around ¥1 trillion a year in the early 1980s. Industry was also financed by the Long-Term Credit Bank, founded in 1952, and the

Industrial Bank of Japan, going back to 1902. They were under government ownership or supervision during the 1950s but continued following MITI's lead even after going private in the 1960s. All these banks provided loans on better than commercial terms.[17]

The Export–Import Bank, established in 1950, was the crucial source of loans for large-scale projects, including sales of ships and turnkey plants. Despite its ambiguous name, the Ex–Im Bank's principal concern was obviously exports and many of the imports were actually related to raw materials or plant and equipment for exporters. By the 1980s, it was also lending ¥1 trillion a year. This time, the conditions were not only better than commercial terms but competitive with foreign counterparts.

Two other financial bodies helped in a different way. One was the Japan Electronic Computer Corporation (JECC) which leased Japanese computers to Japanese acquirers. The Japan Robot Leasing Corporation (JAROC), owned by several dozen robot makers, insurance and leasing companies, did the same thing for robots. Both offered easier terms because they were partly funded by JDB.

Two other organisations were even more unusual. One was the Japan Shipbuilding Industry Foundation, which managed the proceeds from betting on motorboat racing, of which it had a monopoly. Some of the money was channelled to charitable causes but the bulk was used to promote the shipbuilding and shipping industries. Its relations with MOT were obviously close. A similar body was the Japan Society for the Promotion of the Machinery Industry. It was in charge of bicycle and motorbike racing, collecting the betting proceeds which were used to promote the machinery industry. Its relations with MITI were equally close. Given the popularity of betting, the amounts of money contributed by these bodies were substantial.

While all of these institutions were actively engaged in industrial targeting in one way or another, one whose input might be presumed crucial was not. The Economic Planning Agency (EPA) had little to do with the process. It periodically issued plans, which were officially adopted by the government and proudly proclaimed, but which had little impact on events. At best, they created a formal umbrella for long-term macroeconomic policy and contributed to the consensus. But EPA could not implement the plans because no funds were allocated for the purpose. In addition, its staff was too small and top officials were still appointed by MITI. Its bureaucrats, few of whom were actually economists or planners, could hardly impose their will on MITI or, indeed, on any of the other ministries and agencies, which adopted their own sectoral plans and had their own funding.

Unlike EPA, which just did not help much, the Fair Trade Commission occasionally got in the way, the only government agency to do so. It was established in 1948, at American urging, to implement the new Antimonopoly Law. This legislation was designed to prevent a reoccurrence of prewar abuses of economic power by the *zaibatsu* and cartels. Yet, during the new era, there was no shortage of questionable practices like the rise of *keiretsu*, concentration of production, manipulation of prices, control of the distribution system, unofficial cartels and so on. FTC had to prevent this collusion in the private sector and also confront those in the government, like MITI, MOF, MOT and others which encouraged it. More broadly, it differed on certain particulars of industrial policy, the advisability of aiding declining sectors and the validity of administrative guidance.

But there were very definite limits to what the Fair Trade Commission could do. Its staff was too small, its top officials were imposed by MOF, and it simply did not have the necessary political clout. Repeatedly, it had to give in and accept a revision of the Antimonopoly Law that weakened it and numerous waivers for specific industries that were being promoted. Thus, the antitrust laws became rather ineffectual barriers or just irrelevant. As Kozo Yamamura pointed out, 'the basic intent is respected only as long as it does not stand in the way of Japan's industrial policy, especially the activities of the largest firms that are viewed by the LDP, MITI, the larger firms themselves, and by many Japanese as being essential in increasing the productivity and international competitive abilities of Japanese industries'.[18]

After wading through this thick alphabet soup of ministries, agencies, public corporations and research institutes, it must be obvious that MITI is not the only player. In fact, taken together, the others can muster considerably more staff, much larger budgets, more research facilities and even greater political clout. So, anyone who fixates solely or largely on MITI is missing a big chunk of Japan's industrial targeting.

THE BUSINESS COMMUNITY

While most studies of industrial targeting highlight the role of the politicians and bureaucrats, it would be extremely unwise to forget for a moment that there was always a third, vital partner. Nothing much would have come of these efforts if not for the dynamic impulse of the private sector. This must be recalled now and then because businessmen were not only objects of policy but shapers as well.

The corporate participation in each targeting exercise will be amply visible in the individual case studies. Time after time, companies moved into relatively new sectors, raised capital, acquired and mastered technologies, trained personnel and marketed the products. Not all survived, but certainly enough did to give Japan a growing place in the industry. It was the ingenuity of the companies which got them started and the strong competitive urge which kept them going. That much is already known by the general public.

Less widely understood is that companies did not simply wait for the government to target new sectors or introduce additional support. The initiative for this came as often from private enterprise. Ambitious managers knew best which products stood a good chance of rising and what Japan's industrial strengths were. They also knew what kind of support would do the most good.

Naturally, businessmen stressed the patriotic aspect and made a big show of their contribution to the nation's progress. They were also courteous enough to let the government take much of the credit. But, if the business community had not been deeply involved in the whole process, it would not have worked. There is little chance that companies would have followed orders or guidance they strongly disagreed with or thought would fail. What is more, it is unlikely that the right orders and guidance would have been issued without the right advice.

Admittedly, not all companies went along with industrial policy. Some thought the decisions were wrong or that other sectors offered greater promise. Many were too small or insignificant to be involved. Even among those which entered targeted sectors, some came at the invitation of the authorities while others broke in against their wishes. Stronger companies needed less help and disliked the aid given weaker rivals. There was also friction between different sectors. Each felt the others were getting an unfair share of state largesse. If prices were raised in one sector, as a result of government intervention or cartels, those depending on it for supplies would complain.

Nevertheless, most participants accepted – or at least tolerated – both the assistance and the guidance. On balance, they gained more than they lost. And any which were seriously aggrieved could simply go their own way. Thus, the main concern of businessmen was not to resist government action but to help shape it and turn it to their advantage. In so doing, industrial targeting increasingly became a joint activity.

The business input came in various ways. One was through membership in assorted deliberative and advisory councils (*shingikai*) attached to the ministries and agencies. This official channel, however, was the least important. Proposals there came too late and were rarely heeded. Most of the essential spadework had already been done at a lower level. Companies therefore regularly sent staff to consult with the bureaucrats in the relevant bureaux and sections to see what was in the offing. They would draw them out and discuss the merits of one tactic or another. If information and advice were sought, they would volunteer it and thereby shape bureaucratic thinking.

The bureaucrats also cultivated good relations with businessmen. This was important for any project to run smoothly, a matter of no small concern for their career. Anyway, it was the duty of each young bureaucrat to know what was going on in his sector and there was no better source of feedback than those in the field. Thus, they received visitors from the companies or trade associations and occasionally visited them in return. If they were helpful, the relationship could blossom. They would enjoy wining and dining. Key officials could even count on a post-retirement job through the widespread practice of *amakudari* whereby former bureaucrats 'descended' into the private sector.[19]

Since industrial policy and special measures frequently also required formal government approval and some enabling legislation, there were close relations between businessmen and politicians. With economic development commanding top priority, business leaders enjoyed unusually high status and their views on most subjects were heard with respect. Among other things, they stressed the importance of a government with the right attitude and left no doubt that the only viable possibility was further LDP rule. Adding deeds to words, they encouraged their employees to vote correctly and heavily financed the ruling party. This was more than enough reason for politicians, constantly short of funds and frequently running for election, to cooperate.[20]

Obviously, it would have been very hard for the business community to impose its views if it disagreed internally over valid policies or was merely splintered and fragmented. But Japanese companies were extremely well organised at many levels. They possessed a multitude of bodies in which a common position could be forged and presented with considerable effectiveness. This structure was often spoken of as the *zaikai*.[21]

While there is a vast number of companies, 99 per cent of them are regarded as small and medium enterprises. This does not mean that they are unimportant in the economic scheme of things, since they frequently act as subcontractors or suppliers to major companies or provide useful services. But they are certainly of lesser concern in devising and implementing industrial targeting.

The essential core of the economic structure consists of a limited number of companies, a thousand or so by one reckoning. This is not even 0.1 per cent of the total number of companies in Japan. Yet, between them, they account for 6 per cent of the work force, 17 per cent of sales, 22 per cent of paid-up capital and 13 per cent of profits.[22] These are the companies which are sufficiently strong and diversified to move rapidly into new sectors. They are the ones that most aggressively entered the targeted industries and benefited most extensively from the various incentives.

In this group there are two rough categories. One consists of older companies, already rather bureaucratised and often stemming from the prewar *zaibatsu*. For lack of a better term, they may be considered the 'establishment' companies, which usually enjoyed higher priority in government circles. Other companies were relative newcomers, often created by ambitious entrepreneurs who ran them more tightly and energetically. These companies were less privy to government thinking and also less eager to go along with plans rather than trust in their own commercial instinct. They were, however, crucial in expanding the economy and heightening competition, keeping the first group on its toes.

Since these names will come up repeatedly, it might be indicated that the first category includes the likes of Mitsui, Mitsubishi, Sumitomo, Nippon Steel, Nissan, Hitachi, Toshiba and others. Prominent in the second are Sony, Matsushita, Honda, Seiko, YKK, Kyocera and so on. It would be hard to argue that the former were intrinsically 'better' than the latter. But they were probably safer choices for the targeters and enjoyed greater political support.

What is most noteworthy (and fairly typical of Japan) is that these big companies, rather than go it alone, tended to form much larger groups. There are three basic types, all of which are called *keiretsu* or 'linked groups'. First come the horizontal or 'intra-market' *keiretsu*, then the vertical or 'enterprise' *keiretsu*, and finally the distribution

keiretsu. Each type is rather widespread and the well-known groupings provide models which are imitated to some extent throughout
the economy.[23]

The 'intra-market' *keiretsu* are most illustrious. They consist of
leading companies from many different sectors, with as many as a
hundred members in the largest groups. They usually revolve around
a top commercial bank as well as one or more large manufacturers
and a general trading company (*sogo shosha*). The more prestigious
are the ones which can be traced back to the prewar *zaibatsu*, namely
Mitsui, Mitsubishi and Sumitomo. Those of more recent origin were
formed by banks like Dai-Ichi Kango, Fuji, Sanwa, Tokai and
Industrial Bank of Japan.[24]

These *keiretsu* are not just held together by tradition or amity, they
are linked by cross ownership, interlocking directorates, exchanges
of personnel and other techniques. They often have an inner circle of
members which meets regularly in a presidential council. They occasionally engage in joint activities or float new subsidiaries together.
But most of the solidarity takes the form of helping one another
through finance or sales.

The vertical *keiretsu*, basically families of suppliers and subcontractors of a dominant enterprise, exist in a narrower range of sectors.
They are most prevalent in the assembly industries such as automobiles, electronics, shipbuilding, steel fabrication and so on. Most
assemblers have created such a grouping, the best known being those
of Toyota, Nissan, Nippon Steel, Hitachi, Toshiba and Matsushita.
To give an idea of how large they can be, it might be mentioned that
Toyota and Nissan have hundreds of suppliers each.

Links between manufacturers and distributors are also quite common. These vast retailer networks, in which the outlets are controlled
by manufacturers, exist for consumer electronics, household appliances, cameras, eyeglasses, cosmetics and other products. They
can also be amazingly extensive. Matsushita has some 18 000 related
outlets and other electronics firms correspondingly fewer, but still in
the thousands if they are important. Makers of motorcycles and
automobiles also have far-flung dealership networks.

What is most striking is that some major companies are integrated
in all three types of groups. They are part of a horizontal *keiretsu*,
they have created their own family of suppliers and they control a
distribution network. This makes them considerably bigger than they
appear at first sight. In fact, it makes some of them larger than most

competitors they are likely to encounter abroad where such relations are less frequent.

According to Dodwell Marketing Consultants, the top eight Japanese banks (each at the centre of a *keiretsu*) were all among the top twenty banks in the world. Nippon Steel was the biggest steelmaker, Toray the biggest textile maker, Toyota and Nissan the second and fourth biggest automobile producers and Hitachi and Matsushita the third and fifth biggest electronics firms. The ranking in other sectors was only somewhat less elevated.[25]

These are not the only links. Other organisations unite the companies in a given sector. Most noticeable are the trade associations, of which there are hundreds. They form around virtually any product line and include the major producers as well as many smaller ones. The purposes vary but almost always include an exchange of information, attempts to monitor events from abroad and support of measures in the common interest. They may occasionally also involve adopting standards and specifications and, while not strictly legitimate, controlling entry into the sector.

These trade associations are ideal partners for the relevant bureaucracies because they can provide the needed information, offer simpler and more regular contacts with companies in the sector and participate in the implementation of government programmes. But it would be absurd to assume that they are mere tools. To the contrary, by grouping virtually the whole sector, the associations can drive a much harder bargain than individual companies.

In highly concentrated sectors, where there are only a few major producers which control the bulk of the market, there is a tendency for other groups to spring up. They may engage in little more than periodic and informal chats about the situation and what might be done to improve things. Or they can go further. They may make efforts to coordinate price hikes or regulate production or imports. This is not permissible under the antitrust laws and MITI has not seen fit to authorise all cartels. But that does not keep such practices from proliferating.

The corporate community also has a number of more comprehensive organisations which recruit members from all sectors. The broadest is the Japan Chamber of Commerce and Industry (Nissho) which includes companies large and small throughout the country. There is also the Japan Committee for Economic Development (Keizai Doyukai) which attracts more enlightened entrepreneurs, often from more innovative companies. The most formidable body is the Federation of Economic Organisations (Keidanren). It includes the top companies as well as leading trade associations among its membership and is ordinarily regarded as the spokesman of big business.

Keidanren takes precedence over all others. It is generally assumed to embody the will of the *zaikai*. It takes a stand on all economic measures and also political and social ones that can affect the economy. Naturally, it is very attentive to industrial policy. It prods the government to move in directions desired by the business community. And its requests are normally heeded since Keidanren's membership is the primary source of political funds. Keizai Doyukai is of interest since it periodically also issues 'visions' or picks 'frontier industries'. Its lists, by the way, are often assimilated in those of the bureaucracy.[26]

BUREAUCRATS V. BUSINESSMEN (FIRST ROUND)

One crucial aspect in the debate on industrial policy and targeting is who directed the operations – bureaucrats or businessmen. There is a tendency in much of the literature to depict the bureaucrats as out front, giving orders or instructions to sluggish or recalcitrant businessmen for the good of the overall economy. In much of the commentary in the popular media, the bureaucrats are also seen as running the show. Oddly enough, this view is often espoused by both those who support and those who reject targeting.

One explanation for this, a rather special one, may be that most of the books on the subject were written by political scientists. Among them were Chalmers Johnson and Ezra Vogel, who initially set the parameters of study. But even more recent empirical studies were done by political scientists, including David Friedman, Daniel I. Okimoto and Richard J. Samuels. Meanwhile, many economists tended to overlook or scoff at the phenomenon. Consequently, more attention was lavished on the political than on the economic actors and some authors seemed secretly pleased that the bureaucrats were apparently bossing the businessmen about.

Chalmers Johnson is the leading light of the bureaucratophile school. His book, *MITI and the Japanese Miracle*, deals intensively with what the bureaucrats did and makes hardly any mention of how the businessmen reacted. It puts the bureaucrats smack in the centre with other players revolving around them. 'Most of the ideas for economic growth came from the bureaucracy, and the business community reacted with an attitude of what one scholar has called "responsive dependence".'[27] But Johnson was not alone. All too many studies did little more than list bureaucratic programmes and projects, laws and regulations, concepts and visions, with scant concern as to what happened to them in practice.

Fortunately, those who have done serious empirical research paid more attention to the businessmen. They also uncovered serious methodological flaws in the theory of bureaucratic control. According to Friedman, most such studies 'simply assert that a given policy led to desired economic outcomes, assuming that the promulgation of a regulation or law is the same as proof of its effectiveness'. Alas, 'in any given case, directives or legislation might have been wholly superfluous to what industrialists actually did to produce growth. Moreover, it is possible that the bureaucracy's policies were either initially proposed by, or even foisted on, the regulators by firms that the regulators were supposed to be controlling.'[28]

They then went considerably further. In nearly all the case histories, they amassed evidence that the bureaucrats did not run the show and that businessmen were at the very least equal partners. This was expressed in Samuel's *The Business of the Japanese State*. It rejected 'the conventional view of bureaucratic prescience and control' and emphasised 'the constraints upon rather than the power of the Japanese economic bureaucracy'. This weakness of the bureaucracy was largely explained by the private sector's influence which provided a counterbalance. 'This is not the oft-told story of "guided free enterprise", "state-led capitalism" or "bureaucratic dominance". Instead, it is a story framed by a process of "reciprocal consent", in which firms give the state jurisdiction over markets in return for their continuing control of those markets.'[29]

Let us look at the case usually made for the bureaucrats either directing or cooperating in industrial targeting. The main claim to fame is their reputed ability and wisdom. Johnson talked of 'a powerful, talented, and prestige-laden economic bureaucracy'.[30] Macrae said they were the 'most mathematically-minded on earth'.[31] But a more mitigated conclusion was drawn by William W. Lockwood, who observed them in action. 'The industry specialists of MITI, competent as they are in routine affairs, have never given promise of becoming captains of industry with daring and foresight.'[32]

Observers seem unanimous on where that ability and wisdom supposedly come from. Elite bureaucrats are drawn from the finest universities, especially Tokyo University. Quite frequently, they have graduated from the law faculty. But no one bothers proving the connection. After all, Japanese universities are only the equivalent of American four-year colleges; they grant ordinary, not very demanding diplomas rather than a masters or doctorate. Law school imparts some fundamental knowledge, but not enough to practise law. And, anyway, why should such a general or even a legal education prepare one to run (or meddle with) the economy?

True, that is just the beginning. Fledgling bureaucrats are drawn into bureaux dealing directly with the economy and they can learn by doing under the watchful supervision of their seniors. Yet, that learning process is usually truncated by rotation. By the time they know something about, say, steel or machine tools, they will probably be transferred to another bureau in quite a different sector or one that has absolutely nothing to do with industrial policy. These transfers come every two years, although some key bureaucrats may stay on for four or more years. The consequence, as Friedman pointed out, is that 'staff in MITI bureaus frequently do not have personal expertise of any given industry, nor do they have a comprehensive memory of the history of policies applied to a specific case'.[33]

Even if MITI's career bureaucrats were as brilliant as some claim, which has yet to be proven, there were simply not enough to assume the responsibility of running dozens of specific projects, let alone the whole economy. MITI only had about 2500 staff, although other ministries were larger. Its industrial bureaux could only muster two dozen professionals each, hardly enough to supervise the activities of hundreds of companies enrolled in targeting exercises and tens of thousands without. They could not even collect the relevant information or make intelligent decisions, let alone know whether each company was doing what it was supposed to.

While there may be some doubt as to the bureaucrats' technical competence, there is none regarding their zeal and ambition for Japan to progress and, more specifically, to outperform other countries. This arose from a mixture of patriotism, internal esprit de corps and disconcern for what happened to others. Many of the strivings were rather chauvinistic, assuming that local manufacturers could produce anything that was made abroad, only better. But this was clearly tinged with a distrust or dislike of the outside world. Leading targeters often regarded imports as repugnant and foreign capital as menacing. Johnson referred to this syndrome as 'industrial zenophobia'.[34]

Still, one should not exaggerate this patriotism. As noted, bureaucrats were most loyal to their specific bureaux, then to their specific ministries and only last to the nation as a whole. They did not hesitate to compete with other bureaux and ministries even when this was not in the general interest. As Okimoto noted, 'MITI uses industrial policy as a lever to strengthen and extend its power vis-à-vis rival ministries' and more broadly 'to seize the initiative on important issues'.[35] And they were not immune to baser urges. After all, success in helping a given industry enhanced their prospects of promotion and, more insidiously, success in helping a given company assured them of a place to work when they retired. Failure, on the other hand, would be harmful to their career.

The businessmen, whose background is rarely treated with the same awe (by political scientists at least), were actually almost the bureaucrats' equal educationally. Some of them had also studied at Tokyo or Kyoto University. Others came from more practical, more liberal, but academically solid private colleges like Waseda and Keio. Many of them had studied liberal arts or other irrelevant subjects, but some at least had gone through engineering or business courses. Once inducted into a company, they were given far more intensive training in economic and technical aspects of the sector. There was also rotation in the large, bureaucratic companies, but fledgling businessmen kept learning different aspects of the same operations. So there is no question but that they were more knowledgeable than the bureaucrats.

Businessmen were not 'patriotic', not in the eyes of the bureaucrats or the general public. Their focus was rather narrow, to make a success of the company. This commitment, however, was deeper than that of businessmen in virtually any other country since, due to 'lifetime employment', their active career and subsequent pension depended vitally on the company's success. This might cause them to forget the best interests of the industry, or Japan as a whole, or the world, but it concentrated their drive to have the company come out on top.

Given this relative equality, the bureaucrats could only impose their will on the basis of legislation authorising them to either grant or withhold certain things. As indicated, a multitude of laws was adopted and any gaps could be filled in with 'administrative guidance'.

But a careful look will show that the bureaucrats could rarely oblige companies to do anything they did not want to do. The inability to reinforce bureaucratic power, with the failure of the Designated Industries Law, was the pivotal event.

The lack of formal authorisation, while limiting the power of MITI or other ministries and agencies, did not prevent them from accomplishing much of what they wanted. They simply had to adopt gentler, subtler methods. They had to offer a quid pro quo for voluntary compliance. This took the form of goodies that most businessmen were eager to receive: protection from imports, export subsidies, tax relief, public funding, research projects and the like. It is therefore not surprising that they cooperated most of the time. If, however, the bureaucrats tried to impose policies that the businessmen rejected as too costly or harmful, they could be vehemently rejected.

In short, it was a question of leverage. During the earlier period, the one admiringly reported in Johnson's book, the bureaucrats had plenty of leverage. Japan had suffered from the war, there was a shortage of capital, it was hard to acquire technologies, there was a deep-rooted fear that foreign (largely American) manufacturers would conquer the market with better, cheaper goods. Of course, businessmen cooperated then. They were desperate for help.

Gradually, during the 1970s, companies generated their own sources of finance, they improved their technologies and they could do much of their own R&D. They were still happy to have a bit more funding, a bit more public research and some aid in exporting. So they were quite willing to cooperate, but without committing themselves as firmly and without allowing bureaucrats to intrude in vital commercial affairs. Meanwhile, they engaged in much more of their own targeting.

By the 1980s, the Japanese market was formally opened, aside from some quotas, and state protection hardly existed. The government was also under pressure not to subsidise exports or even help out too lavishly with research. Thus, the larger, richer, tougher companies of the time could gain considerably less from MITI or any other ministry. It was only those in depressed industries which were in dire need of help and were willing, although not really pleased, to offer the counterparts required by the bureaucrats.

Meanwhile, the business community was increasing its leverage. Major companies, whether alone or through Keidanren, were heavily financing the ruling party. They bankrolled key politicians who could be relied upon to defend their interests against the bureaucrats. They were also able to subject specific bureaucrats, namely those who counted most, by offering them cosy jobs when they retired. *Amakudari* certainly played into the hands of the businessmen, who could infiltrate and manipulate the ministries and agencies through those former employees who maintained good contacts and those still there who hoped for an equally cosy job when they retired.

In the sections on case studies, there will be ample opportunities to see how the bureaucrats and businessmen interacted in specific exercises, and which dominated. For the moment, however, it seems adequate to stress two things. Without the bureaucrats, there would never have been any industrial targeting. They mobilised support, raised funds and drafted plans. They were usually the initiators and sponsors. On the other hand, without the businessmen, the various exercises would have got nowhere. Their active and intelligent participation was crucial for preparation and implementation. Without it, industrial targeting would never have been a success.

IS THERE A JAPAN, INC.?

At this point, it is essential to consider whether the relations between the Japanese authorities, consisting of both politicians and bureaucrats, and the business community, were not unusually close. This does not mean that one must make a watertight case either for a 'conspiracy' or that the threesome were free agents which just happened to move in the same directions spontaneously. It is quite sufficient to determine whether there was substantially more cooperation, and perhaps collusion, than elsewhere.

In so doing, it is impossible to evade the idea of 'Japan, Inc.'. Originally floated by James Abegglen, a well-known business consultant, it was avidly seized upon by Herman Kahn in his endeavour to explain Japan's success. The idea must have had some validity because it spread widely and became a shorthand formula for much of what was going on during the 1960s and 1970s. Over the years, it has sometimes been grossly exaggerated. But there was more than a kernel of truth. Indeed, when presented by Abegglen, who compared it to a conglomerate, it did explain some interesting features of industrial targeting.

'Japan, Inc.' is a special kind of corporation: a conglomerate in U.S. terms. A conglomerate can channel cash flows from low-growth to high-growth areas and apply the debt capacity of safe, mature businesses to capitalise rapidly growing but unstable ventures. It can move into a dynamic new industry and bring to it financial power that no existing competitor can match. It can increase capacity quickly. The result is that the conglomerate is in a position to dominate a new industry by setting prices so low that existing competitors cannot finance adequate growth. Its costs are so low, compared with the competition's, that it can sell at the going price and earn large profits. In all these senses 'Japan, Inc.' is indeed a conglomerate, a *zaibatsu* of *zaibatsu*.[36]

The more sinister characteristic, however, was the seemingly collusive nature of the relationship. Since outsiders did not quite understand how things were happening, which is not surprising given the efforts not to explain clearly who was doing what, it was assumed that there must be underhanded and tricky things going on. This was likened to a 'conspiracy' and it was pinned to the very bodies which were praised by admirers for their effectiveness. It is not so hard to trace MITI's prominence in this theory to comments by Chalmers Johnson and the MITI boosters. Here is a more nefarious view of the system which was described by Marvin J. Wolf as:

. . . *economic totalitarianism*, a government-directed enterprise in which all the energies of Japan have been mobilised to overwhelm the world competition. It is a national conspiracy directed from a central command post, a squat eleven-story building in Central Tokyo, the headquarters of MITI, the Ministry of International Trade and Industry. The elements that comprise the conspiracy come from every facet of Japanese life: unelected bureaucrats; industrialists; *shinko zaibatsu*, the reconstructed cartels; labor union officials; politicians; and submissive workers. Even co-opted Americans and Europeans contribute to the new power of Japan.[37]

It is just as well to avoid the extremes of adulation and denunciation when considering the relationship. But it should certainly not be played down. It is equally foolish to pretend that there are no special links and attempt to prove this by highlighting some notable conflicts or divergences. After all, the Japanese themselves commonly speak of 'the government hand-in-hand with the private sector' (*kanmin-ittai*).

Basically, it is a question of degree. All that has to be demonstrated is that the cooperation between politicians, bureaucrats and businessmen is considerably closer in Japan than elsewhere. That is not terribly difficult.

The politicians in power, namely those of the ruling Liberal Democratic Party, have certainly backed the business community to the hilt. They have systematically endorsed any measures or policies that could improve the economy in general or aid specific sectors in particular. They have done so even when this conflicted with other popular issues such as housing, amenities, ecology, welfare and so on. They have also withstood the pressure of foreign governments that deemed themselves injured by Japanese trade practices. Only in rare cases, and only after using delay tactics, have the interests of business been subordinated to anything else.

The bureaucrats left no stone unturned to help the businessmen who came under their jurisdiction. They churned out comprehensive and generous programmes, including financial support, protection from imports and backing for research. And they strove to have them implemented as fully as possible. In this, they scarcely showed any concern for the interests of others, whether foreigners or Japanese citizens.

The businessmen also worked tirelessly to strengthen the economy and to improve their own companies' status. But they did not forget their debt to the government. The *zaikai* supported the LDP, providing the funding it needed to win elections and even rallying voters. It provided post-retirement jobs for bureaucrats who had been helpful in the course of their duties. Indeed, they sometimes created specific sinecures for specific ministries or bureaux.

Such links are much closer than prevail in more liberal economies. Most advanced countries also have a political system in which there are more checks and balances. Bureaucrats, who do not wield as much power to begin with, are more carefully supervised rather than freely determining what their prerogatives are. Politicians are more answerable to the electorate and the alternation of ruling parties makes it harder to create long-standing relations. The biggest counterbalance, of course, is the population at large. There is certainly no Western country whose people have as tamely allowed business interests to prevail over popular causes.

Indeed, in some instances such a degree of cooperation between government and business would be illegal or at least unethical. Company financing of political parties would be more strictly regulated and some politicians would be held for bribery. While a 'revolving door' for bureaucrats is not unknown elsewhere, certainly *amakudari* would go against the rules. In addition, many of the relations between businessmen, especially between companies in the same sector, would fall under the restrictions of antitrust legislation and *keiretsu* would not be tolerated.

So, if it is a question of degree, then assuredly the degree is much greater in Japan. But that does not mean that there are no differences or disagreements. They exist everywhere and are also present in Japan.

For example, there are politicians who favour different economic sectors and many who support agriculture over industry. Some have closer relations with specific ministries and back them in any interministerial wrangling. And there is much of that. After all, with a finite budget, it is not possible to get allocations for all desirable projects. The Ministry of Finance is constantly haggling with other ministries to restrict their expenditures. MITI repeatedly insists that more money should be devoted to industry while MAFF grabs as much as it can for agriculture. There are jurisdictional disputes between MOF and MPT as regards the postal savings bank and between MITI and MPT (as well as NTT) on data processing. Even within the ministries there is an endless tug-of-war between different bureaux supporting different sectors.

This sort of conflict is normal. It arises everywhere and certainly also appears in Japan. But it crops up less often so that, rather than having some exceptions to the rule, they tend to confirm it. Moreover, most of these conflicts are either overcome or contained more readily. They have not blocked the process of industrial targeting to any great extent. When they did impose limitations, it was more often on how much could be done, in other words what the resources permitted, than on whether it should be done. There was much broader agreement on the underlying principles.

Part of this cooperation was achieved because the Japanese do have a somewhat less adversarial society and institutional structure. They also regard harmony and consensus more highly. But the primary explanation is that economic progress was a common goal. It was shared not only by the government and business but also by the people, who were willing to make exceptional sacrifices to that end. And it was not always at the expense of one another. By exporting goods massively many internal tensions could be lessened or overcome and the worst problems were dumped on foreigners.

THE PEOPLE

While the politicians, bureaucrats and businessmen actively shaped and implemented industrial policy, the people as a whole only participated passively, more as an object than as a subject. This may appear strange at first, since Japan is reputed to be a working democracy and its citizens have the right to vote. They could, in theory, have blocked industrial policy or replaced it with something else. In practice, although this is government of the people, and conceivably even for the people, it is certainly not by the people.

Most of the essential decisions were taken by the triad that runs the state: leading politicians, top bureaucrats and executives of major companies. This is far from strange since the same historical precedents, cultural habits and social mechanisms which made industrial targeting so natural fashioned a state in which people accepted a relatively dependent status of followers, and only questioned their leaders under extraordinary circumstances.[38]

The electorate was never formally asked whether or not it approved of industrial policy and targeting because they were never formally adopted as state policy. Planning was the official policy, and plans went through the ordinary parliamentary process. But industrial policy and targeting were worked out by the bureaucracy. While there were laws to support rising sectors or depressed industries, they were exceedingly vague and never spelled out precisely what the bureaucrats intended to do.

Of course, there were the numerous deliberative or advisory councils (*shingikai*) and even more plethoric study groups (*kenkyukai*) which were attached to the various ministries. 'People', in the form of academics, journalists, scientists, sometimes even labour, consumer or public interest representatives, attended along with government officials and business executives. They could participate in the discussions and express approval or disapproval. But members were unlikely to do much more since they were carefully hand-picked and not known for imaginative or independent opinions. In reality, as even sympathetic observers had to concede, 'council members merely comment on drafts of guidelines prepared by bureaucrats; serious discussion among themselves rarely takes place. As a result, many council meetings are occasions for authorizing a bureau's or section's policy decision made in advance through informal bilateral consultations between the bureaucrats and private parties involved.'[39]

Admittedly, it can be argued, there was no reason for the citizenry to object since industrial targeting was strengthening an economy from which everyone benefited. People should have been happy that this was achieved whatever the policies. And, for a long time, that was the case. The economy was booming during the 1950s and 1960s and few bothered asking why. In the 1970s and 1980s, however, the economy slipped and there was considerable hardship. But the electorate did not turn on the ruling party or its policies either.

This same passiveness and resignation can be found in countless activities that exerted a significant influence on economic development. Only some of the major ones need be mentioned to grasp the general situation.

People accepted not only the gains but the costs, most directly in the form of taxes. Taxes were gradually raised to foot the bill for industrial policy, the costs of cheap loans, subsidies, infrastructure and so on. It was also conceded that targeted industries should be exempt from paying certain taxes. While one can understand this aspect, another is more puzzling. People did not strongly object to inadequate spending on other items that were of equal or greater importance to them: amenities, education, housing, welfare, etc.

As savers, the Japanese accepted the modest interest rates that prevailed and that sometimes did not even cover the rate of inflation. They voluntarily sank their earnings into the vast pool of savings that was essential to float industries. In so doing, they often favoured the postal savings scheme which offered a marginally higher return. This was particularly noteworthy since that money was fed into FILP which was of direct use for industrial policy. Elsewhere, savers would have insisted on higher interest rates or sent their money out of the country to get better rates, legally or illegally.

As consumers, the Japanese were willing to bear the higher costs of imported goods or go without. This occurred most often for manufactured articles that had been targeted or agricultural produce that was protected. That could be understood since it aided domestic producers even if at some deprivation. But consumers even accepted that goods made in Japan should be directed to overseas markets where they were frequently sold more cheaply. Considering that the purpose of industrial targeting was to foster low-cost producers and not to subsidise exports, one might have expected more complaints than actually arose.

Japan had close to model workers. In order to expand production, they put up with long hours, frequent overtime and short vacations.

In order to keep costs down, they allowed moderate wage hikes even when sales were booming. In times of difficulty, workers agreed to further restraint. When new industries emerged, they underwent training for what might be better jobs. When old industries declined, they accepted retraining for worse jobs or none at all. There seemed to be no conditions under which they asked what was in industrial targeting for them.

Under the banner of 'production first', the Japanese led a fairly dull existence. They were willing to constrain family life, community life, personal interests and leisure to produce yet more goods. They were willing to permit that the landscape be blighted by crowded cities with mediocre housing and even notable degrees of pollution until that became unbearable. Most surprisingly, although they might be expected to make these sacrifices just after the war when they were obviously needed, they continued towing the line even after Japan had become one of the richest countries in the world.

There is not the slightest doubt that such behaviour was a vital contribution to industrial policy and targeting. If it had been lacking, Japan's economic development would have taken very different paths. But there remains an open question as to whether some of the alternatives might not have been more rewarding.

3 Techniques

Most attempts at explaining how industrial policy and targeting work are rather confusing. That is partly because this is a fairly complicated matter involving many different techniques, and variations on each of them, which are used individually or several at a time. Merely listing them does little to clarify the situation unless one also knows more exactly what purpose each one serves. Then it becomes much easier to understand.

This will be attempted here by grouping the various techniques around five basic themes: market, finance, technology, competition and creating a suitable climate. These themes were not chosen just because they manage to cover most, if not quite all, the techniques but because they sum up the various things a company needs to succeed. They are not drawn from economic theory but from the practice of doing business. After all, in case anyone thought otherwise, industrial targeting is not an exercise in textbook economics but interventions in the real world of business.

While the various techniques are separated out and considered more narrowly here, they are obviously combined in practice. Each industrial targeting exercise employs a package of such techniques. The exact contents will vary from one to the other and also from one phase to another. But they never appear alone. And, by combining them appropriately, the overall impact can be greatly enhanced.

Although most of the techniques described here involve action which is taken or influenced by the government, it should not be assumed that industrial targeting can only be undertaken by the public sector. The same ends can be attained by somewhat different means in the private sector. This can happen under two sets of circumstances. Companies can pursue their own industrial policy and target products even if they are overlooked by the government. Or, if they are already included in government plans, the company's action will greatly reinforce the joint effort.

MARKET MANIPULATION

For those living under the logic of a classic, free-enterprise economy, especially if they are in more advanced countries, the market appears almost as if given. It is there and one produces for it. Whoever produces best, local or foreign, has a right to the sales. That logic, however, sounds like folly to people in more backward countries. They know that if their market were thrown open it would immediately be overwhelmed by stronger producers from more advanced countries.

Japan, it must be remembered, was a rather primitive place in the mid-nineteenth century when it was first dragged into international commerce. And it was still relatively backward, especially compared with the occupying power – the United States – when it was brought back after the war. The Japanese authorities were convinced that if the market were truly open there would be little hope for Japanese companies to survive, let alone thrive. Even some American advisors felt that way.

In the logic adopted by latecomers like Japan and many others, the market is not simply there, a free good that one does not have to worry about. It is a positive asset, something one must use and cultivate. It is comparatively 'virgin', as it were, with many consumers who desire many products. If outsiders are allowed to sell before domestic producers are ready, by the time they can finally offer reasonable wares there will be little more demand to satisfy. It is therefore essential to preserve the domestic market for the domestic industry and, if it is not ready yet, then the market has to be kept intact until it is prepared.

The other cause for concern, namely that foreign producers were so much stronger and richer than domestic ones that they would crush nascent rivals, was clearly present as well. Ever since Meiji days, the Japanese had expressed this anxiety and, although the economy was much more resilient by the mid-twentieth century, the fears had not ceased. It was still argued that if domestic producers were not protected they could not possibly withstand the onslaught of American or European companies. It turned out repeatedly that, when the market was opened, they could hold their own. But this was partly because the market had been kept closed so long. Anyway, there is little point in offering rational arguments against fears which obviously have deep emotional roots.

Whatever the reasons, whether to preserve the domestic market or to protect companies against foreign competition, or most often both, Japan's bureaucrats felt it was indispensable to erect an array of protective barriers. It was one of the densest ever, consisting of exchange control, limitations on foreign investment and multiple restrictions on imports including quotas and tariffs. In addition, they proved highly imaginative in creating complicated regulations to inhibit even those investments and imports which were permitted. In the end, even after more formal barriers had been removed, there was still a maze of nontariff barriers.

It should be noted in passing that Japan differed from many developing countries on one crucial point. Most only blocked imports so that domestic companies could sell more. They did not cut off investment, too. In fact, they often encouraged investment as a means of obtaining capital and technology. Japan impeded investment as well. It wanted domestic companies that were truly national, not ones that were run by foreigners. The only concessions were made where essential technology was sought. Even then, the investor often had to accept local partners which usually held a majority interest.

Another salient feature of the Japanese system is the extent to which manipulation of the exchange rate was used to inhibit access to the market. By keeping other currencies artificially high, imports were made much more expensive. In this case, it was not only certain imports which were affected but all imports. The difference in price could be considerable since the yen has repeatedly been undervalued by 20–30 per cent or more. So this kind of protection could actually be greater than mere tariffs. Since this method was less visible, and harder to detect or regulate, Japan could apply it extensively.

This closed economy allowed 'infant industries' to spring up and flourish with little concern for foreign competition from without or within. It was done in a market which remained largely intact until it could be taken over by local producers. This market, it must be stressed, is a very sizeable one of some 120 million consumers by now. That is far larger than most European countries and about half the American or Soviet dimensions. While once poor, these consumers have since become quite affluent and, in so doing, turned Japan into the world's second biggest market. This was very fertile soil in which to grow.

The Japanese government frequently objects that the market is open *now*. The closed market is a thing of the past. That is not entirely true. While the formal barriers are gone, there are still an amazing number of nontariff barriers and the distribution system has its own complexities. Moreover, there is an irrepressible tendency to keep the yen undervalued. So the situation is not really as good as in more open Western countries.

Anyway, the fact that most of the old protectionist legislation has been repealed does not wipe out all the consequences. There are still many serious repercussions for imports even today. During the initial phase Japanese companies were able to sell extensively and satisfied much of the existing demand. By the time others could partake, most consumers had already made their first purchase and would only be interested in buying replacements. Naturally, they were more likely to make subsequent purchases from the same source. Thus, foreign companies operated in a much smaller real market.

In the meanwhile, Japanese companies had improved their production capabilities and the goods they offered were relatively cheap and of high quality. They developed efficient distribution networks which made their goods more accessible than imports. Many of these networks, by the way, were exclusive and could not be used by importers; there were few truly 'independent' channels. So, the key aspect was how long the markets were kept closed. The Japanese managed to hold off longer than others so that, by the time true competitors appeared, there was not much left for them to sell and the difficulties were immensely greater.

While most attention is paid to the general consumer market, it must be recalled that the public sector itself was a major market for many goods. The Japanese government purchased tremendous amounts of ordinary articles, equipment and materials. It also undertook countless public-works projects whose needs were even broader. To help local producers, the authorities practised a staunch 'buy Japanese' policy which was applied at the national, prefectural and local levels. In some cases it was explicitly confirmed by formal laws and directives. Otherwise, it was tacit. That was quite enough since no official would order anything foreign if domestic products were available.

In addition, there were over a hundred public corporations whose combined budgets were half as big as the national budget. Among them were some very large units which provided telecommunications, ran the national railways, constructed highways and bridges, operated public housing and so on. While theoretically autonomous, they followed the government's lead and imposed their own 'buy Japanese' rules. This almost exclusive priority for domestic producers and goods was not formally ended until the late 1970s and it still lingered in many areas into the 1980s and 1990s.

The closed market and a chance to grow were not purely ends in themselves but, rather, tied up to one of the overriding concerns of the targeters. More than others, they realised the importance of scale and strove to forge industries and companies which attained adequate size to benefit from economies of scale. In this way, it would be possible to produce at an optimum level, one where raw materials could be procured in larger quantities and at cheaper prices; where the best, most advanced equipment could be used, thus bringing costs down further. At a suitable scale, it was also possible to organise workers more efficiently, to engage in more R&D and to create a brand image, among other things.

On the vast base of Japan's domestic market, it would be feasible to cultivate large enough companies to rank among the most productive in the world. To see that this base were not unduly fragmented, the authorities actually intervened to regulate the number of players. For, if there were too many, none would attain desirable scales. In some instances, they even specified the acceptable scale and refused to approve facilities that were not sufficiently large.

The importance of protected markets and scale was recognised by other countries which engaged in industrial policy of the import substitution type. Where Japan differed most is that it also insisted on pursuing exports. Exporting had only been a secondary concern prior to this and few other countries even attempted it because they felt they would not succeed.

In Japan, export orientation was actually given higher priority than import substitution, although it was admitted that it could only be undertaken after local industries had been solidly established. The key element here too was the market. It was by selling abroad as well as at home that the largest possible sales, and the biggest possible scales, could be attained. In early years, when the Japanese market was relatively poor and consumers could not afford much, the export market was a precious supplement. Gradually, it became the primary outlet for certain sectors. While it attracted all companies, it was most tempting for lesser firms which had to sell abroad in order to reach the same level of sales and scale achieved by their rivals.

That is why the government adopted another series of measures to promote exports. They included tax incentives, access to cheaper loans, special subsidies and trade promotion bodies. The exchange rate also played a crucial role. By keeping the yen artificially low, Japanese goods cost less in foreign currencies. Finally, as for nurturing domestic industries, exporting was given a patriotic hue and encouraged as a vital means of keeping the nation going.

This 'export-led' growth initially surprised foreign observers. Yet, what is truly strange is not that Japan turned to external markets rather than concentrating solely on domestic sales but that others had not done so as well. Import substitution has repeatedly failed, frequently because the national market was simply not big enough to sustain efficient operations. It therefore made perfectly good sense to export and the real problem was to refine products adequately to be sold. It is only since Japan accomplished this that the potential has been recognised.[1]

What is equally perplexing is not that Japan exported massively to other countries but that it was allowed to do so. After all, it kept its own market firmly sealed for years after it had become a major exporter of numerous products. Yet, the importing countries failed to complain or, if they did, failed to do much either to keep out Japanese goods or to force it to open its market more widely to them. It was not really until the late 1970s, and then again the mid-1980s, that this was perceived as grossly unfair and seriously harmful. But nothing much was done even then.

FINANCIAL SUPPORT

In a still backward country where income levels are rather mediocre, and especially one which has few natural resources and has just been devastated by war, financing development can be an almost insurmountable challenge. It is necessary to collect massive amounts of money from people who often go without, inducing yet more deprivation. Or, and this is the other solution, it is necessary to seek outside financial aid. Japan, given its tradition of isolation and unfortunate experiences in earlier periods when foreign lending created undue dependence in the region, rejected the latter alternative. It was less willing than nearly any emerging country to accept any form of indebtedness.

On the other hand, the government did not hesitate to raise money, almost squeeze it on occasion, from the people. Given certain social and cultural characteristics, institutional arrangements and time-honoured traditions, it could accomplish this amazingly well. In the process, part of the funds was collected and distributed by the state. That is what attracts most attention. But it was actually the smaller portion of a multi-tiered operation.

The government, directed by a pro-business, conservative party, systematically skewed both the collection and allocation of revenue toward economic growth in general. Some of that money was more specifically channelled into industrial policy.[2]

On the collection side, one of the biggest contributions was simply to maintain a low level of taxation. It is hard to exaggerate how much good that can do for business (and consumption). It was very low in relative and absolute terms just after the war and, even four decades later, it was well below the levels in many industrialised countries that Japan competed with. In 1987, Japan collected 38 per cent of national income for taxes and social security while the United States collected 34 per cent, Great Britain and Germany, 51 per cent, and France, 60 per cent.

In levying taxes, the government did what it could to keep the corporate burden as light as possible. This was not done through formal rates, which were almost as high as elsewhere. Rather, it took the form of tax relief with a broad array of special deductions, accelerated depreciation, special write-offs and tax-free reserves. They were clearly related to industrial policy since the best breaks went to sectors which had been targeted and they covered the costs of plant and equipment, R&D spending, exporting and overseas investment. This accounted for as much as a tenth of total corporate tax according to the Ministry of Finance.[3]

Recently, Japanese companies have been griping that they are taxed more heavily than their American counterparts. Taking state and local taxes into account, the level is pretty similar. But the Japanese tax authorities allowed profits to be calculated very loosely and leniently, to judge by the small number of companies which bothered declaring profits and the low levels reported. And they turned a blind eye to massive tax evasion. Under such conditions, it would be hard to imagine that Japanese companies were not doing better than foreign rivals on this account.[4]

When it came to spending, obviously if the government's tax intake was low the outlay was bound to be smaller as well. But it was possible to spend heavily on economic development by scrimping elsewhere. This was done, among other things, by keeping expenditures on education moderate and those on social welfare unusually small. The decisive element, however, was a defence allocation that only amounted to about 1 per cent of GNP. This compares with 4–6 per cent in NATO and even more in the Soviet bloc. If it had been at more normal levels, defence spending would have absorbed a big chunk of the budget or taxation would have had to be increased appreciably.

What is most surprising is that the situation did not change even in the 1980s. According to OECD data, Japan's ranking on government spending as a share of GNP remained very low. Its spending on general administration, education, health, social security and defence were well below average. The only category where it was above average was economic services.[5] As late as 1987, the ratio of outlays to GNP was 15 per cent, compared with 22 per cent in the United States, 27 per cent in Great Britain and 34 per cent in Italy.

It is hard to pinpoint the sources of spending on economic activities since they were widely dispersed and sometimes also camouflaged. As will be seen, some of the ministries and agencies were able to help companies in the course of their normal activities, using their own staff and funding. Two principal forms of assistance were grants and subsidies for research, and aid to small business.

Another form of backup was the creation of a suitable infrastructure. The national budget allocated substantial sums for public works, about a tenth of the total. Public works are undertaken the world over and Japan was only an exception in the extent to which the programmes were slanted toward the interests of the business community. Much more money was lavished on railways, ports and airports, power and utilities, or industrial zones. Less was spent on the roads, public housing or amenities.

The government also established several state-related banks which were indirectly financed and were of use for economic development. Among them are the Japan Development Bank, Long-Term Credit Bank and Export–Import Bank. There were other bodies to aid small and medium enterprises. These banks provided relatively long-term loans at comparatively low interest rates. Such loans were most readily accessible to companies operating in sectors that were being promoted.

The importance of these banks in the early phase of industrialisation cannot be exaggerated. They then represented a fair share of total lending and accounted for a much larger portion of lending to targeted sectors. In addition, what they offered were 'policy' loans for projects that were not judged solely on their economic merits. While the lending was important as such, it was also symptomatic that once industries and companies had obtained loans from such banks it was much easier to get more from commercial banks. Even other companies, in related sectors, could get loans more easily.

There was a variety of other ways in which the government financed business, directly or indirectly. Among the more conventional operations were special bodies established to lease computers or robots on behalf of local producers. More creative were two special private associations which ran the motorboat and motorbike racing. They were allowed to organise gambling and pass part of the proceeds on to industry. For a while during the 1950s, there was a 'link' system under which companies could import goods in short supply and sell them for a profit, using the foreign exchange earned to acquire essential goods or promote exports.

As noted, the government, national and local, and the assorted public corporations, were a major market. But they were not an ordinary market where ordinary prices prevailed. It was possible for them to subsidise domestic companies indirectly by adjusting prices upward to guarantee a healthy profit. This was done to some extent throughout the system. But it was a major source of financing in certain sectors, including targeted ones. Most prominent were telecommunications equipment, computers and railway rolling stock.

This top tier, namely financial resources emanating from the state or directly influenced by it, is where one normally looks to see how much the government is doing to finance business. This is also where one looks to see if it is doing disproportionately more and to criticise any abuses such as excessively low interest rates or exceptionally large subsidies. In studying Japan, most outside observers concluded that it was doing somewhat more than others but not unduly so. The contribution it made was helpful, but hardly decisive.

That is probably so. But it is foolish to look only at the state's direct intervention in trying to gauge its role. There are other things it can do indirectly that might be more dispersed and diffuse but could have an even greater impact.

Of particular importance was how it encouraged and used personal savings. The frugal and thrifty Japanese already had a long tradition of saving and it was not difficult to persuade them to put money aside after the war. However, to provide an added incentive, small savings of ordinary people were exempt from taxation. These sums were placed not only in commercial banks but also in a postal savings system that reached into the smaller and more remote communities and offered a slightly better return. Money also flowed into insurance policies and pension schemes.

Over the years an incredible amount of savings was accumulated. Japan had one of the highest savings rates in the world, ranging from 20 to 25 per cent. This meant that year after year, a quarter and later a fifth of national income was put aside and could be tapped by

Japanese companies. Not only was this a very large pool of savings, it was proportionately larger than savings abroad, where the rate only ranged from 5 to 15 per cent in the United States and Europe.

In addition to their being abundant, access to these savings was relatively cheap thanks to another manipulation by the government. Interest rates on personal savings were kept rather low, below the level for corporate savings, usually only slightly more than inflation and sometimes actually less. Rates to borrowers, especially corporate borrowers, were correspondingly lower. In addition, the city banks which loaned to major companies charged less than the regional ones and *keiretsu* banks gave fellow members the very best rates. This meant that debt financing was comparatively low, little more than half the cost in other OECD countries in the 1950s and 1960s and still cheaper in the 1980s.[6]

This vast pool of savings, ample access through commercial banks, which accounted for 85 per cent of all financial institutions, and cheap interest rates created flows of capital that were extraordinary. This permitted Japan, without foreign borrowing, to devote 20–25 per cent of national income to gross capital formation, and private companies to put as much as 15 per cent of national income into investment in plant and equipment. This was a level that could not even be approached in other industrial economies.

Aside from the normal commercial intermediaries, there was a singular institution known as the Fiscal Investment and Loan Programme. Established in 1953, FILP was fed with money from the postal savings and insurance accounts and state employee pension schemes. It was so large as to be called the 'second budget', disbursing some ¥20 trillion a year by the early 1980s. And it did many of the things that could not be accomplished with the general account budget through lack of funds or because the government did not want to intervene openly.

FILP's funds were pumped massively into economic development, especially during the 1950s and 1960s when it represented a fairly large share of funding.[7] Much of the money flowed into industrial development, export–import loans or assistance to small business, usually at concessional rates. It passed through various agencies, dependent on key ministries, which dealt with public works, regional development and small businesses, as well as the development banks.

Even more veiled and indirect, but incredibly effective as a means of finance, was the power of various bureaucracies to set rates. It was possible to promote nuclear energy by allowing utilities to charge more for electricity, to promote telecommunications by letting the telephone monopoly collect higher rates, to promote airlines by keeping domestic and international fares well above levels abroad. Likewise, by subsidising rice, not only rice production but sales of agricultural implements could be helped. The many official (or tolerated) cartels allowed private companies to manipulate prices on their own. The amounts involved were extremely hard to quantify but once again probably exceeded the more open, direct forms of finance.

There is one last tier, the one that is most often overlooked and least well understood, especially by those coming from liberal economies or blinded by economic theory.

There is no better source of finance for domestic companies, especially those in targeted sectors, than protection. Trade barriers keep out competing products or, at least, raise their prices substantially. Companies therefore not only can, but regularly do, push their own prices close to the import level and even higher if imports are blocked by quotas. If tariff protection is 10 per cent, domestic products can be sold for that much more; if they are 30 per cent higher, then that is the additional leeway; if they are completely blocked, products can be sold for whatever the market will bear.

Naturally, during the running-in period domestic manufacturers could not produce as cheaply and they did not make much money. But they managed to generate sales which financed further rationalisation so that, in due course, costs could be brought down. Eventually, they did become competitive with imports. During the latter phase, domestic producers could make profits which were a function of the degree of protection they enjoyed (10 per cent, 30 per cent, whatever). This profit could then be ploughed back into further expansion. Alternatively, it could finance export production and subsidise exports.

Artificially low yen exchange rates had a similar effect. They made imports, all imports this time, more expensive and permitted domestic producers to raise their prices by the corresponding amount. Since the differential could be 20 per cent, 30 per cent or more, competitive producers earned extraordinary returns. This money could also be used to expand production, boost productivity or subsidise exports. But this time it was across-the-board and not just in certain sectors.

At this point it should be mentioned that there were periods, especially for infant industries, when companies benefited both from a closed market and from the exchange rate. This could boost the benefits to unheard-of levels.

Whatever the money was used for, expansion, rationalisation, exports, it is clear that the amounts involved were vastly greater than either state assistance or the advantages of cheaper borrowing. Moreover, they were income of the company itself, something it owed no one else, did not have to return or account for, and which could be used as it deemed fit. This made the third, and least visible, tier the most valuable.

TECHNOLOGICAL ADVANCE

It is impossible to comprehend Japan's passion for technology without remembering that throughout most of the modern period it was a late developer and it is only in the past decade or so that it has caught up. This explains its very concrete and commercial approach to technology and the kind of emphasis it has placed on research and development.

Nowadays, in the age of high tech, technology frequently implies an ability to fashion sensational new products or do old things in strikingly novel ways. That is what is expected of a frontrunner, and eventually became important for Japan. But, when it first got down to work after the war, what it needed was much more rudimentary. It needed products it could sell. And it wanted to know how to make those products. There was no purpose to inventing them, or figuring out sophisticated ways of manufacturing them, it just had to imitate what others were doing. That is the sense of import substitution or *kokusanka*.

Japanese entrepreneurs thus set about uncovering the wealth of products that had been developed by others. They went overseas, busily visited stores and factories, attended trade shows. They subscribed to professional and scientific journals, carefully examining the contents. They sent employees to study abroad. On finding the right product, they would figure out how it worked. Once they knew that, they could replicate it and perhaps make some minor improvements. This was not done on occasion or haphazardly. Dynamic companies systematically scoured the world for more products and their so-called research departments methodically monitored the literature.

This process was wondrously productive. For a modest investment it was possible to assimilate a tremendous amount of knowhow. It was much cheaper to borrow from others who had hit upon the right product and production techniques than to spend boundless time and money working on one's own. Moreover, it was not certain that, on one's own, one would come up with anything useful; when, with these existing technologies, the result was sure to work. That explains why Japan could already make impressive strides during the 1950s and 1960s when it was devoting only 1–1.5 per cent of GNP to research and development, not even half the level, or a twentieth the amount, spent in the United States.

Of course, this kind of activity did not provide the very best products or the most advanced production techniques. They were more complex and often owned exclusively by leading foreign companies. To really get ahead, that technology had to be acquired through the more onerous method of licensing. This was realised and Japan's almost insatiable appetite for knowhow led it to import hundreds of new technologies each year during the 1950s and 1000–1500 a year during the 1960s. Despite its rising technological level, this absorption did not slacken but actually grew to 2000–2500 a year during the 1970s and 1980s and nearly 3000 in 1990.

The process of borrowing was greatly facilitated by having a closed market. The only way foreign companies could profit from that market was to sell knowhow. By playing one off against another, the Japanese could get a good deal. Then, by holding up approval, the bureaucrats could bring further pressure to bear to ensure that only the best was acquired at the lowest price. According to one authority, Japan's total payments for imported technology from 1952 to 1980 amounted to $45–50 billion. That was less than the United States spent on R&D in 1980 alone. For that price, Japan 'got basically the whole stock of the new technology created by foreign countries'. It was, indeed, 'the greatest fire sale in history'.[8]

For the first two and perhaps three postwar decades, it was ludicrous to speak of research and development in Japan. There was only development. In fact, during the first decade, it was largely copying. But, unlike many others, the Japanese felt a strong urge to improve on what they borrowed. They patiently upgraded the products and refined the production techniques. Over time, they were able to generate articles that were superior in some ways, perhaps with a nicer design, more convenient size, higher quality. Production became more and more efficient, turning out finer products at lower costs. In time, the items that had been borrowed from others could be sold back to them under better conditions than they could be made locally.

The emphasis on development, improvement, even innovation can still be seen clearly from today's R&D statistics. Most of the private-sector work is devoted to application and product development. Even the government institutes and universities concentrate much of their effort on this. The share left over for basic research was under 15 per cent in 1990. Thus, most of the vast increase which brought total R&D expenditure to about ¥12 trillion in 1990 was of direct commercial benefit.[9]

Considering the funding structure, it is not surprising that the commercial side was stressed. By far the largest contribution to R&D spending was made by the private sector. Companies provided 70 per cent of the total in 1990, much higher than elsewhere. Another 18 per cent came from the universities and the rest, only 12 per cent, from the government. By 1980, it was spending over ¥1 trillion a year to promote science and technology and this only increased to about ¥1.5 trillion in 1990. This money was allocated largely to MOE (45 per cent), STA (25 per cent) and MITI (10 per cent).

Since the government's portion was unusually low, it was argued that Japan was not really subsidising research unduly, as foreign critics insisted.[10] Other governments were spending much more.[11] But this explanation is meaningless. The amount could well be smaller because so little of it was devoted to work of a general nature, whether for medicine, social sciences or basic research. And almost nothing went into defence which absorbed much of the Western and Soviet budgets. Nearly all of Japan's public sector R&D had some commercial spinoff.

In addition it should be pointed out that, even in those R&D programmes clearly biased toward development, there was a tendency to stress relatively few topics. Most of the effort was focused on areas that were of special interest at the time. This once included basic materials like steel, other metals, chemicals and petrochemicals. It then shifted to machinery, electronics and computers. Now there is a growing component of biotechnology, alternative energy, new materials and aerospace. This concentration naturally generated results faster and more abundantly than the broader research done overseas.

What is more, it fitted in very nicely with targeting. It is evident from reading the list of projects that they were compatible with the industrial policy of the day. Often enough, the projects were designed to allow Japanese companies or industries to catch up. On occasion, they were to provide a strategic breakthrough or help them pull ahead. They were never undertaken just to acquire knowledge. Actually, often enough, the projects were tied to the introduction or improvement of a specific article, indeed, sometimes of a specific model.

In this process the integration of public and private R&D was exceptionally close. The government, working through the various ministries and agencies, established a dense network of institutes and laboratories. In addition to national centres, there were prefectural and even municipal units. They were all at the disposal of the business community and maintained close relations with the surrounding companies in the given sector. In some cases they would do their own work and allow companies to acquire the knowhow free of charge. In others, they would carry out projects requested or suggested by companies.

While the government institutes did a lot of work for the private sector, specific companies were sometimes brought into national projects. They would be asked to provide researchers to work in government laboratories or carry out research for the government in their own facilities. Frequently, companies were grouped for collaborative research projects. Most of this was partly or entirely paid for out of the national budget. The more abstract a project, the less commercial benefit it offered, the larger the government's share would be.

This distinction between projects affected the methods of financing them. For research with more general goals and limited practical applications, the government would foot the bill by giving companies 'research contracts' or 'consignments' (*itakuhi*). Where a reasonable commercial return could be expected, the government would only provide a 'matching grant' (*hojokin*) and the company had to raise the rest of the money. But this distinction was rather theoretical. While the grants were supposed to be repaid in the event of commercial success, some never were and, in practice, became subsidies.

To outside observers, Japan's narrow focus and limited resources were considered to be serious limitations. That was not the view of most businessmen and bureaucrats, who knew better. By restricting efforts to fewer sectors and a lower level of sophistication, namely application and development rather than basic research, it was possible to accomplish much more with less. Every yen invested had a much bigger payoff. After all, it took relatively fewer researchers to do the work, laboratories could be less extensively equipped and the budgets much smaller.

Equally important, as Okimoto pointed out, is the fact that 'the United States served as the technological pioneer and Japan as the follower. For firstcomers, the costs of R&D are usually far higher than for latecomers, if only because the level of initial uncertainty is so much greater; failures and false starts are almost unavoidable. Latecomers, knowing what has worked and what has not, have a decided advantage in that they deal with less uncertainty.'[12]

Not until the early 1980s did the Japanese admit that they had to do more. For one thing, they were irritated by the charges of being a nation of copiers, capable perhaps of innovation but certainly not of creativity. They were ashamed at having produced so few Nobel Prize winners. But they were much more concerned by the fact that they were running out of technologies which could be borrowed. Foreign companies were no longer as willing to license them and, if they did, demanded much stiffer fees.

It was finally necessary to move from application and development to more fundamental work. If not, Japan could not pull ahead of its Western rivals. That it still lagged far behind in this respect was conceded by the 1981 White Paper on Science and Technology. It noted that, despite any progress, Japan was not doing well enough on 'innovative, creative technology'. Although it had made many 'improvements on existing technology', it contributed a much smaller share of 'epochal breakthroughs' than the United States, Britain, France or Germany.[13]

This atmosphere sparked renewed efforts to raise the technological level and many stirring appeals to show greater creativity. There were some results. By the mid-1980s, Japan was devoting 2.6 per cent of GNP to R&D. By the early 1990s, it was about 3 per cent. That already put it ahead of the United States and everywhere else. Yet, it was planned to boost the level to 3.6 per cent by the mid-1990s. Meanwhile, Japanese patent applications multiplied sharply and more technologies were exported than ever. The technological level of its products and facilities continued rising. And it had more engineers and researchers per 1000 workers than any other country, so the advance could be sustained.

This was all positive. But it was not quite as radical a transformation as desired. The share of basic research actually slipped since the state could expand less because of budget restraints. Private companies showed little wish to do more abstract work and stuck to commercially-oriented projects with a quick payback. They still imported technology and increasingly hired foreign researchers, set up institutes abroad or cooperated with foreign universities to round out their programmes. As for creativity, while it was loudly praised and ardently sought, there was no sign that it was being generated by Japanese society or corporate culture.

THE COMPETITIVE URGE

Nearly all the techniques referred to so far existed elsewhere in other latecomer countries which were seeking economic development and industrialisation through import substitution. There was no shortage of tariffs and quotas in the Third World. The governments not only facilitated loans, they did not hesitate to grant huge subsidies. Technologies were licensed, laboratories opened and foreign companies invited to invest and produce locally.

But the results were wanting. Indeed, in most other countries these techniques have been a formula for disaster. With a protected market, companies did not have to worry much about alternative sourcing and could manufacture mediocre products. The technologies they acquired did not have to be properly assimilated and updated so production remained inefficient. Yet, since their products could be sold at artificially high prices in the absence of imports, companies could make fat profits. Many of them, alas, skimmed off the profits or paid bribes to be covered by more state subsidies.

Japan was not entirely free of such misfortunes, no matter what its supporters may say. This occurred in sectors which remained protected too long or where some few companies controlled the market too thoroughly. It also cropped up in the state corporations which ran the telephone and telegraph networks, the tobacco monopoly and the national railways. But there has been comparatively little.

The best explanation for this superior performance can be traced to an element which was lacking elsewhere and often spelled the difference between success and failure. It is competition. With competition, 'infant industries' had to be sufficiently robust to survive for more valid reasons than import restrictions and government support. Companies had to be well organised and make the best use of capital, technology and labour so as to hold on to sales. Managers had to develop articles which offered better characteristics, higher quality, lower prices, speedier delivery and so on. Realising this, companies (and managers) had no choice but to move up or go under. Helping them excessively only weakened the urge for improvement.

Japan was not a perfect capitalist economy in which free enterprise prevailed, especially not in the first postwar decades. But there was always a degree of competition. It could be real or potential, present or future, spontaneous or contrived, artificially heightened or attenuated. No matter what form it took, competition was a constant challenge.

Some of the competition had perfectly natural causes, such as could – or should – have applied anywhere else. For example, while the market was closed for specific products, the government regularly warned that this was just a temporary situation. In practice, the restrictions were usually maintained for relatively long periods. But there was enough outside pressure for Japan to get into step, so that it was perfectly clear to businessmen that eventually most of the protection would have to go. Any company or industry which did not upgrade adequately to survive in a freer environment would be in trouble.

Moreover, while the domestic market was regulated, external markets were not. They were highly competitive. This was particularly so in the biggest markets to which Japanese companies exported, the United States and Europe. It was also true of the third markets on which Japanese products faced American and European ones. To sell exports, it was necessary to improve products and production techniques to overcome such competitors. So the element of export orientation, which did not appear in the strategies of most late developers, provided a further impetus.

However, the government did not leave it at that. Political leaders ceaselessly appealed to businessmen to expand operations and enhance productivity for patriotic reasons. The only way for Japan to make its mark on the postwar international scene, they said, was through economic progress and proficiency. Japanese products had to be refined since they were a reflection on the nation. Above all, quality had to be improved. Thus, quality standards were adopted and quality marks proudly displayed. To avoid any shoddy goods spoiling the reputation of the rest, certain articles had to meet stringent conditions before they could be exported.

It was further necessary to prevent half-hearted efforts or outright abuses in implementing government programmes. This need was felt most acutely by the bureaucrats who monitored specific industries since they were, in a sense, held responsible for the ability of companies to shape up. A waste of state finances or abuse of protection would reflect poorly on them. If companies failed to withstand international competition when it finally reached Japan, the corresponding bureaucrats would also be criticised. Those in charge of industrial targeting thus did more than simply help the companies, they pressured managers to make the best use of any aid.

In addition, the targeting aspect itself injected a big dose of competition. Once sectors were picked by the government, it was assumed that they would do well and some regarded it almost as a patriotic duty to compete. Since financial and technological support was provided, and the market would be protected, the temptation was even greater. With the stress on scale, it was necessary to get in fast and expand rapidly or be squeezed out. Managers therefore fought aggressively to keep up with the others and a cautious leader was less admired than a highly ambitious one.

Industrial targeting not only generated a particularly fierce species of competition, it conditioned the typical strategy adopted by the Japanese. Since only a few sectors were targeted for accelerated progress rather than advancing more slowly over a broader range, companies tended to concentrate their efforts. Because of the need for huge sales to justify the massive scale, they selected one or two standard products and launched a frontal attack on the market. Weaker companies, domestic or foreign, had to retreat into specialised or higher value added articles. However, once they held the high ground of standard products, the invaders could easily pick off the defenders in one niche after the other.

Yet, this was not enough for the economic bureaucrats. They wanted to mould the toughest, most competitive companies possible. This was not just done in a general way, through kindly advice or stirring exhortations. Full-blown programmes were adopted to enhance the performance of companies in targeted sectors through 'industrial rationalisation' (*sangyo gorika*). This policy had already been applied before and during the war and was revised and updated in the postwar period. Although it had roots in movements in such diverse places as Germany, the United States and the Soviet Union, it became distinctively and emphatically Japanese.

Rationalisation was not achieved through a specific technique, clearly defined by the authorities and then implemented. Instead, it expressed an abiding concern to make Japanese manufacturers competitive and whatever measures were deemed appropriate under given circumstances were used. It gradually developed an international as well as a domestic dimension and could be applied to growth sectors as well as to declining ones.

One set of measures was used to foster strong companies in emerging sectors. As concerned the plant and equipment, no effort was spared to get the best that was available, even if this were not strictly necessary in a country where labour was still relatively cheap. Rather than improve the existing facilities, or replace older equipment with new machinery, the more popular approach was to clear the land and put up brand new plants under the motto of 'scrap and build'. Close attention was paid not only to a plant's design but also to the surrounding infrastructure. The scale, as must be obvious, was as large and as near to the optimum as possible. Then, on a regular basis, the machinery, layout, production processes, supplies, warehousing and so on would be improved. The goal was the highest productivity attainable.

There was also a human side to this. Workers were carefully recruited and trained, they were taught to handle several jobs so they could be moved about from one workplace to another and even from one subsidiary to another. Employees were enrolled in the rationalisation process by being encouraged to suggest improvements, including those which would make jobs redundant. In most factories there were productivity movements and, in many, workers joined QC Circles to understand their functions better.

Other aspects were not as pleasant, often referred to disparagingly by those concerned as 'Japanese-style rationalisation'. Employees had to put in long hours including considerable overtime when business was good. They had to endure less-than-ideal conditions in most factories and downright poor ones with smaller firms. When business was bad, workers would be pushed hard, expected to get by with marginal wage hikes (or wage cuts) and sometimes sent to other, usually lesser, companies or even dismissed.

The goals for declining sectors were not terribly different from those for expanding ones. They still had to maintain reasonable scale and remain highly efficient to hold on to as much sales as possible. This also implied rationalisation, albeit of a somewhat different nature. The older plants and more obsolete machinery had to be scrapped to raise the average level of productivity. While not much new equipment could be acquired, everything was done to work the existing lot efficiently. The harsher aspects, alas, were more in view.

Workers were pushed yet harder, subcontractors were squeezed and managers had to make do on tight margins, if any, while employees were lucky to have a job.

In most of these activities, the company management took the lead and the bureaucrats merely assisted where they could. The government provided the necessary infrastructure so that supplies could be delivered and goods shipped more readily. State banks offered favourable terms for loans to buy new machinery or build new plants as well as to scrap old, excess machinery and close down factories. But they did little more concerning the viability of domestic producers in the national context. Where the bureaucrats intervened most regularly and most decisively was to hold back foreign interlopers. To that end, they protected emerging sectors until sufficient rationalisation had occurred for them to compete against imports and export effectively. And they protected declining sectors until they had solved their problems and could survive in a reduced market.

The fact that competitiveness increasingly meant international competitiveness explains the growing stress on 'industrial structure' (*sangyo kozo*). It was felt that the economy as a whole had to be reinforced. This was done by selecting strategic industries where rationalisation was pursued more thoroughly and forcefully. As one industry became viable, it helped the next which was then targeted and rationalised. It was claimed that the purpose of structural policy was also to hasten the phasing out of older, weaker sectors, which had become a drag. But that rarely happened. Instead, they were usually preserved as long as possible by yet more drastic rationalisation cures.

The last permutation of rationalisation is the most intriguing. In order to make Japan more competitive internationally, it was deemed necessary to regulate competition domestically. This was stimulated by the conviction that there was a deep, almost innate sense of rivalry which prevailed among the Japanese in general and was further intensified by the economic pressures of the business world. Companies saw new possibilities opening up and pounced on them before others could preempt the market. Since there were incentives which made growth easier, they were even more eager to get in. However, since there were soon too many in a given sector, the competition was exceptionally acute. In fact, it was regarded as harmful and perhaps ruinous and stigmatised as 'excessive competition' or *kato kyoso*.

This intense competition actually worried the bureaucrats more than any conceivable lack; they conveniently forgot that much of it was their own fault for pushing size and scale. If it were given free reign, or so they claimed, Japan would remain a nation of numerous, small, weak and quarrelsome firms which could not possibly defend the national market or venture abroad. What is more, the turbulence would inevitably result in bankruptcies, unemployment and social confusion for which they would also be condemned. Cooperation (*kyocho*) was a much better tack, especially while competing with the outside world.

The bureaucrats therefore tried to replace the rivalry with more harmonious relations both among companies and between business and the government. A first step was to organise each sector more strictly. Companies were encouraged to join trade associations which could monitor the situation and promote joint activities. They would serve as a means of feeding information to the bureaucracy and passing along any guidance. In sectors where competition was deemed too strong, measures would be taken to palliate any fragmentation. This might include joint procurement, marketing or research. In some cases, to attain scale, it could involve mergers. Under particularly serious circumstances, it might go as far as cartels.

The most extraordinary idea here was to regulate the number of companies in a given sector, a gross violation of the principles of free enterprise. This arose from the prevailing contempt for small companies, seen elsewhere as a source of ferment and vitality but, in Japan, as symptomatic of instability and weakness. So much can be read from the comments of Yoshihiko Morozumi, then head of MITI's Industrial Policy Bureau. 'The existence of numerous small-scale enterprises never contributes to the development of new technology. When an excessive number of firms, for a given market size, are reduced by means of mergers and unification, it will lead to economies of scale and ability to expand into new technological frontiers.'[14]

In this sense, as Henry Rosovsky commented, 'Japan must be the only capitalistic country in the world in which the government decides how many firms there should be in a given industry and then sets about to arrange the desired number.'[15] Obviously, the control was far from absolute although it worked amazingly well in new sectors which were only just emerging, often under targeting. There, bureaucrats could partially regulate numbers from the start by rationing out technology licences, authorisations of joint ventures, preferential financing and so on. It was much harder in existing sectors or those where entry was easy and cheap. But it was not really so necessary once crowding created an awareness among the rivals that competition was hurting more than helping. In declining sectors, the most congested of all, it was often the companies which turned to the government to help them cooperate in their mutual interest.

The various attempts at moderating competition, not too little, not too much, did not always work. Quite often, companies entered sectors whether they were invited or not, they tried to overwhelm their counterparts by all possible means and they were not much interested in 'live and let live'. But this unruly, unregulated competition actually contributed to 'harmony' in another way. Periodic shakeouts kept reducing the circle of players and the fewer there were, the more they cooperated with one another. Indeed, in some sectors where oligopolies prevailed, they cooperated too much. Nonetheless, competition was able to play an essential part in strengthening the economy.

CREATING THE RIGHT CLIMATE

The last technique is harder to define tightly, and the methods are considerably more diffuse, but there is no question of its importance. Industrial policy and targeting cannot be undertaken unless the crucial actors approve of this approach. And they can be vastly more effective if the population as a whole cooperates or is at least receptive. That cannot simply be assumed. To the contrary, creating the right climate is an activity that must be plugged at constantly.

It can be achieved in many ways, the most evident of which is public relations. The government and its various bodies can go about praising the advantages of growth and, while so doing, play down the benefits or desirability of any other goals which might conflict with or merely get in the way of economic expansion. This was done regularly with an accent on what the Japanese came to call GNPism. To boost GNP, naturally, it was necessary to put 'production first', another once popular slogan.

This provided the framework for more specific action to improve the image of industrial targeting. This was a function of MITI's periodic 'visions' and more frequent reports. They notified the public of which sectors and products were being targeted and therefore deserved higher priority. It was realised early on that dull bureaucratic jargon would not help to get the message across, and the targeters outdid themselves in coining catchy and fashionable phrases.

They offered Japan an 'information society'. They launched a project for a 'fifth generation computer'. They promised a 'technopolis' in which to live.

The bureaucrats also worked very hard at consensus building. They repeatedly met with businessmen to win support for the specific exercises. It did not take long for both cliques to extol the virtues of biotechnology, or nuclear energy or whatever product was the latest to be promoted. Targets were fixed, often implying a doubling in a rather short period, and widely proclaimed. Charts were drawn with a standard onward-and-upward pattern. Then the general public was led to assume that by developing this particular product many more jobs would be created, sales and exports would boom, and life would be infinitely more comfortable and rewarding.

To involve the people in these exercises, the politicians and bureaucrats spawned countless advisory committees and deliberative councils. They met amidst fanfare and endorsed major reports or targets. But it is uncertain whether this stratagem had much impact since the members were not ordinary workaday Japanese but the same old bureaucrats, politicians and businessmen plus a smattering of sympathetic academics who were frequently involved in initiating the very programmes they now applauded. The effect was often, if my zen is not incorrect, the sound of one hand clapping.

The lead role in these public-relations, opinion-forming, consensus-building campaigns was taken by the bureaucrats. They clearly realised the benefits of a favourable atmosphere. It was not hard to bring the business community into line. All businessmen knew that there were concrete advantages to be had. Nor were the politicians unwilling to push for economic growth. That was a positive – and vague – plank that everybody could support. But ordinary people were pulled in various directions. They wanted growth and material goods, they also wanted leisure and security. No matter how much they backed the company, they also had a family to think of. And younger generations were increasingly individualistic and increasingly unwilling to put national interests above personal ones.

Thus, the task all along was to convince broad segments of the population that it was necessary to sacrifice other goals to economic development. This was fairly easy right after the war, when the country was devastated and it was necessary to rebuild in order to survive. The impulse could be sustained later by noting how backward Japan still was and that it had to catch up for reasons of self-respect. Appeals for greater prosperity helped further on. But, as Japan pulled ahead and became a leader in many ways, GNPism became suspect.

Nonetheless, for an amazingly long period of time, the bureaucrats could find new excuses. More recently, they stressed Japan's need to diversify markets and introduce new products in case protectionism got worse. Each time there was a recession at home, or abroad, the dangers of slackening the pace were highlighted. When the yen appreciated, a perfectly natural phenomenon given the circumstances, it was dubbed a 'heavy yen' crisis. This *endaka* implied the need to become even more competitive so that prices could be brought down further.

Still, if production came first, then other things had to come second, third . . . or last. There were a fair number of goals which were actively pursued abroad but neglected in Japan. They included, among others, amenities, the environment, leisure, welfare and social justice. This is the flip side of the stress on economic development and the sacrifices made to keep industrial targeting going.

The most obvious effect of channelling so much finance into industrialisation was that fewer amenities could be built. There was less money for roads and highways, public buildings and parks, even piped water and sewage. With more funds pumped into generating greater output, less could be put aside for health and welfare. Because of long hours at the office or factory, there was less time for leisure. And the environmental impact of new industrial projects was often overlooked in the race to produce more.

This much was realised. And it had to be conceded that fixing priorities implied less attention to these aspects. But the bureaucrats and politicians did not leave it at that. By act and omission, they skewed the situation even more toward growth and away from other concerns. There are endless examples of how this was done, only some of which are mentioned here.

With regard to the environment, MITI and other bureaucrats repeatedly backed business interests in the effort to prevent stricter legislation and stricter enforcement. They allowed factories to be put up almost anywhere, often without taking adequate precautions to avoid damage to the environment. Rather than impose stiff fines for violations of the initially lax laws, they stuck to mere admonitions and warnings. When the first cases of environmental disease broke out, they participated in the cover-up. Only when the situation had become serious and the population pressed for improvement did the government finally create an Environment Agency, which was still kept weak and subject to MITI's views.

The same thing happened with nuclear energy. The bureaucrats initially glossed over the complaints of persons living in the vicinity of new plants. If the opponents could not be convinced by reason, they were often bought off with public monies. Those who continued agitating were then put down by the police. There was a repeat for dangerous products and medicines. They were largely ignored until serious accidents or diseases occurred and even then the bureaucrats had to be pushed to adopt, and then to enforce, stricter rules. Yet, even today, there is no product-liability law in Japan, the only advanced country without it. And the MITIocrats are doing their best to keep one from being adopted.

Just as MITI muzzled EA, it kept the Fair Trade Commission on a short leash. FTC officials repeatedly criticised companies for forming cartels or colluding on sales. Numerous cases of price fixing and gouging were uncovered in the course of the years. But amazingly little was done aside from periodic remonstrations in particularly blatant cases or those which had been played up in the media. Otherwise, the practices continued, frequently in different forms, while the culprits paid a petty fine which was hardly a deterrent.[16]

Since so much depended on a hardworking (and docile) labour force, labour regulations were extremely important and the labour bureaucrats did their bit. The legislation already provided for long daily and weekly hours plus considerable overtime, but even they were not enforced. Workers could be persuaded to work more 'voluntarily' or to give up some of their statutory vacation. The minimum wages were so low as to be meaningless. Even safety regulations were often overlooked until serious accidents occurred. And, while regular employees enjoyed reasonable social benefits and protection against dismissal, little was done for part-time, temporary or piece workers.

At this point, the welfare bureaucrats joined in with the labour bureaucrats to create the ideal atmosphere for hard work. Unemployment relief was restricted as much as possible in terms of numbers of persons covered, amounts granted and length of coverage. If you lost your job, it was best to find another one quickly. As for retirement, social security and welfare remained skimpy, not only in the 1950s and 1960s, even into the 1990s. So employees were not only more dependent on a company pension, they tended to work until much later ages than elsewhere. The reason, as every opinion poll showed, was not that they enjoyed work but that they needed the extra money to get by.

Alongside such broad measures, there were occasionally more specific contributions to sales. For example, all Japanese cars were subject to regular inspections (*shaken*). These were so strict that most drivers bought new cars more often than was really necessary. This was clearly not because the authorities were worried about safety. For the selfsame bureaucrats allowed motos to be driven without a licence. Even repeated accidents caused by inexperienced drivers, many of them fatal, did not result in stricter legislation.

Bureaucrats in the Ministry of Justice also played along. They managed to keep the quantity of litigation comparatively low, which saved companies enormous amounts on legal fees plus any compensation that might have been levied. This was especially helpful with regard to dangerous medicines, few of which cases arose. For antitrust, although individuals could bring complaints, few ever did. Even in the more visible instance of pollution victims, not only were the number of suits quite modest, the trials lasted so long and the awards were so small that this was not a favoured recourse. Incidentally, the lack of litigation was caused not only by cultural hangups or supposed harmony but by a shortage of judges and lawyers, the time and costs involved, and a negative mood instilled by the ministry.[17]

In such ways, the bureaucrats clearly bolstered the sectors they backed or the economy more generally. It would be naive to regard this as anything but intentional. For, even when their attention was called to the dangers and abuses, they gave precedence to production. Nor could it be said that these measures did not affect the targeting exercises or help Japanese companies. Any foreign businessman will tell you how much he would love to have cheaper workers putting in longer hours, less hassle on safety, a chance to collude on prices and, in general, a government that 'understands' his needs and problems.

In this chapter, and the others too, considerably more is said about the role of the bureaucrats than that of the politicians. The reason is quite simple. Japan's politicians had rather little to do with industrial targeting. In fact, they did not have much to do with economic policy, or 'running the country', in general. Even such crucial functions as budgeting, drafting and adopting legislation, and supervising execution of the laws, were left to the bureaucrats by and large. And this was seen by many of the bureaucratophiles as their chief contribution. By staying on the sidelines, politicians did not 'politicise' industrial targeting, did not drag in extraneous matters, did not root for one sector or company over another, did not direct funds toward other, more popular, goals.[18]

If that can be called a 'contribution', then it must be credited to the ruling Liberal Democratic Party which, despite more than four decades in office, never actually 'governed'. But it did pitch in with regard to public relations, consensus building and the like. Its political platform was plainly oriented toward growth, and other planks (ecology, welfare, leisure and so on) were only added slowly and under duress. Even more significant, the LDP managed to keep defence spending down to about 1 per cent of gross national product. That was a tremendous saving, one whose magnitude and significance should not be underestimated. Alas, on the debit side, pet programmes wasted lots of money on the inefficient and costly agricultural, construction and distribution sectors.[19]

While the LDP's Diet members did not know how to run the government, they were extremely proficient at winning elections. Thanks largely to a passive electorate and enormous financial backing from business, most were returned time and again. This provided unequalled political stability ever since the war. That was a tremendous boon to targeters and company executives who could adopt long-term plans with rather little concern that some unexpected political twist might unravel them.

COMPANY TARGETING

Many observers mistakenly assume that only governments engage in targeting and that similar techniques cannot be applied by private companies. When considering the various aspects referred to above, it becomes evident that companies can take special measures that are similar or have similar effects. Indeed, they are doing it all the time. The only difference is that Japanese companies, as latecomers, have a clearer idea of what they are about and they have also polished their techniques to make the exercises more effective.

This sort of activity usually takes place within groups of companies, the group phenomenon being extremely widespread and well adapted. As noted, there are three types of groups and each has its own approach. The first are broad, horizontal groups with members in many different sectors, the 'intra-market' *keiretsu*. The second are vertical groups of suppliers and subcontractors established by leading manufacturers, especially in the assembly industries. The third are networks of distributors controlled by a major manufacturer.[20]

An intra-market *keiretsu*, despite its many ramifications, may feel that the coverage is not complete or that a new sector has opened in which it would like to have a participating company. It could therefore select one of the existing members as its champion to enter the sector and then support it. Or it could take an outside company and integrate it. Or, for a completely new activity, it could create a brand new company as a subsidiary of one or more members. Targeting of this sort was almost systematic under the so-called 'one set' system where each group sought to have a member in every sector.[21]

In a vertical group, the manufacturer may decide that it wants to add a new product to its line and manufacture it internally. If the product becomes important enough, the respective division may eventually be spun off as a subsidiary. For parts and components, it may decide to help one of its suppliers develop them. If there are no suitable suppliers, it could create a new one or absorb an existing vendor. The distribution groups do less of this although they are now increasing the range of 'own-brand' articles, usually supplied by a related or dependent company.

Having targeted and launched a new product, either individually or through their groups, companies can provide roughly the same kind of backing a government does. This can also be summed up under the headings of market, finance, technology, competition and climate.

When it comes to the market, the *keiretsu* is an ideal setting in which to cultivate a promising new product since it can be bought by one or more members. They are not bound to do so. But, if the relations were close, they would certainly give a member company precedence and purchase goods if they were of almost as high quality, almost as cheap, almost as readily available, and so on. This preferential treatment would give the newcomer time and money to improve the quality, price and delivery schedule to compete with others. The temporary loss to group members would presumably be recouped later on and they would at least be pleased to have another useful participant in the group.

For horizontal groups, the situation is much simpler. Each group is run by a major manufacturer which needs a large number of products and parts. If one of its own subsidiaries, suppliers or subcontractors can provide them, it will purchase the goods. It will purchase them in sufficiently large quantities to permit scale economies and at prices adequate to cover costs and make the necessary investments to become a first-rate vendor. These costs will also hopefully be recouped later on when the newcomer is as competitive as the rest. In addition, dividends will go to the mother company if this is a subsidiary.

Sales to individual consumers can be obtained through the distribution networks, which are closely related to leading manufacturers and sometimes dominated by them. Through connections with the wholesalers and retailers, they can be urged not to carry competing products, or, at least, to give them less favourable treatment. In some industries, where exclusive agents only carry one brand and jointly account for the bulk of sales, they can almost exclude outside producers. Meanwhile, the turnover of the captive outlets should be adequate to achieve scale and refine product quality.

An interesting variation arises with the trading companies, whether smaller specialised ones or the huge general trading companies. It works in two directions. The trader may find a foreign market where existing products could readily be replaced by better or cheaper ones, and prevail on a Japanese manufacturer to supply them. Or they may be importing foreign products which could just as well be made locally. They would then ask a related company to manufacture them or set up a subsidiary. Whatever form this takes, trading companies can be extremely effective targeters since they know the markets so well and sometimes actually dominate them.

Finance can also be arranged through the group. Much of the funds needed by a manufacturer come from not just any commercial bank but the one at the centre of the *keiretsu*.[22] From this bank it will get preferential treatment in the sense both of obtaining loans more readily and of getting them on better conditions. Since commercial loans are already relatively cheap in Japan, this makes them exceptionally cheap. Assistance in issuing and placing stock comes from the group securities house. The group insurance company and other related companies will probably buy shares.

Within the vertical groups the relationship is even closer since the parent company owns stock in many of the suppliers which are merely subsidiaries, and controls the others because it is the main – and sometimes only – client. If it is developing a new product itself and needs more funds it can squeeze them by imposing lower prices and delaying payments. If, on the other hand, it is having a new product or part developed by a supplier, it can advance money or guarantee loans with the group bank. Trading companies can do the same with their suppliers.

Japanese companies have little difficulty in acquiring the technologies they need. Two of the methods have been mentioned. Licensing of technology from foreign companies is very widespread and, if it is the only way, a Japanese manufacturer will accept a joint venture. But the most common technique, less often referred to because it is considerably less reputable, should not be forgotten. That is 'reverse engineering'. Companies buy a sample of an interesting product, take it apart to see how it works, and then produce it themselves. They can glean further information from the technical literature or patent applications.

Obviously, there are limits to this approach. It is increasingly essential to upgrade any internal research and development effort. This has been generally recognised and the amount of private R&D has been rising steadily. Large companies in most sectors now allocate 2 per cent of sales, or more, to R&D and smaller firms somewhat less. In technology-intensive fields like electronics, telecommunications and pharmaceuticals, top companies spend as much as 10 per cent of sales. For chemicals, precision machinery and automobiles, it ranges from 3 to 5 per cent. About 500 000 corporate employees are engaged in these activities and the ranks keep swelling. Japan's levels are already higher than the OECD averages and yet they continue rising.

With regard to competition, as mentioned, the bureaucrats' biggest fear was not that it would be insufficient but rather that it would be so intense as to leave companies too weak to compete internationally. They need not have worried. This process, left to itself, quickly weeded out the weaker rivals and left comparatively few, comparatively strong players which were perfectly capable of looking after themselves. Still, the competition was so frenzied on occasion that it did appear ruinous and destructive, meriting its calling of *kato kyoso*.

To understand this, it must be remembered that Japanese competition was not the same brand that prevailed in other capitalist countries. It was not based primarily on profit. Market share and market control were much more significant. This was partially for cultural reasons, since factors like size and ranking were traditionally more respected, while making money was looked down upon. There were also practical reasons. It was necessary to boost sales in order to benefit from larger scale and more efficient production processes. In addition, since the domestic market was relatively empty for most new products, it was possible to expand more swiftly than elsewhere and also advisable to do so smartly before others got in and preempted it. Companies thus paid very close attention to market share, their own and that of their keenest rivals.[23]

This does not mean that profit was unimportant, a company could not last indefinitely without it. But it was much less urgent. In a pinch, Japanese companies would sacrifice profit for market share whereas Western companies would do the opposite. Japanese managers explained that the purpose was actually to maximise long-term profit and, in a sense, they were right. By selling more, even with slimmer margins, it was sometimes possible to have a larger total return. The more pertinent explanation was that, by pushing other companies out of the market entirely, those which remained could pretty well impose their prices and gain a handsome windfall. That is why many Japanese economists refer to the system as 'monopoly capitalism'.

Thus, in the initial phase of an emerging industry, sector or product, companies competed vigorously with one another to obtain more sales. At first, they expanded smoothly enough within the group of related and friendly companies. But, to attain larger scale and more market share, they had to compete more aggressively on all aspects, including price. They would offer their goods at whatever price was necessary to sell more than the next. As this degenerated into *kato kyoso*, many succumbed. Those which survived were usually those with the largest secure market and the strongest financial support. Quality, service, delivery and so on were of some interest but not as decisive as market and finance.

Once things had been sorted out somewhat and there were only a dozen or so remaining companies, the competition often entered an even more acute phase. For it was no longer a general melee but a matching of rival companies one-on-one. It became almost personal, with the few top companies trying to gain an edge over one another, the middle runners trying to push into the front ranks, and the laggards struggling to keep up. The fiercest contenders were usually smaller firms which feared that if they lost any more market share they would disappear. The battle was only intensified when companies represented different groups.

Only when the pack had thinned yet further and there were only about half-a-dozen remaining makers of any size did the competition slacken. By then, each had a pretty good idea of its ranking and the chances of improving it were smaller. The costs of gaining market share were so high that renewed competition was not really justified by the potential benefits. At that point, in an oligopolistic (and sometimes monopolistic) setting, there was a marked willingness to limit competition to such things as quality or service . . . but not price. The time had come to rake in the profits that had been foregone for so long.

Yet, while things were calmer on the domestic market, they might be heating up elsewhere. Companies which had lost market share at home still needed adequate scale to produce efficiently and thus strove desperately to increase their exports. Leading companies, afraid they might be outflanked abroad and thereby give their rivals another chance on the home market, also stepped up their efforts. Unseemly competitive battles then erupted overseas. Since foreign companies insisted on profits they often lost market share to the Japanese who were so obsessed with the prolongations of domestic rivalries that they hardly noticed they were crushing the foreign industry. When they finally had enough market share to satisfy them, or when foreign governments acted to restrict market penetration, this side of the competition might be stilled.

Thus, Japan underwent cycles of competition and coexistence or cooperation which closely followed the rhythm of industrial policy and targeting. When a new sector was picked, the existing companies were quickly joined by new ones set up by groups or leading manufacturers who wanted to expand their product range. There were soon too many for the market and, in one round of *kato kyoso* after another, the number decreased. Some went bankrupt, others just withdrew with losses, and a few barely held on by exporting. Only when a small band remained did things calm down in that sector. By then a mad dash had begun into other sectors that were targeted.

When it comes to creating the proper climate, businessmen almost outdid the bureaucrats. By stressing how imperative it was that the company succeed, they enrolled workers in quality-control circles and productivity drives. They got them to work fully not only during normal hours but even after hours, whether in the QC Circles, or coming up with more suggestions, or participating in supposedly social activities with fellow employees which always had some payoff for the company. Then, as each new product was launched, this was proudly announced on bulletin boards and in newsletters and employees were urged to buy the company or group brand. It would be hard to imagine a Seiko employee wearing a Citizen watch or a Toyota worker driving a Nissan into the company parking lot.

Why management had so much leverage was not hard to figure out. It had wed its destiny to that of the staff more tightly than anywhere else. The key was 'lifetime employment', at least for those who had it. Since they would be with the same company throughout their career, and then depend on its pension, employees could only prosper if the company did so as well. This potently drove employees to work harder and think more deeply of company interests than in places where a job was just a job and a clear line was drawn between working life and personal interests.

Part II
Case Studies

4 Risen Sectors

The initial stage of postwar industrial policy was devoted to the restoration of a number of industries which had been pioneered and developed ever since the Meiji era. Most of them had risen to some prominence before the war and several received special support from the militarists, because they were regarded as providing either the sinews of an armaments industry or, more generally, the backbone of a strong, modern economy.

Thus, the task consists of two phases: rehabilitation and further development. Most liberal governments faced with similar situations stopped after the first and left the businessmen to proceed on their own. In Japan, the truly remarkable effort was related to the second, when the state continued working to make these leading sectors. Officially, they were given priority because they were basic industries which supplied essential inputs for many others. There were manifold linkages which could be exploited. These were sometimes also relatively labour-intensive sectors and thus had employment effects. But there is no doubt that the authorities still considered them the core of any modern economy to judge by the great store that was set in the catch phrase 'heavy-and-chemical industrialisation'.

The bulk of the exercise took place during the 1950s and 1960s and the lead was clearly taken by the government. It provided amazingly complete protection in the form of exchange control, tariffs, quotas and restrictions on investment. It also pumped in considerable funds, largely through long-term, low-interest loans but occasionally by outright subsidies. And it backed some useful research. On this rather solid foundation, private initiative could build.

The sectors which are dealt with here include basic materials like steel, aluminium and petroleum plus textiles. Other branches processed these materials into key products, such as ships and petrochemicals. But there was more to it than just manufacturing. The same practices favoured services like banking and insurance or shipping. A further, not so terribly different effort was directed toward agriculture. While not mentioned here, other sectors also benefited from this process, including nonferrous metals, heavy machinery and electrification.

COAL, OIL AND PETROCHEMICALS (1)

Right after the war, no challenge was more urgent than to secure sources of energy, without which it would be impossible to restore the economy. In Japan, bereft of other alternatives, this boiled down to rescuing the coal mines. They had been worked exhaustively during the war with little concern for maintaining the shafts and equipment. Production only remained high because of ruthless pressure on a workforce consisting largely of poor or minority Japanese and forced labour from Korea. It was hoped that production could be continued by pushing the miners yet harder, since funds were lacking for mechanisation. But the Koreans revolted and not enough Japanese volunteered to replace them.

This left the economy in dire straits since coal was necessary to generate electricity, fuel certain industries, heat homes and offices and so on. In particular, the steel mills could not be operated without coal and so a plan was devised of linking coal and steel. Steelmakers would get more coal, to produce more steel, to mine more coal. Both the mills and the mines enjoyed special support from the Reconstruction Finance Bank. They could also draw on the commercial banks or group members. This linkage, known as the 'priority production system' (*keisha seisan hoshiki*) was the first act of targeting.[1] It was fairly successful in that, by the early 1950s, there were 864 mines with 450 000 workers producing 50 million tons or more a year, which covered about three-quarters of the nation's energy requirements.

By the mid-1950s, however, this success began to sour as domestic coal encountered competition from foreign coal and, more significantly, much cheaper oil. The Ministry of International Trade and Industry then had to intervene for less laudable reasons. It had the Diet adopt a Coal Mining Rationalisation Law in 1955. Based on the concept of 'scrap and build', funds were raised to buy out and close down more inefficient mines and modernise more promising ones. This was organised by a Coal Mining Facilities Corporation under the supervision of MITI's Coal Industry Rationalisation Council.

No amount of rationalisation, however, could bring coal prices down sufficiently to compete with oil. MITI therefore adopted the questionable stratagem of raising the cost of oil. It had the Diet adopt a Heavy Oil Boiler Control Law which taxed boilers using oil and placed heavy duties on imported fuel oil. It was aided by the Suez crisis from 1956 to 1958, which cut off supplies of cheap oil from the Middle East. But the flow was restored and prices continued declining. In 1959, it was admitted that coal production would have to be stabilised at about 50 million tons and oil would cover a larger share of energy needs.

Finally, in 1961, oil imports were fully liberalised. This gave the oil refining sector a long awaited chance to develop properly.[2] The problem here was that MITI could not create a genuinely national industry because the supplies of oil were controlled by foreign oil companies, especially the majors. Many of the refineries were thus built by joint ventures with foreign technology and management. Not until the 1960s did MITI have a chance to break this hold. As Middle Eastern oil producers sought new customers for increasingly abundant supplies and also tried to free themselves from the majors, they turned to Japanese firms like Idemitsu and Maruzen which were strongly supported by the government.

For petrochemicals, the approach was more conventional. Regulations made it hard for foreign companies to invest dⁱrectly in the sector and they found it easier to sell their technologies and equipment. This provided an impulse for Japanese companies which benefited from the full range of support – cheap loans, government procurement, tariffs and other protective measures. They were coordinated in two major plans for 1955–60 and 1960–65. During the first, the number of entrants was restricted but during the second newcomers were allowed.

Meanwhile, other projects were launched to promote downstream sectors which used the basic petrochemicals. Makers of synthetic fibres, rubber, plastics, dyes and so on were encouraged by MITI to acquire technologies and expand production. Further on, makers of fine and special chemicals enjoyed similar backing. A special effort was made for fertiliser and ammonia production, this time under the auspices of the Ministry of Agriculture. In the more specialised downstream sectors, the manufacturers were often small and medium-sized operations, while the basic petrochemical companies were larger, including big names like Mitsui, Mitsubishi and Sumitomo.

These exercises were an apparent success. Production rose rapidly and soon covered all domestic needs with a surplus left over for exports. By the 1970s, chemicals became the fifth largest industry, accounting for about 10 per cent of total shipments, half of this coming from petrochemicals. In fact, Japan's chemical industry was second only to that of the United States.

THE STEEL INDUSTRY

Steel was the first major modern industry to be targeted by the government and no other sector enjoyed as strong and sustained promotion during the early stage of postwar development. Steel was regarded as an essential industry in itself since it was a major supplier of products and work. Immediately after the war, it was even more vital since it was necessary to reconstruct factories, housing and infrastructure. Further on, steel provided indispensable inputs for other key sectors, such as shipbuilding, machinery and automobiles.

Already, under the Occupation, the government intervened to rescue the industry on the basis of the above-mentioned priority production system whereby coal was used by steelmakers to boost production. The additional steel was used by the coal industry to mine more. This coal then flowed into the steel industry, permitting further expansion. Substantial funds for this came from the Reconstruction Finance Bank and steel production was partially subsidised. This allowed the steelmakers to recover and helped other sectors as well, although it sparked a bout of inflation.

MITI's goal, however, was not mere recovery. It wanted to turn steel into a powerful and dynamic industry. This was to be done through the modernisation of technologies, renewal of equipment and installations and an increase in scale. Included were a conversion to more efficient LD converters, improvement of sintering and other equipment, the introduction of continuous rolling, and building larger blast furnaces in integrated mills, many of them 'greenfield' works. To this end, it adopted a First Rationalisation Plan for 1950–54 and then a Second Rationalisation Plan for 1955–9.[3]

This exercise, undertaken at a time when MITI still had little experience in industrial targeting, was certainly audacious. It clearly went against the existing comparative advantage, since steel required enormous capital and advanced technologies. So the effort and cost would be tremendous. That is why targeting steel was questioned even by MITI bureaucrats and more openly disparaged in MOF and BOJ for financial reasons. But it was decided to go ahead, partially because the alternative was even less appealing. As one analyst put it, 'if the steel industry's development had been allowed to be shaped by markets rather than plans, at best only a few firms would have survived, while at worst the entire industry might well have been wiped out by competitive imports.'[4]

These plans would have been futile if MITI had not taken stringent measures to protect the steelmakers during the initial period when they were not competitive. The most effective move was simply to close the market by erecting tariff and other barriers to imports. This reserved the existing and potential market for Japanese producers. Given the size of the population, the need to make up for wartime damage and then develop further, and the number of steel-based industries targeted, this was to become the world's third biggest market.

But the steelmakers, with outmoded machinery and small capacities, could not have expanded without very broad financial support. This came in several ways. One was the provision of tax relief so that more of any earnings could be reinvested. The Ministry of Finance was quite generous, allowing rapid depreciation of equipment, exemptions on reserves for price changes and bad debts, and duty-free import of necessary equipment. Far more important was that, in a protected market, steelmakers could charge much higher prices and thus have greater earnings.

Even then, companies still needed massive loans. MITI was again instrumental in encouraging state-related banks to direct a large share of their lending to steel. In addition, these loans were on very favourable terms. The Japan Development Bank, Export–Import Bank, Industrial Bank of Japan and Long-Term Credit Bank obliged, and between them provided 40 per cent of the necessary financing during the 1950–55 period and still 12 per cent for 1956–60.[5] Thereafter, they could be supplemented and substituted by commercial banks. With state backing and actual or tacit guarantees, the larger companies had no trouble obtaining all the credit they wanted. In fact, they thrived off loans with a 12:1 debt–equity ratio well into the 1970s.

MITI was also helpful in obtaining the necessary technologies, partly by being unhelpful to outsiders. Foreign companies were not allowed to export to Japan or to set up local production. All they could do was license technologies. And the bureaucrats carefully controlled the authorisation of licences and inhibited competition among Japanese steelmakers. This forced foreign companies to sell their technologies at lower prices. At the time, of course, they did not realise that they were creating dangerous rivals for the future.[6]

Armed with cheap funds and advanced technologies, Japanese steelmakers forged ahead. Old and new producers joined the race for modernisation, hoping to gain an edge, with Kawasaki, Sumitomo, Kobe, Yawata, Nippon Kokan and Fuji in the lead. They put up one large-scale state-of-the-art mill after another. Soon Japan boasted eight of the ten largest works in the world. Steel production rose from 5 million tons in 1951 to 41 million tons in 1966 and then 100 million tons by 1972. Since mills were located along the coast, it was easy enough to receive raw materials and export finished products. Sales were facilitated domestically through membership in *keiretsu* and tighter enterprise groups, and exports were channelled through related *sogo shosha* and other traders.

It was not long before the major steelmakers ceased needing MITI's aid. And there was not that much MITI could do for them. Nonetheless, it decided to intervene again during the trade liberalisation of the 1960s. It insisted that another round of rationalisation was essential to withstand the expected onslaught of imports. It also pressed for consolidation of the industry to strengthen companies. While its loans were accepted and further upgrading took place, managers resisted most attempts at matchmaking, preferring to maintain their independence. The only result was a merger between Yawata and Fuji Steel to create Nippon Steel, Japan's largest and also the world's largest steel company.

MITI need hardly have worried. Japanese producers were already more than competitive. They could not only defend the home market from imports, they were able to export high quality, low cost steel to other industrialised countries which had not modernised as extensively. Indeed, stuck with huge capacities that often exceeded domestic demand, they were forced to export. In order to break into new markets, they charged low prices which brought only moderate profits, and occasionally engaged in outright dumping. This aroused resentment abroad and provoked trade restrictions or calls for restraint. To still these complaints and impose some discipline, MITI had to organise and supervise an endless series of export cartels.

The trouble was not that MITI did not do its work well enough. Where the worst problems arose was when it and the steelmakers were too ambitious and effective. It was easier to get them going in the 1950s than to slow them down in the 1960s and 1970s as more steel works, often with larger capacities, continued being erected. MITI tried to channel the process through meetings with executives of major companies, joined together in the Japan Iron and Steel Federation. Producers were to submit their plans for the coming year and a sub-committee of the Industrial Structure Council would indicate whether they seemed appropriate.

While the steelmakers were amenable to guidance during the

earlier period, when they depended heavily on loans and tax relief, they no longer cared by the 1960s. For some additional time, by allocating iron ore and coal, MITI could subtly bring them into line. But it was not able to stop aggressive companies that wished to boost sales, such as Sumitomo. This only provoked the others, who sought to maintain their own market share.

Periodically, the steelmakers went too far. Demand could not keep up with capacity and fierce competition set in. Price cutting ensued and, still deeply in debt, the producers were in trouble. MITI might then intervene to encourage cuts in production which would sustain prices. Or it could turn a blind eye to private arrangements to that effect, something which irritated the Fair Trade Commission. During the recession of 1964–5, MITI intervened forcefully with the specialty steelmakers, first suggesting voluntary production cutbacks, then introducing a formal production cartel and later a price cartel. With MOF, it had to save some smaller companies from bankruptcy.[7]

Yet, even the 1973 oil crisis did not put an end to the urge for expansion. MITI warned that demand would be softer and companies should be more cautious. But some still proceeded with additions or whole new plants, hoping to pull ahead of competitors. And the industry as a whole remained incorrigibly optimistic. As late as 1980, the Japan Iron and Steel Federation projected that steel output would reach 120–125 million tons by 1985 and 130–140 million tons by 1990.[8] In fact, it stabilised at about 100–110 million tons and showed little sign of improvement. Meanwhile, trusting in these and other rosy projections, capacity had been raised to some 130 million tons.

SHIPBUILDING AND TRANSPORTATION (1)

Impressive as MITI's targeting of steel was, it was actually upstaged by the promotion of shipbuilding and shipping undertaken by the Ministry of Transport. MOT provided more nurture and protection, more direct and detailed guidance and more support than MITI over a considerably longer time. It operated primarily through its Ships Bureau in liaison with the private sector, largely through a Shipbuilding Rationalisation Council and a Shipbuilding Technology Council.[9]

Despite the insistence of the Occupation authorities that Japan's shipbuilding capability should be limited after the war, MOT lost no time in initiating its plans to restore (and ultimately reinforce) the industry. Much of the existing shipping had been destroyed, which created a need. Part of the existing shipyards, on the other hand, were still in decent shape, which meant the need could be met. That is, it could be met if the companies were reorganised and sufficient funds provided to prime the pump.

Through a scheme known as 'planned shipbuilding', a government-run Shipping Corporation ordered and bought ships which were then leased to shipping companies. With money earned from operating the ships, shippers could pay the lease and these funds could be used by the corporation to have more ships built. Initially, the funds for this were supplied by the Reconstruction Finance Bank. It was soon replaced by the Japan Development Bank and commercial banks.

Planned shipbuilding was only intended to get the industry moving again and, although it had financed some 1150 ships by 1980, it was just part of the effort. Much broader financial support was provided in other ways. The Japan Development Bank devoted a large share of its loans to shipbuilding. They represented a third of the total during the 1950s and 1960s and amounted to nearly ¥2.7 trillion by 1981.[10] These loans were granted at low interest rates with long repayment periods. JDB lending served as a signal to commercial banks to advance additional funds, if not much below going rates, then certainly at reasonable levels.

Other financing came from various sources, some of them quite novel. One was a 'link' with sugar imports whereby shipbuilders were allowed to import sugar which was then being rationed, to sell it at exorbitant prices on the market, and to use the profits to subsidise export ships. The Japan Shipbuilding Industry Foundation, which holds the motorboat racing monopoly, used some of its winnings to promote shipbuilding. Since the take was good this added up to some ¥377 billion from 1962 to 1981. During the earlier period, when domestic steel was expensive, the Japan Development Bank subsidised steel purchases.

Meanwhile, shipbuilders were allowed to hold on to more of their profits through a bevy of tax benefits. These included tax-free reserves for price fluctuations, a large special depreciation account, export and investment loss reserves and tax and other fiscal incentives for overseas market development. Since they depended heavily on purchases by Japanese shipping lines, they benefited indirectly from another batch of tax breaks for the shippers.

Another form of support was the valuable research work done by the Ministry of Transport through its Ship Research Institute. It kept abreast of foreign developments and encouraged shipbuilders to exploit the new technologies, which MOT then proceeded to promote with assorted assistance and guidance.

In some ways, nothing was more crucial than the aid related to exports. In earlier years Japanese ships were not that desirable and could only be sold at low prices, prices so low that they had to be subsidised. This was done partly through the Export–Import Bank, which charged very low interest rates to foreign buyers. Some 40–60 per cent of its total loans were tied to such sales during the 1950s and 1960s. Indirectly, export sales were subsidised by domestic sales since Japanese shipping companies paid as much as 15 per cent more per ton.[11] This permitted dumping on the grandest scale ever.

What must be remembered, of course, is that these considerable benefits were not dispersed among the dozens of shipbuilders in the country. Instead, they were concentrated on what ultimately was a small number of large concerns. They were carefully picked by the Ministry of Transport and enrolled in its various programmes, without which they would not have received the assistance. Since MOT's goals coincided pretty much with their own, there was minimal resistance and, if anything, they tended to advance too vigorously on their own.

The ten top companies were reduced to seven through mergers and counted Mitsubishi, Ishikawajima-Harima, Kawasaki, Hitachi, Mitsui, Sumitomo and Nippon Kokan. From their names, it is evident that they belonged to the leading *keiretsu* and sometimes headed their own enterprise group. Some were also steelmakers. In this way, they had all the necessary contacts to do well. They had access to financing through a major bank, they had access to steel, machinery and other inputs, and they could sell their ships to the group's shipping lines.

Encouraged by an ongoing series of rationalisation programmes, the shipyards (of these companies at least) underwent dramatic changes. First, electric welding, automatic gas cutters and block construction methods were introduced. Then special fitting and welding-block methods were adopted. Parts and whole ships were standardised. The speed with which vessels could be completed increased and the number of man hours needed for the job fell. At the same time, new types of ships were launched, car carriers, container ships and especially oil tankers.

But the changes were particularly striking since they were not just incremental. It was a question not of improving and expanding old shipyards so much as of constructing huge new ones. The concept that pervaded the Ministry and industry was 'scrap and build', tear down inefficient yards and build more productive ones. The new installations were not only modern but built to unprecedented scale to handle the ever larger supertankers that became popular in the 1960s. Soon Japan had a dozen such mammoth shipyards, while Europe had none.

Throughout this period, production mounted swiftly. From a negligible quantity shortly after the war, it rose to 5.3 million tons in 1965, doubled to 10.5 million tons in 1970, and hit nearly 18 million tons in 1975. About three-quarters of this output was exported. During this period, Japan's share of worldwide production rose from 25 per cent in the early 1960s to 50 per cent by 1975. Japan was not only a leading shipbuilder, it was not even merely the top shipbuilder, it produced as many ships as all other countries put together.

The rise of shipbuilding was paralleled to some extent by shipping. From the start, the two were linked since one produced for the other and the Ministry of Transport controlled both. This control, however, was exercised more often in the interest of the builders than of the shippers.

As noted, Japanese shipping lines were expected to purchase Japanese ships under the Planned Shipbuilding scheme. At times, they were expected to buy ships, that were not as good as foreign ones and not as cheap as used ones, at unusually high prices. This was only partly compensated for by the cheap loans they received. The rest had to be passed on to their customers in the form of higher freight charges. They were therefore fortunate that MOT guidance to trading companies and other potential clients urged them to use Japanese bottoms as much as possible.

Thus, the Japanese merchant fleet continued growing as well. It expanded to handle Japanese imports and exports, most of which it carried. Meanwhile, it picked up third-party business by discounting rates. By the end of the 1970s, Japan boasted some 40 million tons of shipping that was second only to Liberia, which was a flag of convenience rather than a national flag.

The Ministry of Transport also engaged in industrial policy for the airlines, especially the national carrier Japan Airlines (JAL), but also All Nippon Airways (ANA) and Toa Domestic Airways (TDA), which it initially restricted to domestic routes. It did this, first, by impeding foreign competition as much as possible. Given the principle of reciprocity, this was harder to do. But MOT always found one pretext or another to delay granting rights to the more attractive routes at the more convenient times. Meanwhile, it set uncommonly high rates within Japan and from Japan. Thus, for example, a round-trip flight between Tokyo and New York departing from Tokyo could cost 20–50 per cent more than the same flight departing from New York. Domestic flights could run to as much as twice the price per kilometre as similar flights in the United States.

This naturally enriched the airlines which could expand rapidly and, unlike the shippers, did not have to buy domestic aircraft aside from one case. JAL was soon one of the world's leading carriers although it was not overly efficient and was also slated for privatisation. ANA and TDA went international as well, benefiting from a strong domestic base. But this 'success' was paid for by countless Japanese and foreign passengers who, for decades, had to put up with inadequate services and excessive prices.

TEXTILES (1)

Textiles are not what foreigners usually think of when they consider industrial targeting. Yet, this sector was one of the principal beneficiaries and it was nurtured and promoted for a long, long time. That was partly because it was a traditional industry which had already been backed in Meiji days. But it was also in constant evolution with new kinds of fabrics and fibres and new end products emerging all the time.

During the war, Japan's textile industry suffered almost as severely as the steel industry. Many of the larger factories and much of the machinery had been destroyed or was simply broken-down and antiquated. It was necessary to restore production promptly to provide work and earnings. Since this was a peaceful pursuit, and one which matched the existing comparative advantage based on abundant competent but poorly paid workers, this was done with the blessing and support of the Occupation authorities.

In fact, the recovery can be traced directly to American initiative in helping a former enemy. As of 1947, spinners could draw on a special credit line, known as the Cotton Revolving Fund, amounting to some $210 million. In addition, large quantities of raw cotton and cotton yarn were shipped so that the raw material was also available. No less relevant, the US market was opened to Japanese exports and this became one of the first and most substantial earners of foreign exchange.

Rather than allow the industry to progress on its own as of then, the Ministry of International Trade and Industry adopted a long series of laws, encouraging and regulating the sector, which stretched from the 1950s to the 1980s. Indeed, there were so many that it proved hard to coin enough names: Old Textile Act, Textile New Act, Special Textile Act, Temporary Textile Act, Exceptional Textile Act, New Textile Act . . .

While some of the efforts were devoted to traditional activities like spinning and weaving and traditional fibres like cotton and silk, much more was turned toward the new and exciting area of man-made fibres. Japan had missed out on much of this development and,with the sole exception of Kurashiki's process for producing vinylon from carbide, the essential technologies were invented and controlled by foreign companies, mostly American and some European. MITI therefore acted to facilitate the transfer of technologies both by encouraging Japanese firms to license valuable ones and by making it difficult for foreign firms to enter the market.

In the early 1950s, MITI launched a crash programme to promote synthetic fibres. It targeted production of nylon, vinylon and vinylidene chloride initially and then followed up with acrylics and polyesters. The goal was to establish large-scale modern plants and, to this end, it had the Japan Development Bank provide generous loans for the purchase of facilities and equipment. MITI also organised a scheme to train production workers for the new techniques and was helpful in obtaining the necessary raw materials.

The key, however, was to keep out the foreign manufacturers who not only had far more experience in making these new fibres but also ran larger plants and enjoyed access to cheaper raw materials. Imports were thus restricted to ensure the Japanese makers had a huge captive market. They made good use of that to bring most of the spinners, weavers and other direct users under their control. For good measure, the government ordered civil servants to purchase uniforms made of Japanese synthetic fibres.

With this, the industry grew by leaps and bounds with export growth outpacing and pulling along output growth. By 1970, it produced some 750 000 tons of natural fibre and 1 290 000 tons of man-made fibre. It also employed over 1 750 000 people. This made it not only one of Japan's biggest sectors but the second biggest textile industry in the world after the United States.

FARMING

One would be very mistaken to assume that 'industrial' policy could only be applied to manufacturing industries. It could also be adopted elsewhere. The broadest, most lavish and longest-running exercise actually took place in agriculture. It is not unusual for governments to intervene here and Japan had as many 'valid' reasons as another. It was important to maintain food 'security' for the good of the population. In a pinch, the country could not really count on imports, it was claimed. Moreover, farmers were still a large share of the population, so it was necessary to improve their living standards. More to the point, they were the main supporters of the ruling Liberal Democratic Party. Yet, the chief reason was probably that the bureaucrats also found it in their interest.

During the entire postwar period, agriculture has rarely operated under a free market system. Most crops, and certainly the more significant ones, have been subject to government price policies and guidance on production. The farmers have enjoyed various forms of support or, more rarely, been subject to constraints. Only for relatively secondary crops, or those that did well spontaneously, have they really been left to their own devices. Otherwise, the Ministry of Agriculture, Forestry and Fisheries decided what crops should be grown and which strategies adopted to promote the farming sector.

The most urgent challenge in the late 1940s was to restore food production in a country that was faced with severe shortages due to wartime disruption and defeat. This was all the more daunting in that Japan had never been able to feed itself at an acceptable level before. The key, or so it was assumed, was to boost rice output since it was the traditional base of the farm economy and the staple food. This assignment was tackled vigorously by MAFF. Thanks to improved techniques, more irrigation and fertiliser, greater mechanisation and artificially elevated rice prices, it was achieved during the 1950s.

But the 1960s saddled Japan with what turned out to be a far more intractable problem. Rice production now exceeded the needs of a population that was shifting toward other foods and wanted a more balanced and appealing diet. Thus MAFF had, on the one hand, to stabilise or reduce rice output and, on the other, to diversify production. This goal was laid down in the Basic Agricultural Law of 1961. To attain it, the bureaucrats targeted a number of new crops that should gradually replace rice. They included other grains (wheat, barley, soybean), fruits (oranges, grapefruit), dairy products and livestock, tobacco and sugar.

To accomplish the shift, MAFF had to do more than merely guide the farmers. Most of the crops were unfamiliar and they had to be taught how to cultivate them. In some cases, they needed new machinery and equipment as well as basic infrastructure. In the case of fruit, in particular, they had to get through a period until trees matured and the first crops could be harvested. For milk and beef, there was the problem of improving the strain of cattle. For these and other tasks, the bureaucrats supplied appropriate extension services, sponsored long-term, low-interest loans, lobbied for public works and so on.

But it took more than this. To encourage the farmers, the government provided special incentives. First came a subsidy for those who took land out of rice production and let it lie fallow or put it to other uses. Further benefits were offered to switch to more desirable crops. There were price supports for wheat, barley, soybeans and sugar beets and subsidies for milk and eggs. In addition, protection kept out or limited imports of most competing products either throughout the year or during peak seasons. Exceptionally high tariffs and particularly tight quotas were applied to meat and fruits.

In this sheltered environment, it was possible to boost output of the alternative crops. Japan was soon producing more wheat, barley and soybeans, more oranges and grapefruit, more milk and meat. But even this success was mitigated. The quality was not always adequate in the case of tobacco and some citrus fruits. Or domestic production required other imports. For example, massive amounts of foreign feed had to be processed by Japanese cattle. For most crops, while yields were high, they did not quite reach European levels. And per capita production was distressingly low.[12]

Moreover, the whole exercise was incredibly expensive. First of all, it was costly to the consumer. The prices for most foodstuffs were far higher than elsewhere and it would have been much cheaper to import them. The differentials were not moderate, ranging from two or three times the international rate for milk and certain fruits and grains, to four or five times the international rate for beef. Even rice was far costlier than abroad and had to be sold at a reduced price.

This meant that the Japanese people could afford to eat less and enjoyed a less varied diet than elsewhere.

Meanwhile, as taxpayers, they had to foot the bill for various forms of assistance. One was to employ a huge specialised bureaucracy. Another to pay for innumerable public works. Most irksome was the seemingly endless demand for subsidies. It included the support for production of alternative grains, milk and eggs. For rice, it was necessary to cover the difference between the government's purchase price and its lower sales price as well as the cost of collecting the rice and then storing it. This burden was about twice as high as in the European Community.[13] All these costs ran into several trillion yen a year and there seemed to be no end in sight.

Looking back, it could hardly be argued that targeting was a success in purely economic terms. Japan still suffered from an excess of rice production and had insufficient supplies of other crops. Despite tremendous efforts, the level of agricultural self-sufficiency dropped substantially from 90 per cent in 1960 to 73 per cent in 1980. And even this was tenuous. If the price supports, subsidies, tariffs and quotas had been taken away, most farmers could not possibly have survived. There was hardly a crop for which they were competitive internationally, not even rice. The end result was to maintain an inefficient farming sector at great cost to the consumers and taxpayers.

FINANCIAL SERVICES

'Industrial policy' could also be applied to services. While less often recognised by outside observers, this was done quite frequently. It occurred most extensively in the financial sector. One way or another, just like MITI or MOT, the Ministry of Finance fostered viable companies in the various branches under its supervision: banking, insurance, stock brokerage and so on.

In order to control these branches, and maintain closer supervision, MOF drew strict boundary lines between the activities of each type of financial institution: banks, insurance companies, stock brokers, etc. It also made other distinctions within the categories, such as consumer finance and trust banking or, on a geographic basis, (national) city banks and local banks. Then it adopted very detailed regulations defining what each category could do and according to which procedures. The rules were not always perfectly logical and there were ways of getting around them. But, by and large, the financial territory was relatively well policed as concerned who did what and how.

The purpose was not only to maintain an orderly sector, one where MOF bureaucrats knew just what was going on. It was much more. First of all, it provided a means of moving these institutions in directions the government (or MOF) felt were correct. When policies were adopted, the bureaucrats wished to be certain that private enterprises would fall into line. The second reason was to encourage greater specialisation, allowing companies to know their field well and not disperse their funds and personnel. This made them stronger, for the good of Japanese development, to defend their turf once the market had to be opened up and to project a Japanese presence abroad.

While not strictly necessary in economic terms, there was the same overwhelming urge to expand scale. Often, this was not directly sought by ministry policy and arose spontaneously from the earlier existence of *zaibatsu*-related banks, insurance companies and securities firms that regrouped after the war or emerged within the newer *keiretsu*. On occasion, it derived from policies that promoted mergers (formation of the Dai-Ichi Kangyo Bank) or tolerated them to avoid bankruptcies (Sumitomo's absorption of Heiwa Sogo). At any rate, it was quite evident that banking was dominated by the six major city banks, stock brokerage by the Big Four and insurance by a handful of giants.

To be certain their wards prospered, the bureaucrats provided an exceptionally propitious context. For example, the spread between bank borrowing and lending rates was kept wide enough to generate handsome profits. The rates for various insurance policies were kept high enough to guarantee equally handsome profits. The securities firms could obtain fat commissions from both selling stocks and launching new issues. Part of this took place under the so-called 'convoy system' whereby rates were adjusted to keep the least efficient entities afloat, since the government abhorred bankruptcies. But this meant that more efficient, usually larger, players could obtain even bigger profits.

This comfortable arrangement, which prevailed in its more pristine state during the early postwar decades, was basically designed by the Ministry of Finance. It was done pretty much on its own, with only occasional reference to the political authorities or Diet. But MOF did have to cooperate with other bureaucracies. One was the Bank of Japan, which possessed certain powers regarding monetary policy and set the discount rate. It also dealt with the Ministry of Post and Telecommunications, which promoted its own postal savings scheme. While there was little friction with a normally docile BOJ, relations with MPT were often tense since it pressed for higher interest rates for its depositors, diverting funds away from the commercial banks.

Actually, where the nastiest conflicts usually occurred was within the Ministry of Finance itself. Each bureau had a different clientele, one looking after the banks, another the securities firms and a third the insurance companies. Each wanted the best for its specific sector, trying to increase any advantages or expand the sphere of interest. Nothing was more remarkable than the tug-of-war between the banks and securities companies, and their respective bureaux, over what each should be allowed to do.

The point on which everyone agreed, of course, was that this cosy relationship should not be upset – nor the increasingly lucrative market spoiled – by foreign interlopers. The postwar exchange control and prohibitions on investment kept the market hermetically sealed for almost two decades during which time local institutions could arise and consolidate. As of the 1960s, however, there was a gradual process of liberalisation as foreign companies saw the merits of doing business in Japan and complained that Japanese financial institutions already had a far greater presence abroad.

As in other sectors, it took much time and coaxing to open the market. Some few foreign banks had been allowed in during the 1950s. But the others were only permitted as of the early 1970s. Consumer finance, however, was not opened until the late 1970s and trust banking, the mid-1980s. Foreign stock brokers first came in the 1970s, but the larger contingent only arrived in the 1980s. While life insurance firms came a bit earlier, non-life operations were quite restricted until the 1980s.

Entering the market, as in other sectors, was only the very first step. Foreign companies were stymied at every attempt they made to grow or increase market share. There were many nontariff barriers, as for insurance companies that were only allowed to sell exactly the same policies as their Japanese competitors rather than more innovative ones they had developed abroad. Consumer finance companies could not advertise. Foreign banks were not permitted to open branches in order to increase local deposits and thus had to rely on scarce and costly sources of funds.

Beyond the NTBs were the marketing constraints. The most significant ones derived from the fact that the newcomers were not members of the various industrial groups or *keiretsu*. They did not have close relations with other companies which almost automatically did business together, for old time's sake or more practically because of cross shareholding and interlocking directorates. Thus, foreign banks, securities houses and insurance companies only occupied a small corner of the market which was shared between more and more of them.

While creating a stable financial sector and hardy Japanese institutions, the artificial protection and arbitrary control were unable to induce efficiency. Much of the competition was limited to 'service' in the most superficial forms, namely smiling and bowing girls in uniform or luxurious offices. There were, for example, few current or money-market accounts, little choice among alternative insurance policies or even 'package' policies covering multiple risks. Worse, the rates were clearly very high for the consumers, who paid more than elsewhere for insurance or earned less than otherwise on savings.

A rigid industrial policy had its limits and it was necessary to undertake far-reaching liberalisation of the financial sector if it were really to modernise. This was not conceded voluntarily by MOF. It also had to be inspired by foreign pressure. Other countries complained that Japanese firms were raising money in their markets while the Japanese market was closed to foreign companies and governments. When banks, insurance companies and others invested massively in American securities, sending the dollar up in the early 1980s, Washington insisted that the time had come to liberalise Japan's interest rates. Meanwhile, the unceasing struggle between banks and securities firms was eroding some of the barriers.

As a result of flagrant inefficiencies, and under growing foreign and domestic pressure, the Ministry of Finance gave up or modified some of its cherished policies. The domestic financial market was opened. Foreign entities were allowed to raise money. Interest rates were gradually liberalised, first for large depositors, then even for ordinary savers. Banks and securities firms expanded their range of activities, using offshore ventures as a testing ground. And, in general, regulations and red tape were reduced. But it was not as if MOF had ceded all right to intervene. Its bureaucrats took advantage of every opening or crisis to reimpose control or at least guidance.

Although the Japanese market was now officially 'open', foreign banks, securities firms and insurers still found it extremely difficult to expand market share or simply obtain clients among large companies, especially those related to the *keiretsu*. Meanwhile, their Japanese rivals were expanding rapidly abroad. They set up branches and full-fledged offices, acquired local banks and brokerages, poached trained personnel and sometimes engaged in financial dumping (charging exceptionally low interest rates or fees to attract new customers). By the 1990s, Japanese financial intermediaries were among the largest in the world.

5 Rising Sectors – Public

Once the basic industries had been restored and could shift nicely for themselves, the targeting operation became even more focused on rather different kinds of sectors. These were not labour-intensive and, in many cases, not even capital-intensive like the first batch. Rather, they were extolled as knowledge-intensive and consequently deemed ideal for Japan because of its highly educated workforce. They brought other advantages as well: they promised high value added, they were relatively non-polluting and they enhanced the nation's prestige.

No matter how appealing many 'high-tech' sectors were, and despite a general feeling that they were appropriate for the existing (or coming) comparative advantage, it must be admitted that Japan got into them at a rather late date. By the 1960s and 1970s, when most of them were targeted, the products had already been invented and the technologies developed by other countries. Japan was merely copying, although it did its best to add worthwhile improvements. Indeed, it did so well over this period that some of the products were thoroughly assimilated by Japanese companies and became almost archetypical 'made-in-Japan' articles.

During this phase, the initiative was often taken by the private sector in the sense that entrepreneurs discovered the products and realised their value well before the bureaucrats caught on. But the government quickly mobilised to support any further development and in many cases played a crucial role. While there was still some financial assistance, if considerably less, and the market was closed, albeit less hermetically than before, the main thrust became heavily subsidised research projects.

The sectors that were cultivated during this period were often vital for further economic growth, such as machine tools to help other industries gear up, and telecommunications equipment to bind the country together. Pharmaceuticals also arose to salve a more aged and affluent population. The crowning glory was the more sophisticated forms of electronics such as computers and semiconductors. But there were other sectors of lesser note, including precision machinery, optical goods, medical equipment and many more.

COMPUTERS

Of the recent targeting exercises, none has assumed the scale and intensity of the drive to establish Japan as a major supplier of computers.[1] There were certainly good reasons for it. Computer sales were rising steadily abroad and should follow along in Japan, the product could be manufactured by existing electronics companies, computers could be used to rationalise other sectors and this was an article requiring fewer natural resources and more high-quality human resources. Yet, there was much fumbling and hesitation at the outset.

Computers were already being developed actively and successfully by American companies, led by IBM, a decade before they attracted widespread attention in Japan. The Ministry of International Trade and Industry hardly noticed and had to be alerted by electronics companies. In 1955 it organised a Research Committee on the Computer to monitor American progress. Its Electrotechnical Laboratory also ran a few minor research projects. But MITI did not even have a special office or any appropriate legislation. Indeed, the basic law for the whole electronics industry only came into effect in 1957.

Computers were included among the products encouraged by the Electronic Industries Promotion Law (Denshinho) of 1957 and its successor, the Electronics and Machinery Industries Promotion Law (Kidenho) of 1970. The position was further enhanced under the Specific Machinery and Information Industry Promotion Law (Kijoho) of 1978. These laws authorised MITI to engage more actively in industrial policy, including funding of programmes, coordination of research and development, waiving of anti-monopoly laws and application of administrative guidance.

MITI supervised this work through its Electronic Industry Division, which was superseded by a more specialised Machine Information Industry Division. It was advised by an Electronic Industry Council. To improve and institutionalise its relations with the private sector, MITI helped establish several organisations with which it worked closely, including the broader Japan Electronic Industry Development Association and, for specific projects, various bodies such as the Electronic Computer Basic Technology Association and Institute for New Generation Computer Technology.

Yet, even after adoption of the legislation and creation of the institutional machinery, MITI did not play a very active role for several years. It encouraged local companies to look into production but permitted limited imports of IBM and other computers because they were so much better. In fact, it even allowed IBM to set up a wholly-owned subsidiary, a rather exceptional move at the time. It was made against the wishes of potential rivals and many MITI officials. But there was a significant counterpart: IBM had to open its basic patents to licensing by Japanese manufacturers. Then, to provide a balance and attract yet more technology, MITI encouraged local companies to enter into tie-ups or licensing agreements with other American makers like RCA, Honeywell and Sperry-Rand.

To keep foreign firms from dominating the emerging market, IBM was still treated like an outsider and did not benefit from industrial policy. This was done despite the fact that it opened a Japanese subsidiary with Japanese staff. The other foreign companies were only allowed a minority position and had to leave control over local production to the Japanese partner. Meanwhile, the market was closed. There were stiff foreign-exchange restrictions and a requirement that importers obtain MITI's permission. Tariffs remained high and quotas tight while, with the government and more broadly, an official 'buy Japanese' policy was enforced. This protective covering was not peeled off until the late 1970s and early 1980s, slowly and grudgingly, layer by layer.

As the Japanese industry gradually evolved and reasonable – if still not first-rate – products were put on the market, more financial assistance was provided. This included various tax benefits. To encourage R&D, there was a special write-off for general expenditures and accelerated depreciation of any facilities used to attain 'newly developed technologies'. There was also a reserve fund for the return of computers and another for development of software. To stimulate sales, purchasers of computers could get accelerated depreciation and deductions from local taxes. There was briefly even a subsidy of 50 per cent of development costs for new machines.[2]

Even more significant was the creation of the Japan Electronic Computer Corporation (JECC), established in 1961 by the computer makers with MITI support. JECC bought computers and then leased them to users at subsidised rates. Only domestic computers were covered and this excluded imports, local products with too much foreign content and even products of IBM-Japan. The operation was financed by the Japan Development Bank, by far the biggest contributor, and commercial banks. One advantage was the promotion of sales of locally-made computers. Another, no less important, was for the companies to thereby offer terms as good as or better than IBM and to be paid promptly in cash.

While these measures helped the nascent computer industry, the quality and cost of domestic models simply could not compare with those of IBM and other American makers. They could be sold, especially to the government, if they were almost as good or benefited from special financial advantages. But Japan was not catching up and each time its makers came out with an improved model it still lagged far behind IBM's next offering. Indeed, if something drastic were not done, Japan's computer industry could have succumbed like those of Britain and France.

It was this recognition and IBM's takeover of France's Machine Bull in 1964 that finally galvanised MITI. Everybody realised that the technological level of Japanese computers had to be enhanced dramatically if the industry were to succeed in any real sense. At the suggestion of its Industrial Technology Council, MITI's Agency of Industrial Science and Technology introduced a series of major research projects, some of them carried out directly by its Electrotechnical Laboratory and others under a special Large-Scale Project Office. The need was further confirmed by MITI's Electronic Industry Council, which gave computer research the top priority.

These projects took many forms and were financed in many ways, each being almost a special case. In general, however, the more theoretical or basic the research, the more was done by government laboratories at government expense. The closer it came to application, the more was done in cooperation with company researchers, in either government or special cooperative laboratories. When the commercial interest was particularly high, the private sector might carry on alone. For the former, the government covered most of the expenses and had specific work done under 'research contracts'. For the latter, companies received 'grants' (*hojokin*) which were supposed to be repaid but were not always.[3]

This already varied arrangement became even more complicated in practice because of the difficulties of working with individual companies that were arch rivals in a rapidly evolving field. MITI tried to keep the number of participants small to concentrate the effort and build strong, internationally-competitive players. It even sought to bring about mergers. In fact, it initially tried to create one firm out of the six leading contenders and later forced them to cooperate in three teams of two. But, in the end, it could only obtain a limited degree of practical cooperation.

While, in theory, MITI was simply targeting computers in general, in practice it had targeted IBM and desperately sought to replicate existing or expected IBM models and eventually outdo them.[4] This made the research work more focused and, for that reason, somewhat easier than trying to produce an article which could take many different forms. On the other hand, it made the Japanese into slaves of IBM's own strategy and unflagging, if sometimes frustrated, copiers. Most decisive, it drove some Japanese companies to opt for 'plug compatibility', meaning that they produced computers compatible with IBM machines and could be thrown if IBM changed its basic architecture.

Ever since the mid-1960s, there have always been one or more programmes underway, many of a quite impressive scale.[5] The first notable one was the super-high-performance computer project which ran from 1966 to 1971. It aimed to design a computer that could compete with IBM's then existent mainframe. But, despite all hopes and a last ditch effort to increase the memory capacity, it was immediately superseded by IBM's newest model. MITI did somewhat better in the next round, from 1972 to 1976, producing what it called a '3.75 generation' model to match IBM's latest series, which was proclaimed to be merely a '3.5 generation' machine. This time, Hitachi, Fujitsu, NEC and Toshiba, in one group, and Mitsubishi and Oki, in another, managed to turn out rather good counterparts.

While these programmes dealt with the basic hardware, another series of projects was run from 1976 to 1983 to overcome certain weaknesses that emerged, so as to create a 'fourth generation' computer. The first worked on very large-scale integrated circuits and is described under the semiconductor industry. Another tried both to improve the quality of standard peripherals and to limit the makers to fewer, more specialised firms. It dealt with magnetic disks, bubble units, printers and so on. The final aspect was software, where a special effort was made for language processing, including Japanese language capability.

Aside from this project, software was given particular attention as of 1970, when the Information Technology Promotion Agency (IPA) was established. It was designed specifically to promote software and services through a broad array of tools. It commissioned firms to develop useful computer programs and then leased them to computer users, it maintained a register of general-purpose software programs, it facilitated credit to software houses and it encouraged cooperation among leading firms in solving general problems like production, storage and standardisation. Finally, a Software Technology Center was formed to engage in R&D.

This initiative was taken a step further with the Software Development Project which was to develop computer-written applications software and ran from 1976 to 1980. Later on, MITI launched the SIGMA software project of joint research over the 1985–92 period. These exercises, however, were more difficult than hardware because they required a creative element that was harder to foster. Just how poorly they fared was summed up by Okimoto, referring to the first project. 'Although an effort was made to cast the results in a positive light by referring to the "library of working aids for programmers" that had been developed, no amount of window dressing could disguise the fact that the project had fallen short of the goals that had been set. Only about 20 per cent of the software packages developed . . . have turned out to be commercially useful.'[6]

Having fostered companies that could produce viable mainframe computers, it was not necessary for MITI to help out much when they branched into smaller computers. The personal computer and microcomputer segments got by on their own. But MITI did step in to give local makers a much needed boost in their effort to design supercomputers. From 1981 to 1989 it ran a project to develop a high-speed computer system for scientific uses. The goal was not only to make faster computers, faster this time than those of Cray and Control Data, but to adopt new solutions such as the Josephson junction and gallium arsenide.

Nothing was to be grander than the 'fifth-generation computer' project which MITI scheduled from 1982 to 1991. It was to be designed by a special Institute for New Generation Computer Technology (ICOT) which would enjoy relative freedom in its research activities. ICOT was staffed with about fifty young (and hopefully innovative) researchers drawn from both the public and private sectors, and would be amply funded. Its exact goal always remained rather sketchy but there was no doubt that this time it was expected to push beyond existing frontiers of knowledge and fashion a truly unique computer. It was hoped, among other things, that the machine would be capable of pattern recognition and artificial intelligence.

This project was announced with greater fanfare than usual, MITI priding itself on the new role of pioneer. It was also taken up by enthusiastic foreign 'experts', like Edward A. Feigenbaum and Pamela McCorduck, who wrote *The Fifth Generation: Artificial Intelligence and Japan's Computer Challenge to the World*. Again, without bothering to look at the exact contents of the project or how the aims could be achieved, the stress was on Japan's will to succeed and its supposedly proven ability to do so when facing a daunting task.[7] Many Japanese, however, remained sceptical and compared ICOT to the supersize battleship *Yamato*, which was built but little used before being sunk in the Pacific War.[8]

As it turned out, the Japanese sceptics were right and the foreign admirers wrong. When the ten years were over, ICOT had yet to unveil any fifth-generation computer. It had come up with interesting improvements on existing techniques and made worthwhile contributions to theory. But there had been no breakthrough and there was no commercial product or even one on paper. But this did not faze the MITIocrats. They quickly regrouped and launched a sixth-generation computer project dubbed New Information Processing Technology (NIPT). Its goals, while still rather vague, were intended to be more modest . . . and achievable.

Although MITI played the leading role in upgrading the computer industry, it was not alone. Nippon Telegraph & Telephone had a considerable need for computers and data processing and therefore set technical specifications, designed hardware and software and ran advanced research in its laboratories. Moreover, it helped its suppliers produce the necessary material. On occasion, it also launched larger projects which closely paralleled MITI's. From 1982 to 1986 it worked on an improved 'fourth-generation' computer. This was to be succeeded by its own 'fifth-generation' computer. While the continuous institutional rivalry dispersed the bureaucratic effort, it actually contributed to the industry's progress since the same makers were usually enrolled in both teams.

It is very difficult to calculate exactly how much the government spent on promoting the computer industry. For R&D alone, from 1966 to 1985, MITI provided at least ¥100 billion in direct expenditures and ¥420 billion in subsidies. NTT's expenditures were also substantial, and impossible to estimate. To this must be added the cost of funding JECC's leasing operations and IPA's credit guarantee system. Then come assorted loans from JDB and FILP. Finally, there are the tax rebates.[9] All in all, the funding may have approached ¥1 trillion, a massive effort. It was particularly important during the earlier phase, when the makers were struggling to design acceptable products. Although now dwarfed by company spending, this aid is still a valuable contribution, especially since it usually goes into general or theoretical research that the companies do not want to spend their own money on.

Thanks to both the protection from foreign competition and intensive government support, Japanese companies did emerge as strong contenders. The nucleus naturally comprised those which had benefited most from MITI's projects and, for some, NTT's computer work. They included Fujitsu, NEC, Hitachi, Toshiba, Oki and Mitsubishi Electric, in that order. The latter two eventually restricted their mainframe activities. Fujitsu, Hitachi and NEC also produced supercomputers. But there were a number of others that manufactured smaller computers, including Matsushita, Sony, Sord and Sharp.

Thus, while government backing was helpful, it was neither decisive in guaranteeing that a company would succeed nor did exclusion keep dynamic companies out. But it is obvious that this boost accelerated the industry's rise significantly and was decisive in keeping foreign companies from dominating it. While IBM and other foreign makers held on to a slice of the Japanese market, they were gradually passed by domestic players. Once having developed good products, and brought costs down, the Japanese proceeded to export and encroach on American and European markets.

During the late 1970s and early 1980s, the industry gathered speed. Production and domestic sales kept increasing by 20–30 per cent a year while exports expanded almost twice as fast. By 1985, production had easily passed the ¥3 trillion mark and exports were nearly half of that. While IBM stayed the world leader, several Japanese companies were closing the gap. Fujitsu was already number three and NEC number five in the ranking. The Japanese share was still smaller, but growing much faster. How far they could go remained to be seen. But there was no doubt that Japan had caught up and might push ahead.

SEMICONDUCTORS

Even after the Ministry of International Trade and Industry realised, somewhat belatedly, the great potential of computers, it failed to grasp the crucial role of semiconductors. This component, destined to replace the vacuum tube and thereby dramatically reduce the size and expand the power of future generations of computers, was developed in the United States. Texas Instruments and IBM took the lead, but there were many other companies that moved in, such as National Semiconductor, Intel and Motorola.[10]

Japanese companies again had much keener foresight and began developing their own capabilities in order to produce smaller, better or cheaper consumer electronics. Whenever they lacked technologies, they turned to American companies which usually licensed them. In this way, Sony pioneered the use of the transistor for radio and television after its importance had been overlooked by American firms and questioned by MITI itself. Sharp pursued its work on integrated circuits (ICs) in order to produce desk-top calculators, which it did by 1967. Soon after, ICs were used for colour television. And they continued showing their versatility as they were incorporated in one product after another.[11]

In fact, when it came to commercial applications, Japan quickly pulled ahead of the United States. This was largely because many IC makers were also producers of consumer electronics. The top five were NEC, Hitachi, Toshiba, Fujitsu and Mitsubishi. But many others manufactured for in-house use, including Sharp, Sanyo, Sony, Matsushita and others. This gave them two advantages. First, they had a large captive market for whatever they produced and any additional sales were icing on the cake. Secondly, they could shift funds from divisions that were doing well selling mature products, to invest in the essential R&D to develop semiconductors.

In the early years, MITI did not do much to promote the industry in any constructive sense aside from minor research projects. But it did not fail to protect the emerging makers as soon as it saw the possibilities. This was done in various ways. One was to prevent foreign makers from setting up shop in Japan and preempting the sector. Only Texas Instruments was allowed in, in 1965, but it had to accept a joint venture with Sony and also open its basic patents to other companies. The restrictions on foreign investment were not lifted until 1974, at which point local companies already dominated the industry.

More important, semiconductor imports were strictly controlled until 1970 and then only liberalised in stages. This left a rapidly expanding market for the Japanese to divide among themselves. Only more sophisticated articles were sought abroad, and those in small quantities and only until local producers caught up. Even after the sector was opened, Japanese makers were able to keep out imports by cooperation or collusion between suppliers and users. Many of the users were actually part of the same company or dependent subsidiaries or affiliates. Others belonged to the same industrial group or *keiretsu*. And the biggest single purchaser (about 10 per cent of the total) was the public corporation NTT, which rarely bought anything from outside of its 'family'.

Finally, in the late 1970s, MITI took a more dynamic approach. This was partly because semiconductors were intimately related to its ongoing computer programme. Japanese companies still lagged behind in the production of semiconductors for computers. In addition, they sensed that the fourth generation of computers would be powered by very-large-scale integrated circuits (VLSIs) which would replace the existing large-scale integrated circuits (LSIs). IBM was already working on them and, after having struggled so hard to close the gap, the Japanese did not want the Americans to pull ahead. To preclude this, MITI launched a high profile VLSI project that ran from 1976 to 1979 at a cost of ¥29 billion to the government and ¥43 billion to the cooperating companies.

Direction of this project, entrusted in MITI's Agency of Industrial Science and Technology, was not quite as easy as for the computer projects. This time, the companies were more advanced and harboured strong suspicions of one another. While there were potential gains, some aspects were too sensitive commercially to be shared with others. And the most advanced companies were the least interested in cooperation. Eventually, NEC, Toshiba, Hitachi, Mitsubishi and Fujitsu signed on, with the first two forming one team and the others a second. It took some doing to establish a VLSI Technology Research Association and, even then, they continued to disagree on how closely they should cooperate. In order to overcome the qualms, the project was disarticulated in certain ways.[12]

Part of the work was of a general and relatively theoretical nature and was undertaken in a common central laboratory with a hundred researchers, most from participating companies and a token few from the Electrotechnical Laboratory. Applied work was done by researchers from the specific companies in two independent laboratories. Even more commercially useful work was actually done in the individual companies. Ultimately, over a thousand patents were taken out on the results of the research, but the bulk of them were held by the respective companies. While certainly improving the technological level, the R&D results were not 'earthshaking' and failed to make any state-of-the-art breakthroughs.[13]

While receiving much less publicity, Nippon Telegraph & Telephone also undertook a VLSI project at roughly the same time.

Running from 1975 to 1981, and costing ¥40 billion, it was focused more on developing VLSIs for telecommunications gear such as microwave systems and switching equipment but also for its own computers. NTT cooperated with three close members of its 'family' of suppliers, NEC, Hitachi and Fujitsu, all of them also in the MITI project. They worked together with NTT engineers and, while paid nothing for their assistance, could count on major orders in due course.

After these projects, the government ceased playing a major role in promoting the semiconductor industry. MITI decided to encourage more advanced integrated circuits, known as 'new function elements', and initiated three specific programmes to last through the 1980s. They focused on grid superchips, environment-resistent reinforced chips and three-dimensional circuit chips. To this was added a special project on optoelectronic devices for the decade 1986–96. But these R&D projects were fairly modest and a small supplement to the work the companies were doing on their own. Far more significant was the fact that they now had R&D budgets that exceeded even American levels and absorbed more than 10 per cent of sales year after year.

But one should not underestimate the value of past government intervention. It came at just the right time, when Japan was behind, and allowed it to leapfrog from the then state-of-the-art 16K DRAM chip to the new standard, the 64K DRAM chip. The private sector could take it from there. Japanese companies had already made considerable inroads into the world semiconductor market in the late 1970s and soon controlled some 40 per cent of the American market. The demand for the new chips was even greater and only Japan was in a position to meet it rapidly. As orders poured in, and American makers could not fill them, the Japanese took advantage of the situation and quickly captured about 70 per cent of the 64K DRAM segment.

This gave the Japanese the edge they needed to stay ahead. They could now develop new generations of semiconductors on their own and managed to come out with key products months, and even years, before most foreign rivals. This happened with the 256K DRAM chips in the early 1980s, the 1M DRAM chips in the mid-1980s and then the 4M DRAM chips in the early 1990s, and so on up. In all cases, they swept the markets, making it very hard for foreign competitors even to get in. The success was so great that the American makers cried foul play and even Japanese firms regarded the competition as too rough. This was because certain companies pushed resolutely ahead no matter what the economic situation indicated. When there was a gradual rise in sales, expecting more to come, they expanded their capacity and output far more than prudent rivals. Even when there was a recession, and most foreign companies cut back on production, the Japanese pressed on assuming that the next upturn would revindicate them. Sometimes it did. Sometimes, it did not. The outcome was a sudden and drastic fall in prices due to oversupply. For example, prices of 64K DRAM chips plunged so steeply that they temporarily slipped lower than those for 16K DRAMs. During 1985, the price of 256K DRAMs dropped by 90 per cent.

At such prices, it was obvious that many companies were taking losses on the new products, which replaced one another at a dizzying speed. Relatively few, according to industry sources, were making profits.[14] None of them could really claim to have gained much after subtracting the costs of R&D and unused capacity. But this did not faze them. What was far more important was that weaker companies were driven out and the circle of semiconductor makers gradually narrowed. Many of those which fell by the wayside were foreign and even the few which remained were reeling from the price competition.[15]

It was obvious that American and European companies could not sustain this sort of race. They had to make profits or pull out of loss-making lines. The Japanese, on the other hand, could afford to lose money on any products they really wanted and cover this with profits from more mature products. They could also fall back on their bank and, if worst came to worst, the government.[16] Anyway, their real goal was market share and predatory pricing or dumping were among the most effective means to that end. Realising as much, American and other producers accused the Japanese of dumping and often enough subsequent investigations confirmed this. Any relief, however, usually came too late.

In fact, by the mid-1980s it looked as if the American semiconductor industry could be seriously impaired. In response to complaints by the American Semiconductor Industry Association and key players, it was decided to work out a special arrangement to set floors on Japanese prices and open the Japanese market to American makers.[17] This led to long and painful negotiations which resulted in a 1986 agreement that satisfied no one and failed to achieve its purposes. Despite the unmistakable evidence of a crisis, the Americans (and Europeans) could not come up with any way of reversing or even slowing down the ominous trends.

It was probably too late anyway. The Japanese companies had gained a decisive edge and could proceed on their own, with or without government support, with or without predatory pricing or dumping (which were almost inevitable given their own fierce competition). This was crucial, for the semiconductor industry was growing at a remarkable pace, often expanding by 20 or 30 per cent a year and reaching ¥3 trillion in 1985. Exports expanded even more rapidly so the Japanese share of the world market kept rising, passing the United States by the late 1980s and holding a commanding lead by the 1990s. By then the top three chip makers were Japanese.

But this was not a normal race, not judging by the time, effort and money the Japanese players put into it. It was not one in which American companies, for example, could pull ahead further down the road. Having lost out for the major products and the technology-drive lines, there was little hope of getting back in without incurring unacceptable expenses. Hiding in 'niche' products might tide them over for a while. But the future of the semiconductor industry, one they had founded and developed, was now clearly in the hands of the Japanese. And that is fateful for it is the key to the coming 'information age'.[18]

TELECOMMUNICATIONS

No matter how impressive MITI's industrial policy and targeting occasionally appeared, it was nothing compared to NTT's campaign to restore and strengthen the telecommunications industry. This it did in a sustained way, day by day and year after year, from its inception until the present time. It was not undertaken through special projects or under special legislation but as part of the regular and ongoing business. And it did not involve just key products or specific breakthroughs but the initiation and expansion of production of virtually any and every item that went into running a telecommunications system.

Nippon Telegraph & Telephone was established in 1952 as a public corporation. This status gave it considerable autonomy from the government and permitted it to operate pretty much on a commercial basis. On the other hand, it enjoyed extremely close relations with the Ministry of Post and Telecommunications and also the innumerable politicians who wanted telecommunications improved in their electoral districts. In addition, it was a monopoly. It controlled the nation's huge telephone and telegraph network, aside from international communications, provided by Kokusai Denshin Denwa (KDD). It handled all common carrier transmissions and licensed all private communications.

As the purchaser of two-thirds or more of the total national demand for telecommunications equipment, NTT had a keen interest in the sound development of domestic vendors. Its market position, and its financial standing, allowed it to direct and support favoured companies to an extent that was quite impossible elsewhere. This power was used actively and aggressively.

The first thing that MPT and NTT did was to close the Japanese market to imports, aside from crucial articles which could not be produced domestically. This occurred not only for the products that NTT absorbed itself on the basis of a stark 'buy Japanese' policy. It also applied to the rest, since strict regulations were adopted for just about every item and existing standards somehow facilitated sales of national goods while impeding those of imports. Since other telecommunications markets were also reserved abroad, this was relatively easy to get away with.

But NTT went a step further. Like MITI or MOT, it did not promote all telecommunications-related companies but a restricted circle of some three hundred, four of them being particularly favoured: NEC, Fujitsu, Oki and Hitachi. They formed what was known as the 'NTT family'. The companies were selected not only because of proven competence, surely not in the early days when production was beginning. There was a dose of faith and also personal interest. For example, those companies had close relations with NTT or MPT officials and hired them for post-retirement jobs.

Having closed the market to imports, it was essential for NTT to improve the technological level of its wards or it would not be able to put together a first-rate system. It therefore encouraged technology transfers and licensing to the necessary extent. Then it prompted domestic companies to adapt their products ɯ its specific needs and sometimes improve them or come up with new models. Its engineers worked closely with company engineers to determine the exact requirements and specifications in return for a promise to purchase the products once approved.

In certain cases, NTT went considerably further. It has several

special laboratories of its own with over 3000 scientists and researchers (about three times larger than MITI's Electrotechnical
Laboratory). R&D operations were exceedingly well funded, con-
suming ¥70–100 billion a year in the early 1980s. And it knew exactly
what it wanted. There was little time wasted on general or theoretical
pursuits and more devoted to development, and later research,
related to the products needed for NTT's five-year plans.

After NTT had done most of the basic work, the results were
handed over to the private companies which had to design specific
products or components. In earlier years, such knowhow might be
given to one particularly favoured company. More recently, it has
been distributed more widely within Japan, but not abroad. Meanwhile, Japanese companies eagerly acquired patents from Bell Laboratories, which were more readily available.

NTT's research work saved its suppliers precious resources and
permitted them to expand their range of goods and rise along the
learning curve more swiftly and cheaply than otherwise. But the
financial assistance did not end there. Until quite recently, almost all
of NTT's orders were negotiated with specific companies rather than
being thrown open to general bidding. It was broadly felt that the
prices agreed were more than generous.[19] Not only that, companies
knew roughly how much they could sell and could therefore invest
rationally in installations and often attain scale, given NTT's considerable needs.

While this system worked to the entire satisfaction of NTT and its
'family', there were certain shortcomings. One was that technological
development sometimes lagged since most of the new products and
technologies were still invented abroad and it took some time for
Japan to catch up. This applied to quite ordinary things like digital
telephones, mobile telephones, citizen-band radios and cable television. More significant for business, NTT's control over data transmissions and jurisdictional disputes between MPT and MITI slowed
down the spread of information processing.[20]

Not to be outdone, NTT launched a series of major programmes in
the 1980s to usher in the 'information age'. One prong was to
upgrade the system with digitalised equipment, fibre optics and
satellites, drawing the nation into a denser telecommunications network. Another was to provide linkages between different services
like telex, facsimile and computers. For companies, value added
networks (VANs) would be opened. For the ordinary citizen, the
stress was on a teletext system called CAPTAIN. Yet, despite the

public relations blitz, it was obvious that none of these things were radically new and Japan was just getting in step.[21]

The other problem, at least for consumers, was that NTT's services were relatively expensive and KDD's, on occasion, grotesquely so. As monopolies, they could decide the rates and they merely needed political support to impose them. This left the cost of local calls and especially international calls exceedingly expensive for such a small and compact country. There were also definite inefficiencies and waste in the system for, despite its huge revenues, the financial situation deteriorated. While NTT once made substantial profits, it was no longer flourishing and it was feared that it could one day become a burden on the national budget.

But the domestic dissatisfaction had less direct impact than foreign complaints. At a time when Japanese products were entering other countries in increasingly large quantities, it was insisted that telecommunications should be liberalised there. That was particularly urgent since some foreign companies still had a technological advance and supplied equipment which could be sold in Japan, if given a chance. Those complaints were echoed by Japanese companies which were not among the existing suppliers and also wanted a chance to sell to NTT.

The mounting pressure ultimately brought about changes in the telecommunications sectors. In 1981, Japan agreed to apply the provisions of the Government Procurement Code to NTT, thereby opening its market in exchange for greater possibilities of selling abroad. NTT was given a new president who was committed to making more foreign purchases. In 1985 NTT was turned into a private company. In addition, several 'second NTTs' sprang up, promoted by other companies, occasionally with backing from other ministries.

This put an end to the phase of rampant industrial policy, but it did not halt the practice entirely. Despite the fanfare, NTT's purchases of foreign products were quite minor, only a few per cent of the total. And certain products encountered nontariff barriers in the private market. More progress was made by other Japanese companies which were in a better position to benefit from the opening, like Matsushita, Mitsubishi Electric and Toshiba. There was increased public tendering, but there were also remnants of the close cooperation which maintained earlier, long-standing relations.

If there were any doubt as to whether targeting survived in the sector, and in a privatised NTT, that was laid to rest by the case of mobile telephones. Motorola, which developed the technology and captured much of the US market, was initially inhibited in selling its products in Japan by regulations, which were eventually adjusted to permit sales in part of the market. Only after strong American protests was it allowed, in 1989, to sell everywhere. This delay gave NTT time to come up with its own, smaller models, which were developed with and manufactured by Fujitsu, NEC and Mitsubishi. By leasing rather than selling, and having access to NTT's thousand sales offices, these competitors enjoyed a distinct advantage. This blocked Motorola, which could have swept the market if it had not been held back earlier on.

There was no need to worry about most of the members of the old 'NTT family'. They had had almost four decades to grow in a sheltered and enriched environment and were now rather advanced and competitive. They had already begun selling to other Japanese clients and, during the 1970s, they expanded exports as well. In both cases, their secure and lucrative business with NTT provided the necessary base and helped subsidise initial sales. By the 1980s, Japan was the world's leading exporter of telecommunications equipment and the industry was turning over more than ¥1 trillion a year.

MACHINE TOOLS

There has never been any doubt about the pivotal role of machine tools in the industrialisation process. They are known as 'mother machines' because they make the great mass and variety of machinery that is indispensable for all other sectors. Yet, for a decade after the war, the machine-tool sector was neglected by a supposedly prescient Ministry of International Trade and Industry. To replace the old and sometimes broken-down machinery of the war years, leading manufacturers imported better and cheaper foreign models. Not until the mid-1950s, when economic development speeded up and huge amounts of machinery were required, was the need for a strong domestic industry recognised.

By then, MITI had completed its most urgent programmes for promotion of the basic industries and could devote more personnel and funds to other sectors. The machinery industry was singled out and, in 1956, a special Promotion of the Machinery Industry Law was adopted. It was renewed twice and then converted into a Promotion of the Electrical Machinery Industry Law in 1971. As of 1978, this became the Promotion of the Information Machinery Industry Law. From law to law, the range of machine tools covered expanded and MITI's intervention intensified. The thrust throughout, however, remained the replacement of imported products by domestically made ones, a classic case of *kokusanka.*[22]

During these several decades, MITI tackled various essential tasks. None was more important in the early years than to prevent foreign makers from swamping a still weak and fragmented domestic industry. Appeals from local companies, faced by stronger, richer and more technically proficient competitors, helps explain the response. As long as specific machinery could not be supplied locally, it was imported. As soon as it could be made by a Japanese producer, even if the article were not quite as good and a bit more expensive, foreign imports were cut off.

This could be done very handily until 1962 through the use and abuse of exchange control. Japanese manufacturers wishing to import equipment had to apply for the necessary foreign exchange and, if MITI felt the machinery could be obtained locally, the permission was not granted. Meanwhile, tariffs were used to protect the domestic market. They were lower where imported machinery was still useful, higher where local production was scheduled to take over. Each time a specific category was targeted, for example, numerically-controlled machine tools, the tariffs went up. Foreign makers frustrated in attempts to export hoped to get around this by investing in Japan. But that was prevented until 1970, at which point it was too late. So, they were essentially limited to joint ventures or licensing technology.

To strengthen the industry, the government – guided in this by MITI – lavished financial assistance on the makers. The resources made available rose steadily during the 1960s and into the 1970s, when this came under harsh foreign criticism and was muted. The aid took a variety of forms, tax incentives, cheap loans and R&D assistance, and was provided to the machine-tool makers and their customers, domestic and foreign.

Domestic makers benefited from numerous special tax measures, including accelerated depreciation, R&D credits and export deduction. Domestic purchasers benefited from special depreciation rules adopted to promote sales of Japanese-made machinery. Meanwhile, exports were encouraged by other tax rebates including an export income deduction, export accelerated depreciation, export loss reserve system, overseas market development reserve and so on.

Substantial loans were granted, naturally at low interest rates and with lenient repayment schedules. They came from the Japan Development Bank and Small Business Finance Corporation primarily, the former providing some ¥74 billion from 1956 to 1969. This assistance was channelled to the makers. But they also benefited indirectly from other loans. During the late 1960s, the Industrial Bank of Japan and the Long-Term Credit Bank offered loans to domestic purchasers of Japanese-made machine tools. For exports, the assistance was even greater. The Japan Export–Import Bank financed the purchase of turnkey plants involving a broad mix of products, many from the machinery industry.

Even more attractive than loans, which had to be paid back, were certain rather unusual forms of free assistance. One was a slice of the sugar linking system, whereby the trade association could import sugar at the international rate and sell it at the much higher domestic rate, using the proceeds to subsidise exports. Another was special grants from the Bicycle Rehabilitation Association (BRA) which put some of the earnings from bicycle and motorbike racing into the industry. This was done through a Japan Society for the Promotion of the Machine Industry, theoretically independent but attentive to MITI's wishes. These were not paltry sums, estimated at as much as ¥22 billion a year by the 1980s.[23]

Equally significant were the grants and loans for research and development. MITI's Agency of Industrial Science and Technology provided matching grants for specific research projects undertaken by individual companies or groups of companies. The JDB and SBFC supplied loans for major research projects, again on very favourable terms. And the BRA granted additional amounts. The overall level of assistance was considerable, estimated at ¥8–10 billion in grants and ¥8–9 billion in loans, or some 10–15 per cent of all research and development spending.[24]

This assistance served multiple purposes. Most evidently, it financed and strengthened the industry, which was the formal goal. More subtly, it increased industry indebtedness to and dependence on MITI, which was instrumental in obtaining it. This was particularly important here because MITI was not on very good terms with the makers to begin with. Unlike steel and chemicals, machinery makers were relatively small and fractious firms, many of them family-based and most very independent. They were suspicious of MITI for having neglected the industry for so long and also disliked any interference in their business.[25]

Yet, MITI's hidden agenda consisted largely of a 'rationalisation', such as had been imposed elsewhere and would not necessarily appeal to many makers. In its view, the industry could not succeed until companies were larger, financially stronger and more advanced technologically. Only then could they gain economies of scale and raise quality to an internationally competitive level. To attain this, it tried to induce cooperation among the makers and worked, as much as possible, with the Japan Machine Tool Builders Association (JMTBA) which encompassed the larger firms.

It was hoped that natural selection would lead to a shakeout, with weaker companies falling by the wayside. To some extent, it did. But there were still too many in its view and MITI therefore pushed for mergers and regroupings. This was done by verbal admonitions and, more effectively, by promoting joint research and joint investments with more and bigger loans. In 1965, through JMTBA, about forty leading makers were talked into forming ten groups to share information and enhance cooperation. That being a recession year, they accepted. As soon as the economy improved, they returned to thoughts of individual progress.

A more promising tack was to let the companies remain autonomous but increase the specialisation among them. In 1956, JMTBA's members reached a product-allocation agreement that was formally approved by MITI and administered by the trade association. But little came of it since producers wanted to make as many articles as possible, especially the more lucrative or advanced ones. In 1964, again at MITI's insistence, JMTBA's members agreed to concentrate their production. They would drop subsidiary lines and only make machinery for which they had 5 per cent or more of the market, or if the product represented 20 per cent or more of their output. While not always obeyed to the letter, MITI could wrest some compliance by its right to approve new products (the stick) and its ability to grant assistance (the carrot).

Specialisation brought definite advantages. For the first time, by concentrating on a few products instead of many, companies could refine their designs and bring down costs through greater economies of scale. They could increasingly standardise, making a few multi-purpose models rather than many special-purpose ones. Instead of waiting until they got an order, they could launch models that fitted general needs and then seek customers. No less beneficial, by selling fewer different models they had fewer competitors and could beat those remaining in narrow niches.

Naturally, this further enhanced the quality of Japanese products, which was an underlying goal. From the start, MITI established performance and quality standards which it imposed on the industry domestically and, even more strictly, with regard to exports. These standards were announced in advance and makers were given several months to attain them. No sooner had one set of standards been reached than tougher ones were proposed.

Over the years, MITI encouraged a broadening and deepening of the product line. Under each new basic law, it targeted additional items. Back in 1956, it promoted simple machinery and machine tools before moving on to lathes and drilling, boring, grinding and milling machines. More complex tools, combining more functions, were introduced in the 1960s, including machining centres. Then came the turn of complex assemblies of machinery, integrated plants and turnkey factories. In 1971, electronics-based machinery was given priority. In fact, MITI decided that 50 per cent of machine-tool production should be CNC (computer numerical control) by 1977. This goal was adopted before foreign makers even realised the importance of such equipment.

This upgrading process was expedited by extensive research and development, part of it carried out or funded by the government. The Agency for Industrial Science and Technology played a key role since it had several laboratories doing work of interest to the sector, especially the Mechanical Engineering Laboratory with a staff of 300. The Japan Society for the Promotion of the Machine Industry, funded by bicycle racing proceeds, also had two research centres. The Technical Research Institute was oriented toward practical projects while the Economic Research Institute gathered broader information. As already noted, AIST, JDB and SBFC provided matching grants or loans for R&D.

The bulk of the R&D was conducted by private companies. They had to match the grants and pay back the loans. They also tended to indicate in which directions the R&D should be guided, since they had the best idea of how the industry was evolving. Unlike the government-related bodies, they were much less interested in basic research than in practical applications leading to commercially viable products. And they were extremely leery of one another, which explains why joint research was so hard to foster and leading companies refused to cooperate in what, to their lights, was helping the competitors.

With all due respect to their efforts, early research and development was not of a very high calibre. Sometimes it involved licensing and adapting foreign technology. More often, it could be character-ised as 'reverse engineering'. Companies and laboratories would purchase foreign machinery, take it apart, and see how it worked. They would then figure out how it could be replicated, incorporating enough changes to get around the patent laws and perhaps outdo the originator. In this sense, the targeting was very concrete.[26] And foreign makers were deeply resentful of the process, although there was not much they could do about it.

However, by the 1970s, enough progress had been made for the government's research laboratories in particular to move on to more general projects, such as machining technology, accuracy of machine tools, computer-aided design and production and CNC-machines. In the 1980s, two national projects were launched which were at the cutting edge of technological advance. One was to develop flexible manufacturing systems (FMS) which are supposed to create tomorrow's 'unmanned factories'. Another was working on complex manufac-turing systems which include the combined use of machine tools, robots, lasers and other new technologies.

Not content to boost the industry by replacing imports with dom-estic products, MITI soon began promoting exports. As early as 1962, it set a goal of exporting 20 per cent of machine-tool production by the 1970s. It was eagerly backed by the makers who formed the Japan Machine Tool Trade Association which, in addition to collect-ing information or organising trade fairs and display rooms, could group makers for large deals, coordinate policies and liaise with the government. Although ambitious makers threw themselves into ex-port campaigns, they only gained a modest share of the world market in the 1960s and early 1970s. Since they received subsidies and cheap loans and engaged in aggressive price cutting, they also attracted charges of dumping and calls for restraint. To calm the tension, MITI had to enforce floor prices through an export licensing system.

By the late 1970s, however, the situation had changed. Thanks to specialisation and standardisation, prices were coming down sharply and quality was still rising. The makers knew foreign markets better and were recognised by local dealers and buyers. Some set up their own distribution and service networks or even local factories. The tide turned with the introduction of numerically-controlled machine tools, where Japan had a definite edge. With this, exports grew more rapidly than domestic sales, reaching a third of total production by the early 1980s.

Thanks to their inherent abilities, and the big help they got from the government, the machine-tool makers had managed to catch up. Far behind American and European rivals in the 1950s, they drew abreast in the 1970s, and then pulled ahead in one segment after the other. They were acknowledged as producers of good and cheap machinery, not mere copies but advanced articles as well. By the late 1980s, Japan had already passed Germany and the United States to become the world's top producer and exporter.

PHARMACEUTICALS

There has always been some question as to whether the pharmaceutical industry was targeted. That is doubtlessly because the Ministry of Health and Welfare, the principal agent here, was more discreet in its activities than MITI and others. It played a more passive role, limiting itself to protecting rather than directly promoting the industry. Yet, although the means were less striking, they were no less effective.

Few industries were sheltered for as long as pharmaceuticals. For three decades after the war, until 1975, it was impossible for foreign companies to go into the business on their own. And it was hard for them to send exports. These faced an impregnable battery of tariffs and quotas which only came down during the 1970s. The nontariff barriers, even more extensive and insidious, remained well into the 1980s with some vestiges still in the 1990s. Using one regulation or another, MHW blocked the acceptance of foreign drugs even after they had been approved in other advanced countries.[27]

Among the nontariff barriers, cited here just to show how prohibitive they could be, were several that obliged producers, basically, to repeat the approval process in Japan. It was necessary to redo the clinical tests locally because, or so it was argued, racial differences might cause different reactions. The insistence on redoing preclinical tests did not even have a scientific basis because they were conducted on mice and guinea pigs. Since there were no written guidelines nor a generally accepted code of Good Laboratory Practice, applicants were dependent on the good will of MHW bureaucrats, who did not have to give any justification for their decisions.

These various barriers had several baneful effects for foreign makers. They raised the price of imported drugs, because of tariffs, or reduced the number that could be shipped, through quotas. The additional testing and strict adherence to safety regulations also added to costs, sometimes substantially. Far more important, they kept new products off the market for years while Japanese competitors could develop their own. And shortened the period they benefited from patent rights, should they be so protected.

The foreigners' loss was clearly the Japanese makers' gain, and this was the key to MHW policy. Since they could not export or produce locally, the only way to get into a promising market was for the foreign firms either to license production or to go into joint ventures in which they could only hold a minority interest. On either basis, it was the Japanese partner which marketed the products. In most cases, it was also the Japanese partner which manufactured the products. In this way, local firms learned how to make a broad array of medicines, at negligible cost to themselves, and controlled the distribution channels so that they could easily insert their own products when desired.

Over the years, literally thousands of products were licensed and about 150 foreign firms entered into joint ventures. Some of their partners were already pharmaceutical firms whose technological level was much lower to begin with but grew rapidly. Others had been mere distributors until they learned by doing. Many more companies, by buying or borrowing knowhow, also entered the industry. Only after 1975 did they face any genuine threat from foreign companies, some of which finally set up their own production and marketing arrangements.

Helping local companies manipulate the market was only one contribution of the Ministry of Health and Welfare. No less crucial was its surreptitious financing of the industry. This was done largely through the national medical insurance scheme under which MHW bureaucrats set the prices for some 15 000 products. These prices were particularly high in the early years when production had just resumed. Even during the 1970s, prices were kept high although enhanced productivity and scale lowered the production costs. Not until the 1980s, and the financial crisis, were prices cut substantially.

Meanwhile, ignoring practices that would have been regarded as abuses anywhere else, MHW encourage the overmedication and excessive use of medicines that have become characteristic of Japan, making it the second biggest market overall and the top one in per capita consumption. Rather than having drugs distributed by independent pharmacists, most of them were sold by the very doctors and hospitals that prescribed them. By obtaining these products beneath the official rate but selling them at MHW's approved rate, they could make as much or more money than they did practising.

What with one thing and another, pharmaceutical sales grew at an incredible pace even by Japanese standards. Production rose by 10–25 per cent a year during the 1960s and 1970s, exceeding ¥1 trillion in 1970 and ¥4 trillion in 1983. Pharmaceutical companies regularly made huge profits, higher than any other industry and three or more times the level of manufacturing in general. This naturally encouraged the rise and expansion of companies, numbering about 2000. Equally striking, these larger and financially stronger firms were soon coming out with more new products on their own, as much as a quarter of the new products launched. While still only a minor player abroad, domestic companies recaptured half of the domestic market by the 1990s.

This was certainly an achievement which even MITI might envy. But it was not without its costs. No one shed a tear for the foreign companies which were kept out or hemmed in. But there were – and still are – patients who suffered and perhaps died for want of proper medication. All patients paid more for whatever medication they got and, as noted, they certainly got more than they should. What happened was a clear transfer of resources from the patients to the doctors, hospitals and pharmaceutical companies, namely MHW's clientele.

6 Rising Sectors – Private

It was not only the government which singled out attractive products and mobilised its resources to promote them. This was done throughout the postwar period by the private sector, often with striking success. In some of these exercises, the public role was secondary, minor or negligible. But this did not keep the businessmen from pushing ahead. The goal they had in mind, although not always stated publicly, was not so much a strong economy or international recognition as market share and sometimes profits.

Thus, for these branches at least, there was less concern with dynamic comparative advantage even if some more enlightened entrepreneurs had their eyes on the future. They conformed more closely to the existing resource endowment, only moving calculatingly from labour-intensive processes to capital-intensive and finally knowledge-intensive ones. For some, this was done while producing the same articles, upgrading them or switching to new-fangled versions of the same thing. For others, it involved a diversification into other, more promising sectors.

While government aid was smaller, it was not entirely lacking and could, on occasion, be critical in assuring the sector's success. But most of the credit certainly goes to private companies for finding ways to improve on any products they targeted and especially for their ability to manufacture them more efficiently and guarantee greater reliability and quality. Although not all managed to do this, those which survived and expanded were exceptionally astute.

It would be impossible to embrace the immense range of products that were developed primarily by the private sector. Only some of the more characteristic ones or outstanding success stories are included here, such as automobiles, motorcycles, consumer electronics, sewing machines and watches. There are many, many more worthy of note, like cameras and film, glass and ceramics, audio equipment, measuring instruments, household appliances and processed foods. Most services also derived from private initiatives such as real estate, warehousing, leasing, printing, publishing, advertising, tourism and leisure.

AUTOMOBILES

It is often claimed, most vociferously by the companies concerned, that the automobile industry emerged on its own with only minor government assistance. In fact, it is added, the government was against 'us'. Only strong-willed and self-reliant efforts were responsible for the rise of what has been one of Japan's most successful industries. While there is a degree of truth in this, it is far from being the whole truth.[1] To understand the situation better, it is necessary to go back to prewar days.

Initially, passenger cars and trucks were imported from the United States and Europe since local indigenous attempts at production were an utter failure. Realising the market's potential, both Ford and General Motors set up assembly plants and quickly dominated sales. Soon after, in 1926, MITI's predecessor, the Ministry of Commerce and Industry began what could only be regarded as industrial targeting. It appointed an Industry Promotion Committee which undertook a study of the motor vehicle industry and ultimately recommended that the struggling local automakers jointly design a single model to compete with the foreigners.

Nothing came of this until the 1930s, when the country began preparing for war and the military needed a national industry that could make trucks and other vehicles. The spillover on the commercial side was, first, an attempt to merge three existing companies, which failed. Then major *zaibatsu* like Mitsui, Mitsubishi and Sumitomo were approached, but refused since this was not a money-making proposition. Finally, two new entrants – what became Nissan and Toyota – were backed as national champions. To make sure they succeeded, Ford and General Motors were forced to close down and high protective tariffs went up.

Admittedly, after the war, production slipped drastically and many of the facilities were in poor condition. But an industry still existed and the task at hand was not to create one out of nothing but to restore it. At the time, this did not look very easy. The country was again overrun with foreign vehicles that were vastly better, and considerably cheaper, than local models. Thus the automakers could not even sell what they produced and the costs of production and inventory were undermining them. In an attempt to rationalise, they laid off workers and strikes broke out at Nissan and Toyota.

Meanwhile, given the industry's abject state and certain theoretical considerations, a debate raged as to whether Japan should even manufacture passenger cars. On the basis of comparative advantage, some insisted, it should not tackle such capital and knowledge-intensive activities. Others added that the costs were too great and would drain essential capital away from more useful projects. This side was led by the Bank of Japan and financial circles. The Ministry of International Trade and Industry had very different views. The abstract argument was concluded in 1950, when the Korean War broke out and the automakers were flooded with orders.

Prior to this event, there was every possibility that the automotive industry would have collapsed or at least been stalled for a consider-able time. But the financial resources, the increasing experience, the occasion to attain greater scale economies and a chance to show what they could do led to a resurgence. Much of the further progress must be attributed to the entrepreneurs who held tight under adversity and then seized the passing opportunity. But a very crucial residual share of the credit goes to government support.[2]

First of all, the industry enjoyed financial backing. It was a major recipient of low-interest loans from the Reconstruction Finance Bank which also absorbed earlier loans with commercial banks right after the war. It also obtained funds from the Japan Development Bank. Equally important, it benefited from tax breaks which permitted special depreciation of property and facilities. This was particularly important since rapid depreciation of machinery made it cheaper to change models. By the 1960s, these were less and less essential as commercial loans and retained earnings grew.

The government supported R&D as well, partly by encouraging it with tax write-offs, partly by actually carrying it out. MITI's Motor Vehicle Technology Institute worked on engines, transmission gear and other parts as well as standardisation. Other projects were carried out by laboratories of the Ministry of Transport and the Japan National Railways as well as trade associations and universities. Most significant in early years, this did not actually phase out, as later studies were done on anti-pollution and safety devices. In addition, the Agency of Industrial Science and Technology promoted electrical motor vehicles. Still, again by the 1960s, the automakers assumed the bulk of the R&D burden.

However, before they got down to truly independent research the automakers absorbed as much as they could from abroad, since foreign competitors were far ahead technologically. This was facili-tated by MITI's policy of encouraging tie-ups such as arose between Nissan and Austin, Isuzu and Rootes, and Hino and Renault. This brought a valuable transfer of technology in return for licensing fees. Toyota, both before and after the war, insisted on going it alone. But it was not above copying foreign makers' parts or taking their models apart to see how they worked. Nor were any of the other Japanese makers.[3]

MITI occasionally engaged in more specific industrial policy and targeting. As early as 1948, it adopted a 'basic policy for the motor vehicle industry' which laid down production plans and set goals that were never reached. It then promoted a 'people's car', as of 1955, which was to be small, cheap and mass-produced. Once the design was approved by MITI, production would be subsidised. Nothing ever came of this because the specifications were impossible to meet and the makers opposed the plan.

During the 1960s, to create stronger companies, MITI pressed for specialisation and tried to keep out new entrants (namely Honda). This failing, it sought to bring about mergers into three major groups, each specialising in a certain type of car. That was not much more palatable to the companies and only had modest results. Prince was absorbed by Nissan and later on Nissan took an interest in Fuji, and Toyota in Hino and Daihatsu.

Last, but certainly not least, MITI and other ministries protected the market. Strict quotas were only lifted in 1960 for trucks and yet later, in 1965, for passenger cars. But there were still substantial tariffs, as much as 40 per cent for smaller cars, with the level gradually declining until it reached zero in the late 1970s. All this while, and until the present day, MOT maintained numerous intricate and questionable nontariff barriers that made importing time-consuming and costly. Just how decisive this was is mentioned by Michael A. Cusumano in a comprehensive study of the industry's development.

> Public officials had less influence on the automobile industry than on sectors such as iron and steel, shipbuilding, or electronics. But a single policy – protection against imports – turned companies that would surely have been business failures into highly profitable operations.[4]

MITI not only adopted measures to keep foreign autos out, it adopted even stricter ones to keep foreign automakers out. Restrictions on investment, in either local production or existing firms, were preserved until the 1970s. Once withdrawn, some of the weaker

Japanese firms opted for foreign partners rather than come under the control of domestic rivals as Chrysler bought into Mitsubishi, Ford into Mazda and General Motors into Isuzu and Suzuki. Bans on investment had a subsidiary but far from negligible effect of making it impossible for them to open dealerships on their own. Foreigners not only had to export, they had to pass through Japanese intermediaries that often boosted the prices yet further and were sometimes seen as the most insidious nontariff barrier of all.

The authorities also promoted sales in a rather devious manner. They insisted that automobiles undergo strict inspections (*shaken*) every two years, inspections so stiff that many owners bought new cars sooner than they would otherwise have done. Yet, this could hardly be explained as concern about safety because the bureaucrats were less rigorous in their demands on the quality of new cars. Frequently models which were regarded as defective abroad, and which had to be recalled for safety reasons in the United States, continued being driven in Japan. Indeed, a consumer movement which tried to repeat the exploits of Ralph Nader in showing just how dangerous Japanese cars were – in early years, they were hardly flawless – was blocked. The relative absence of recalls and product liability suits was a tremendous saving.

Nothing was more important to the ultimate success of the Japanese automotive industry than this long period of incubation.[5] Without it, foreign makers would probably have set up local production facilities that dominated the market and/or invested heavily in domestic makers and dominated them. They would also have established distribution channels. Faced with massive imports, it would have been impossible to attain reasonable scales for Japanese models since, less well designed, with poorer technology and uncertain quality and reliability, they would not have been popular. Instead, potential purchasers had to buy Japanese or go without while the manufacturers gradually overcame the defects and drawbacks.

Meanwhile, profits, even on the originally mediocre Japanese cars, were gratifying. By the late 1960s, when the automakers had already resolved most of their production and design difficulties and were exporting, the gains were even greater. They could then produce cars cheaply and sell them for as much as 40 per cent more as a result of tariffs. Fortunately, most of the earnings were ploughed back into new plant and equipment, more R&D and especially export promotion. As the Japanese market ceased growing rapidly, the urge to export only mounted. For the earlier models, which were not quite as good as American or European cars, it was necessary to stress the price advantage. Any savings for foreign customers were undoubtedly compensated for by higher prices to ordinary Japanese.

Japanese companies did not like MITI's meddling in business or calls for cooperation or mergers. But they did appreciate the aid and protection. Individually, and jointly through the Japan Automobile Manufacturers Association (JAMA), they lobbied for more. By the 1960s, however, they realised that they would soon have to stand on their own and were increasingly in a position to do so. They worked tirelessly to produce the best cars, offering the most features and finest quality for the lowest price. They never hesitated to upgrade technologies and equipment, improve the use of human and financial resources and develop a network of equally proficient suppliers.

In fact, in their drive for expansion, company executives frequently engaged in industrial targeting that would have put MITI officials to shame.

First of all, every maker had comprehensive plans for production and sales of motor vehicles, not just in general but categorised by type and model and even market. They could calculate how many of a given model, comparable to other makers' models, could be sold in Japan and abroad, further breaking this down by Japanese prefectures and cities and even foreign countries and cities. This was the basis for other plans, often quite long-term plans, for plant expansion, renewal of machinery, employment of personnel and so on.

Secondly, while each maker specialised in given models, they were always eager to make more. Toyota and Nissan gradually introduced larger, flashier cars to compete with American and European makers. They also launched smaller models or cooperated with minicar makers like Hino and Daihatsu. As these possibilities ran out, they targeted other sectors they could enter, whether more closely related, like fork-lifts for Toyota, or somewhat further afield, like aerospace for Nissan. Each of the new ventures was subsidised by the old.

Meanwhile, and throughout the period, they saw to it that their suppliers also targeted the essential parts and components. This last aspect is perhaps the most interesting because subcontracting of parts production is so important not only for automobiles but for most leading Japanese industries. Thus, assemblers would only import parts as long as they could not be supplied locally, an internal 'buy Japanese' policy of sorts.

To get what they needed, assemblers would cultivate existing suppliers or create entirely new ones. They would urge them to acquire any necessary technologies and do the basic research. But, to get the best, assemblers might also do some of the R&D, provide advice on manufacturing and management, purchase in large enough quantities to justify valid scales and even offer or guarantee loans to make the essential investments. In return, they had readier access to the full range of parts and could raise the quality and reduce the cost of these essential elements.

While the plans and targets were not always met, and sometimes did not even come close, they did provide a firmer basis on which to work. Without them, the rapid expansion would have been impossible. So would much of the later cost-cutting. How smoothly the system could run was shown by the just-in-time system which was based on annual, monthly, weekly and even daily production targets which determined the rate at which suppliers should deliver parts to the assembly line and themselves procure raw materials to make more.

The only drawback was that occasionally the automakers got carried away by the urge to meet ever more ambitious targets. Corporate machismo tended to override more sober economic calculations as each company vied to expand market share while its rivals, to preserve what they had and perhaps gain an edge, did the same. This was a constant factor in the relations between Toyota and Nissan but it affected smaller companies even more since they could less well afford to lose even a bit. The intense competition would have resulted in the disappearance of second or third-ranking makers if not for the possibility of boosting export sales.

These rivalries therefore extended abroad since, in Europe or America, Toyota would still compete with Nissan while Honda, Isuzu and Mazda would sell all they could to maintain production scale. When Toyota decided that company policy was no longer merely to outdistance Nissan but to overtake General Motors, the situation became more acute. If Toyota were to grab 10 per cent of world sales, its officially proclaimed goal, other companies would have to lose. The most likely candidates were foreign because they cared more about profits than market share and, to preserve profits, would perhaps keep losing market share until they simply vanished.

The unsettling encroachment on foreign markets led MITI to intervene in the industry's affairs once again. This time it was not to promote expansion but to defuse endless trade conflicts caused by massive Japanese exports, and promise further efforts to truly open the Japanese market to imports. Neither of these activities was appreciated by the automakers, although they conceded that a trade war would be even more distasteful. To improve relations with the United States the industry accepted 'voluntary export restraint' as of 1981 and MITI assigned the makers export quotas based on past performance. They also tacitly accepted tight quotas in various European countries and then a European Community limitation.[6]

To get around these barriers, the automakers began production in the United States and Europe in the 1980s and sought to expand further in the 1990s.[7] This move overseas was taken not only by the larger companies but by the smaller ones as well, afraid of falling back. They carried their rivalries with them, Toyota trying to outpace Nissan, Honda trying to make up for a weaker position in Japan, and so on. Since they continually expanded production and frequently cut prices, the competition for local makers was intense. It was estimated that, between imports and local transplants, Japanese makers would hold a third of the US market by the mid-1990s. It might hit half that level in Europe.

This was an incredible transformation for a sector which was only revived in the 1950s and started exporting in the 1960s. By 1990, it was about as large as the American industry, producing some 13 million motor vehicles at home and another million abroad. However, while the US makers were in some difficulty and clearly contracting, Japanese makers continued expanding and were bound to reach the number one position sooner rather than later.

MOTORCYCLES

Japan's emergence as the principal manufacturer of motorcycles was certainly much more a result of entrepreneurial efforts than in the case of automobiles. Initially, even scooters had been regarded as too much of a luxury to waste scarce resources on, and the Occupation authorities actually forbade production. When Japanese industrial policy was resumed, motorcycles were definitely not regarded as a strategic sector and there was little concern about it.

While the industry was not promoted, it was protected and that made a big difference. It benefited from exchange-control rules which made importing foreign products impossible, and later, tariffs which made it costly. Foreign makers could not invest to open their own factories or even create a proper distribution network. As for everything else, skewed exchange rates made imports more expensive and exports cheaper. Also, not to be forgotten, the authorities allowed people to drive smaller scooters without a licence and did not recall models that were deemed hazardous abroad. Japanese consumers thus paid for part of the learning process, occasionally with their lives.

Still, it was the individual entrepreneurs, relatively few of them with any experience at making motorcycles or running a business, who took the lead. Many began by tinkering with broken imported models, seeing how they functioned and replicating them. Others simply put motors on bicycles and worked their way up. This activity only really got underway in the 1950s, and yet, within a few years there were almost a hundred motorcycle companies.

Naturally, they could not survive without dramatically improving the quality of their products and bringing down costs so that they could compete with more sophisticated and cheaper foreign models. To do so, they did not hesitate to engage in massive reverse engineering. This much was conceded by a MITI insider. Companies 'had few scruples in choosing models to be imitated, whether they were American, British, German or Italian. Patents and priorities were systematically held in contempt . . .'.[8]

In this turbulent atmosphere, some companies proved tougher or more imaginative than others and gradually increased their market share. In fact, within little more than a decade, most of the initial contenders had fallen by the wayside and only four remained. Honda, with prewar antecedents, was the leading firm, with over 50 per cent of the domestic market. Yamaha, an offshoot of the musical instrument firm, was second, with only about half as much. Then came Suzuki, which also made minicars. And finally Kawasaki Heavy Industries, more committed to shipbuilding.

Having improved the quality and design of their motorcycles and consolidated their position, all four makers began exporting massively. To some extent, this was in order to earn valuable foreign exchange and expand scale. But it also derived from the continuous rivalry between the makers, Honda trying to maintain its lead abroad and others seeking to outflank it. In so doing, they were eventually exporting more units than they sold at home. In the course of time, they also took up overseas assembly and production.

Since competition is such a significant aspect of this and every other industry, it is worthwhile examining a specific case in more detail. The most serious recent bout occurred in the early 1980s, when a new and ambitious president of Yamaha decided to close the gap with Honda. By launching more models, and covering more categories of consumers, he was able to gain market share per cent by per cent. Then, attempting a greater leap, he invested heavily in a major plant that could almost double output. With this sharply increased production on the way, Yamaha tried to pull ahead and lowered prices to do so.

For some while, Honda was too busy improving its own passenger-car operations and trying to broaden its small niche in the domestic market. But it could not risk losing more motorcycle sales and reacted no less aggressively. It stepped up production and turned out fifty different models in one year, twice the normal rate. It also sold them more cheaply. The offensive was so forceful that it left Yamaha and the other two makers reeling. And it shook the industry as a whole. For the makers were stuck with almost a million unsold units.

What became known as the 'H–Y war' hurt all four makers, none of which made any meaningful profits and some of which made remarkable losses. Yamaha was worst hit since it had expanded production more and was stuck with more inventory. It also had to pay for the loans it had taken out to build the new plant. In the end, it ran losses of over ¥24 billion and had a debt of ¥105 billion. It had to give in or risk destruction. In 1983, it cut back sharply, reducing production by more than half despite the massive overcapacity. It also dismissed or transferred part of the workforce and dropped the overly ambitious president.[9]

What is particularly interesting is the role of price during the competition. The initial attempt by Yamaha to catch up consisted of targeting successful Honda models and turning out something along the same lines. As production mounted and units had to be sold, prices were cut abroad . . . but not in Japan. Even when financial difficulties arose there was no desire to upset the comfortable price structure which was imposed on domestic dealers by the makers. Costs were cut instead, including personnel and even utilities, with factories working unheated in the middle of the winter. Finally, with unsold units piling up, it was necessary to sell them locally at deep discounts, a most unusual occurrence in Japan. Once the competition ceased, however, the prices went back up to recoup losses.

It is not surprising that this kind of rivalry devastated foreign makers. The Americans and many Europeans had more open mar-kets where Japanese motorcycles could readily penetrate and sell at low prices until they gained a reputation for quality. In Japan, it was hard even to find dealers that would handle any but the most exceptional foreign makes. Once the Japanese foursome, especially Honda and Yamaha, shared a vast domestic market, they could easily keep prices lower abroad by keeping them higher at home. Ultimately, the only foreign makers which survived were some of the top German ones, Harley-Davidson (thanks to special protection) and some of the Italian ones, since they also looked after their domestic producers.

Thus, by the mid-1980s, four Japanese companies not only shared 99 per cent of the national market, they also held about 70 per cent of the world market. This enabled annual production to rise to over 6 million units, which is an impressive level. And it was done with hardly any help from above.

CONSUMER ELECTRONICS

Consumer electronics is another of the sectors that the Japanese manufacturers opened up and developed largely on their own. Yet, even here, there was some government assistance in the initial phase which should not be overlooked, especially since it was this early boost which got the industry going.[10] It was then much easier to continue improving old products, adding new products, enhancing quality, reducing price and expanding markets. This is most noticeable for four major products which became the industry's mainstays: radios, black-and-white televisions, colour televisions and video cassette recorders. Such a base made it simple enough to absorb other articles, some a bit further afield, including tape recorders, video discs, microwave ovens and refrigerators.

Aside from rice cookers and *futon* driers, there was virtually no product that originated with the makers. They had all been invented somewhere else, they had then been tested and improved, and even markets had been created before the Japanese stepped in. Radios go all the way back to Thomas Alva Edison. The Americans pioneered black-and-white television and RCA had a workable colour system by the early 1950s. Video cassette recorders were developed by Ampex in 1956. Holland's Philips was also a source of products including a variety of VCR and the compact disc player.

What the Japanese did, basically, was to improve on what they found. For example, for radios, Sony used transistors (also an American invention, from Bell Laboratories) to produce smaller, even portable models. Sony also developed the Trinitron picture tube which enhanced the quality of colour television. Both Sony and Victor Company of Japan (JVC) miniaturised video cassette recorders, sharply reducing not only size but cost, so they could become commercially accessible to the general public.

It was certainly easier, faster and cheaper to improve on old products than to invent new ones. It was just necessary to acquire foreign technology somehow. The more reputable way was to license it, and literally hundreds of technologies were adopted year after year, both for complete products and for the necessary components. Companies needed no encouragement to do this, realising the potential themselves or copying rivals whom they did not want to get ahead and preempt the market. The other technique, less defensible but still applied, was reverse engineering.[11]

This does not mean that improving on what they found did not require intelligence and ability, indeed, a kind of genius. Some of the modifications involved designing components and products with better performance or more features. Others were to reduce the number of components, thereby making goods cheaper to produce and less likely to break down. Miniaturisation was a constant feature, since the smaller, the cheaper, and also the smaller, the handier and more likely to be used widely. Obviously, quality was the key to much of this. So was manufacturing technology. With a smarter use of personnel, increased automation and efforts to prevent defects from occurring, it was possible to turn out better, cheaper and more reliable products.

This continuous and meticulous improvement explains much of the steady progress of the industry. But there were periods when it spurted ahead, passing the originators and sometimes actually driving them from the market. This was often related to a crucial breakthrough. For example, again with radios, the use of transistors rather than vacuum tubes. For television, it was the greater use of solid-state technology and integrated circuits. For VCRs, it was the miniaturisation, which really came into its own with the Walkman.

While the technology transfer was largely a result of private initiative – Japanese companies contacting more advanced American or European ones and working out a deal – there was a government role. MITI saw to it that the deal was more acceptable than might have been obtained by a weaker and supplicant local partner. And it did its best to have any knowhow disseminated widely. Moreover, by preventing foreign investment, it left licensing, technical assistance and joint ventures (with the foreigner as minority partner) as the only alternatives.

There was also some official support of basic R&D. A MITI-financed project as of 1966 helped makers develop television receivers using integrated circuits. Another worked on solid-state devices for components. More recently, the Agency of Industrial Science and Technology, in cooperation with several firms, studied video discs. Of particular importance during the whole period was the effort of the Japan Broadcasting Corporation (NHK) to upgrade the industry. Its laboratories made notable contributions to all sorts of technologies, including magnetic video-recording, high-performance VCRs and high-definition television.

After all, although they tended to forget it, the electronics companies were also covered by the three special laws on the machinery, electronics and information industries. Indeed, even before they were adopted, as of the mid-1950s, MITI was channelling assistance. Some of this took the form of direct grants and low-interest loans, for either research, commercialisation or modernisation. The Japan Development Bank provided many of them but even commercial banks favoured producers of the then 'strategic' articles.

Nothing was more precious than reserving what was to become the world's second biggest market for national manufacturers. MITI used the whole array of barriers to keep television imports out: foreign-exchange control, quotas, tariffs, NTBs. Thus, even less satisfactory and more expensive locally-made sets could be sold when America was still producing the best. When Japanese companies became more proficient and could match foreign products in quality and price, the barriers had another effect. Local makers could still sell at higher prices, indeed, as high as the tariffs permitted, and collect fat margins.

In this sense, trade barriers were a much bigger contribution to company finance than were tax rebates, R&D subsidies or cheap loans. For example, with duties on imported televisions of 30 per cent until 1970, television manufacturers could earn 30 per cent more than otherwise on what were, by then, quite substantial sales. Fortunately for Japan, these profits were not dissipated but used to finance the next generation of products. Thus, radio sales subsidised television development, television sales subsidised VCR development, VCR sales subsidised video disc development and so on.

These extra earnings did one more thing. They subsidised exports. The government provided special depreciation for manufacturing capacity needed for exports, and other exemptions for cultivating foreign markets. There were also cheap export loans. But this was nothing compared to the financing derived from selling on protected markets. In this sense, for example, televisions sold more expensively at home subsidised sets sold more cheaply abroad. And, when higher prices were not assured by tariffs, collusion among makers kept prices relatively high. Even the Japanese consumers noticed this, although only in 1970 did they react angrily with a boycott of expensive colour TVs.

It was this combination of improved products at lower prices – products which were improved and whose prices were kept down through government–business cooperation – that enabled the consumer electronics industry to export massively abroad. As of the late 1960s, at a time when its television tariffs were still much higher than American ones, Japanese TVs gained a major share of the US market.[12] In fact the rise was so sharp and precipitous that most American makers (including those who had invented the product) were in difficulty and sought redress. The charges of dumping were ultimately vindicated, but by then most had gone under and major Japanese companies had local factories.[13] The same process then occurred in Europe and elsewhere.

Many American government officials, businessmen and academics felt that this was not terribly unsettling.[14] It was normal that Japan, with its cheaper labour, should take over such products. What they did not realise was that, once having taken over certain products, it was much easier to dominate others. The best example is video cassette recorders. They require many of the same components and, having given up on TVs, no foreign manufacturer could make VCRs cheaply or efficiently. More insidiously, the more consumer articles they had in their product range, the more mature ones could subsidise newcomers. This meant that government aid and protection was no longer necessary, the companies could target new products and cross-subsidise them on their own.

While it is obvious that American and European firms fell under the blows of Japanese export drives, it is often forgotten that a large number of Japanese companies also disappeared in this fierce and unforgiving competition. The several hundred radio makers, the several dozen television makers and the broad ranks of VCR makers were quickly narrowed down. The survivors of the early shakeouts were naturally in a better position to get through later ones so that, by now, there are only about a dozen major manufacturers left. They are strong, integrated and diversified companies like Matsushita, Hitachi, Toshiba, NEC, Mitsubishi Electric, Sanyo, Sony, Sharp and JVC.[15]

It is interesting to note that, having taken the lead for consumer products, the Japanese did not radically change their business practices as one might have expected. They still engaged in targeting, only this time they copied each other. There was a small group of more creative, imaginative and innovative firms that first saw the potential of novel products and came up with marketable models. Most prominent was Sony, the originator of the transistorised radio, Trinitron picture tube, Walkman and Beta-format video cassette recorder. Another was JVC, which developed the VHS-format VCR. Other firms were more conservative, cautious and slower; but had greater marketing capabilities, like Matsushita; better *keiretsu* connections like Mitsubishi, Hitachi and Toshiba; and also greater financial resources. The latter often waited for new products to prove themselves and then came in massively.

This happened for transistorised radios, colour televisions and the Walkman, of which there were dozens of replicas within a few years. But nothing compared with the intense competition over video cassette recorders, initially launched by two smaller companies, Sony and JVC, and eventually licensed by many more. From year to year, copying from one another and improving on one another, the performance rose, the number of parts and size decreased, the quality and versatility were upgraded. Meanwhile, prices plummeted. This was partly because smaller size and larger scale permitted price reductions. But it was primarily to drive the weaker makers or the opposite team (VHS versus Beta) out of the market. In the end, it was the stronger marketing power and financial backup of the VHS team that won, and Sony's Beta-format, judged technically superior by most experts, that lost.

By the mid-1980s, consumer electronics was one of the biggest industries in Japan. Defined to include audio equipment, video equipment and household appliances, it generated over ¥7 trillion in sales annually. The hottest items were now VCRs, although televisions, tape recorders and stereo sets held their own and it was hoped that video discs, compact disc players and high-definition television would be the rising stars. In nearly all cases, exports exceeded domestic sales, often by two or three to one. For some articles, like VCRs and compact disc players, Japan was almost the only source.

Strangely enough, despite the evidence that the consumer electronics industry could get along on its own, and the fact that it had been largely ignored until then, in the late 1980s MITI decided to target high-definition television (HDTV). This was partly because it was looking for something to do but also because the same technologies could be used for computers, medical, defence and other products. 'That', according to Peter Groenenboom, head of Philips's international consumer electronics division, 'is why the Japanese have targeted HDTV as a key strategic industry. They wish to dominate tomorrow's economic world.'[16]

Indeed, MITI's Masahiro Hashimoto claimed that the high-definition market could reach $34 billion by the turn of the century. However, while MITI was serving as organiser and cheer leader, much of the actual research and support came from NHK and private companies. By 1990, Sony, Matsushita and others were selling sets which would at first be too expensive for most but whose price could be brought down to two or three times that of a conventional receiver by mid-decade. Meanwhile, although there was hardly any demand yet, NHK began broadcasting high-definition programmes so that there would be something to view. The rest of the world was already being left behind.

CONSTRUCTION EQUIPMENT AND OFFICE AUTOMATION

One of the more instructive areas in which to see how Japanese companies have carried out their own targeting is construction equipment. The sector was never targeted as such, although it definitely benefited from the broader industrial policy which restricted imports and investment. There was also a very definite tendency to procure Japanese products for use in public-works projects. But any lacks were overcome by the domestic manufacturers, who managed to close the rest of the market by themselves and induce any necessary technologies. This was done in anything but a haphazard manner and the achievements of this somewhat neglected sector were as impressive as others on which MITI lavished much time and effort.

The key to the process, as must be realised by now, was keeping foreign companies out long enough to permit local makers to develop the basic products and knowhow to get along on their own. In this sector, it was particularly easy because of the close relationships existing within the groupings or *keiretsu*. Each major group had one or more members which produced – or could produce – construction equipment. They also included, and this was crucial, members which constructed buildings and public works (contractors), sold or leased buildings (real-estate firms) and financed construction (banks). It was not really that difficult to convince the contractors to use, and the real-estate firms or banks to recommend, use of products provided within the group.

It was obviously not a strict rule and every Mitsubishi construction firm did not exclusively use Mitsubishi products. But it was easier to sell them. An outside manufacturer, one with no links to any grouping, was in a considerably weaker position. This much was admitted by foreign makers who opted for cooperation with Japanese companies as opposed to attempting to penetrate the market on their own. The most intriguing case is Otis, which had a joint venture with Toshiba from 1958 to 1965. When its elevator sales slipped, it again opted for a joint venture with Matsushita, in 1974, rather than try to work the market alone.

Realising their marketing clout, the Japanese companies offered this, in exchange for technology, to outside companies that had something they wanted. Shortly after the war there was a lot to be learned and numerous companies licensed technologies or went into joint ventures. Among the most prominent were the Caterpillar Mitsubishi joint venture and Komatsu's tie-ups with International Harvester and Bucyrus-Erie. This was not done for everything, but particularly for strategic items like tractors, power shovels, wheel loaders and so on. There were also the Otis joint ventures.

In these cooperative arrangements, whether licensing or joint ventures, it was the Japanese company which handled not only the marketing but also the production. It was carefully and comprehensively instructed on how to make the products, how to apply the technologies and how to maintain quality. There was nothing theoretical about this, technicians were sent by the foreign partner to show local personnel exactly what had to be done. Japanese engineers, technicians and workers, as well as managers and researchers, learned by doing.

It apparently did not take long for them to know how to do everything quite nicely on their own. If the foreign partner kept adding to its line and upgrading its technologies there might be enough more to learn to keep the pupil satisfied. If not, the partnership tended to languish. Worse, the Japanese pupil often began improving on the original product, adding new features, making smaller models, adjusting to local conditions, using more electronic devices and especially refining quality. Since it could now produce independently and controlled the market, nothing was easier and more tempting than to shed the foreign partner.

Foreign managers usually envisaged this possibility and prudently incorporated in the agreements stipulations about termination, so that it could not be done unilaterally by the Japanese partner, and about sales and exports of improved models. While they were willing to concede the impenetrable Japanese market, American and other companies had no desire to let their partners export similar (let alone better) products throughout the rest of the world. But the Japanese often managed to slip out, as did Komatsu with International Harvester and Bucyrus-Erie. It is interesting to note here that the Fair Trade Commission, which paid little heed to massive violations of antitrust law, was insensed by these restrictions on Japanese licensees and joint venture partners, which, it argued, were not valid.[17]

Thus, by the 1970s, Japanese manufacturers were recovering the domestic market from foreign interlopers. Otis's share of elevator sales plummeted from a high of 80 per cent to a low of 10 per cent. The slack was taken up by broad-based manufacturers like Toshiba, Hitachi, Mitsubishi Electric as well as specialised firms like Fujitec. Komatsu relentlessly expanded its position until its local sales were almost four times larger than those of second-ranking Caterpillar Mitsubishi. The next step, in the 1980s, was to expand overseas. Fujitec took the surprising step of moving its headquarters to the United States, its prime market. Komatsu, hoping to beat Caterpillar on its home base, also set up production facilities in the United States. By the 1990s, the Japanese were well on their way to success as American competitors came on bad times.

The turnaround in the office-automation sector was even more extraordinary. OA only became a slogan for Japanese companies in the early 1980s, when many of the products were already fairly mature. Until then, they had been rather minor players with a very small share of the market. Yet it took no longer than a decade to rise to the top for a string of significant products which were targeted, one after another, including photocopiers, electronic calculators, electronic cash registers, word processors, typewriters, facsimile machines, computer systems, and so on.

Only for computers did Japanese companies obtain direct and substantial assistance from the government. So it could be said that the greatest credit for any success must be attributed to the private sector, which is true. Still, it would be unfair to totally discount the backing of the public authorities since they helped put the companies in business for many of their other products, including consumer electronics, telecommunications, computers and semiconductors. This laid the foundation on which they could engage in their own targeting exercises.

By the time the Japanese got into the business the products they selected were well known and the technologies tried and true. So, there can hardly be talk of foresight. It did not take much imagination to realise that there would be a mass market, especially if costs could be brought down. To obtain technologies, Japanese managers approached Texas Instruments, Xerox, NCR and others which were tops in their fields. As we already know, lacking any other way of getting into the Japanese market during the 1950s and 1960s, they accepted the provision of technical assistance, licensing of technologies or entering joint ventures.

Only a small portion of the research was supported by the government, especially NTT's work on small facsimile machines. The overwhelming majority was launched by companies that were behind and determined to catch up. They managed to make the necessary improvements in design, performance and quality. They reduced the size, weight and, especially, cost. More decisively, they adapted these products to the electronics age thanks to knowhow acquired in other sectors. It was again the use of solid-state technologies and semiconductors, namely the addition of electronics to products which were once primarily mechanical, that enabled them to draw ahead.

Coming after trade liberalisation in most cases, the market was no longer closed by tariffs or quotas. But there were occasional nontariff barriers, some thrown up by NTT. Far more important was that by then the major electronics companies controlled the distribution system. They either owned or dominated the wholesalers and retailers and in some cases had vast networks of specialised outlets that sold only their goods. In addition, they had privileged access to the *keiretsu* and other groups. It was quite impossible for a foreign company to penetrate the market except through a Japanese partner, another reason to accept risky tie-ups.

Once again, the competition was fierce among the rivals for each product and few remained after the shakeouts. Four companies (Tokyo Electric, NCR Japan, Casio and Omron Tateisi) controlled 70 per cent of the electronic cash register market. The top five

(Canon, Ricoh, Fuji Xerox, Konishiroku and Sharp) held 75 per cent of the photocopier market. Casio, Sharp and Canon had 74 per cent of electronic calculator sales and Brother and Silver Seiko held 70 per cent for electronic typewriters.[18]

This was an impressive, and increasingly excessive, concentration of sectors which elsewhere might have disturbed antitrust authorities. But it was passed over by the Fair Trade Commission, which also tolerated market manipulation to fix prices and keep new entrants out. MITI, on the other hand, was pleased with the situation since it now had a small number of very strong players on the international market.

It is obvious that Japanese exports did well because the products were carefully designed, of high quality and accessibly priced. But it is no less clear that, by controlling a huge domestic market, it was possible to attain considerable scale safely and use domestic sales to subsidise foreign sales. For diversified producers, which the companies were in most cases, earnings on earlier products even more effectively subsidised the development, manufacture, domestic sales and export of the latest hot items.

The result was usually predatory pricing and sometimes crass dumping, which allowed the makers to enter foreign markets. Once established, they followed somewhat more normal pricing practices although, in a pinch, they never hesitated to undercut the competition. With time, there were not many foreign companies left. Some went bankrupt and others took the more comfortable way out, selling Japanese products under their own brand name. By the 1990s, most of these products were almost a Japanese monopoly.

One unexpected success was typewriters, whose recent history typifies the process. Typewriters had once been entirely neglected by the Japanese and left to American and European companies including IBM, Xerox and others. For decades this industry was nurtured and developed by these companies until, in the early 1980s, it was realised that electronic typewriters could be better and cheaper than mechanical or electric ones. Then the Japanese jumped in massively, a dozen companies entering the sector and expanding production at an incredible pace. To sell this huge inventory, prices were marked down sharply, often below cost, and typewriters were sold in ordinary stores or through catalogues when traditional retailers proved inadequate or recalcitrant.

The Japanese could keep prices low not only because of large-scale production or simplified models but because they produced many of the electronic parts in-house. But that was not enough and recurring losses had to be covered temporarily by other products until the competition died down. Then the makers would have not only a new product line but one that consumed chips, which would thereby permit larger scale in that sector. With electronic typewriters gradually merging into word processors, the motivation grew even stronger. The smaller foreign firms were quickly swamped or had to sell imported typewriters and even the larger ones were in trouble. Within a decade, Japan's market share rose from negligible to dominant.

SUNDRY

Not surprisingly, less glamorous articles tended to be overlooked by the bureaucrats and targeters. Nonetheless, they emerged as major Japanese products as a result of the ability and determination of private entrepreneurs. Sewing machines, watches, zippers and musical instruments are just a few but they sum up the situation fairly well.

Admittedly, even they sometimes benefited from the broader industrial policy and obtained long-term, low-rate financing on occasion. The Japanese market was closed to almost everything in the 1950s and 1960s, and these products were frequently included. Of particular concern was to keep Singer from either exporting or producing sewing machines locally. Just as often, however, the products seemed so unimportant that foreign manufacturers neglected the Japanese market, given its notorious complexities. Zippers, among others, surely gained from that indifference.

Nevertheless, the articles existed. The technologies were available. Markets at home or abroad were receptive. A smart entrepreneur could take the technologies, apply them in Japan, and sell to the expanding markets. This was realised by several sewing-machine companies that had been nibbling at Singer's market share before the war; the K. Hattori company, which made watches the core of its activities; and a small zipper maker named Tadao Yoshida, whose factory was bombed during the war but who made a comeback under the brand name of YKK.

These entrepreneurs were all visionaries. But none of them were so visionary as to bet on some future, dynamic comparative advantage. They realised that after the war the only thing Japan had in abundance, and cheap at the price, was skilled and hardworking labour. The products they chose, and for good reason, were then exceedingly labour-intensive. Sewing machines, rather small items as such, still incorporated hundreds of parts which had to be made carefully and assembled painstakingly. This was even more acute for mechanical watches. Zippers absorbed more labour for a modestly-priced article than anything.

That the key was labour, and not capital, and not technology, was perfectly clear to all concerned. So the sectors were vulnerable. To beat the Japanese competition, Singer opened its own factories in Taiwan to use yet cheaper labour. In order to survive, the Japanese had to do the same. Even while Hattori's Seiko was undermining the high-cost Swiss watch operations, it was being undermined by masses of tiny sweat-shops in Hong Kong that could turn out workable, if rudimentary, watches at half the price.

As Japan gradually lost its comparative advantage for labour, and acquired one for capital and technology, the manufacturers reorganised their operations . . . without need of bureaucrats to preach rationalisation. They invested in more machinery and automated processes to an unheard of degree. Seiko factories were soon working night and day with hardly any personnel to service them. Zippers were barely touched by human hands any more, except to check their quality. Metal and textiles were fed into one end of YKK's production lines and came out as an endless strip of zipper at the other.

In some cases rationalisation took another form. Major manufacturers were actually only assemblers and the mass of parts and components was made by small suppliers and subcontractors. This was done for sewing machines in a rough-and-ready way until MITI had a brilliant idea. If, rather than each manufacturer having its own suppliers, they were to pool the orders, enabling larger, more efficient suppliers to arise, everyone could benefit. The suppliers could attain larger sales and become more proficient; the assemblers could have better and cheaper parts. While this did not entirely appeal to them, since each company wished to maintain its distinctiveness, cooperation was deemed necessary to compete against Singer's giant operations.

Makers also increased expenditure on R&D. Most of the budget originally went into development, improving on existing products, technologies and manufacturing processes. But ever more went into research. In some cases this was decisive. Japanese watchmakers recognised the potential of quartz technologies and digital watches well before the Swiss, who mastered and unwisely stuck to the intricate techniques of mechanical watches. Quartz, as it happened, was the wave of the future and the Japanese rode it hard. As solid-state components penetrated consumer electronics, they also had spinoffs for sewing machines which could now be computerised and programmed faster by the Japanese.

But, as so often, it was the marketing end (plus financing) that was crucial. The makers began establishing wholesalers and retail outlets. Some had extensive networks of door-to-door salesmen, as for sewing machines, others opened shops in as many neighbourhoods as possible, as for watches. YKK seemed to have distributors everywhere, some of them former competitors which earned more selling than making zippers. Ultimately, consumers bought Seiko watches or YKK zippers not only because they were good and priceworthy but because it was so convenient and, to tell the truth, so hard to find competing (especially imported) products.

Financing was necessary to create this far-flung marketing apparatus, which often involved long delays in the payment of goods. It was also essential for the endless bouts of competition. These commercial wars were not easy to avoid. With rivals constantly boosting scale and capacity, supply had to exceed demand on occasion and price-cutting was essential to unload excess inventory. But these losses were made up later when makers colluded on prices, which was increasingly the case as the sectors consolidated.

From year to year the number of domestic competitors dwindled. The process went amazingly far in these three sectors, further than even MITI would have recommended. There were ultimately only two major sewing machine makers, Brother and Janome. Seiko, Citizen and Casio, but especially Seiko, dominated the watch industry. YKK managed to corner 90 per cent of the market, an exceptional achievement even for Japan.

Having taken over the Japanese market, it was much simpler to conquer foreign markets. With massive domestic sales, the makers did not hesitate to offer their products at extremely low prices to gain market share. But they did not do this across the board. They nibbled at smaller markets first and stuck to a narrow range of articles. Once they had a foothold, they expanded. They went after larger markets and moved up from relatively ordinary, cheap models to more luxurious ones. Unwary competitors went under, including Singer and many Swiss watchmakers, although the latter counterattacked. For zippers, it looked as if YKK might eventually have a worldwide monopoly to go with its domestic one.

Before closing, there is one last company which must be mentioned because it epitomises more than any other what company targeting was about. That is Yamaha, the world's leading maker of musical instruments and more. Before the war already a producer of pianos and organs, this company has undergone a striking evolution over recent decades. Taking advantage of Japan's cheap labour it was the first to 'manufacture' pianos using mass-production and assembly-line techniques. These cheap pianos were sold to music shops and schools which might want other instruments, which Yamaha soon provided. Eventually selling nearly the whole orchestra, it was possible to price the latest instruments added to the line very cheaply to win market share. Just to be certain its products were suitably marketed and serviced, Yamaha opened its own stores and schools.

Then Yamaha went up-market, creating an electronic organ, the 'electone', which carried its activities into a new dimension. Soon it was producing all sorts of electronic equipment, not only audio and video sets but the integrated circuits that went into them. Since music was part of the leisure industry, the next steps were into sports and recreation, with centres, equipment and clothing for tennis, skiing, golf, and so on. Used to fashioning wood for pianos and guitars, it took to making other wood products, like skis, but also furniture. In this amazing progression, the old ventures cross-subsidised the new, pianos helping guitars, electones backing ICs, the lot supporting leisure. As for exports, how could the relatively small foreign companies specialised in pianos or guitars, skis or furniture, even video or ICs, compete with such a giant when it had targeted a specific market segment?

7 Sectors Slated to Rise

It is more than slightly misleading to assume – as some observers claim – that the day of industrial policy has passed and now the government entrusts the economy to market forces. What has happened is simply that different sectors are being targeted and are receiving substantial aid, but in somewhat different ways. Upon closer scrutiny, one could actually say that there is about as much effort to boost the economy to a higher level as there ever was. This time, however, the desire is not only to catch up or even pull ahead but to take the lead.

Talk of the public authorities withdrawing from active involvement is equally erroneous. In most of these frontier sectors, the government plays an eminent role and, in some, private companies can only be coaxed into cooperating because of this support. It continues providing ample funding, although more in the form of loans than grants. It also offers tax benefits. But the primary thrust now is support of basic research and practical R&D. While this sort of thing also occurs in other countries, it is not as sharply focused or as directly linked to commercial spinoffs.

This phase of industrial targeting began gathering force during the 1980s, when many new sectors were picked as showing promise and being somehow appropriate to Japan's comparative advantage, or where it wished to be some years (or decades) hence. It can be assumed that it will continue beyond the end of this century and well into the next, to judge by certain pronouncements. At any rate, we already know that some of the specific projects are not scheduled to finish until the late 1990s.

Among the sectors that were targeted are some which merely represent an upgrading of what already exists, such as the move from ordinary materials to 'new materials' or from machine tools to robotics. Others involve a bigger shift, as from pharmaceuticals to biotechnology. And a few imply a dramatic step into a wholly new realm, such as nuclear energy and aerospace. While the most significant sectors are included here, there are others, such as solar energy or undersea mining.

Here we will deal first with the more commercial sectors where private companies merely need encouragement, like new materials, robotics and biotechnology. Then come those where little would be done without strong government backing, like nuclear energy and aeronautics, or where the government basically carries the ball, namely space technology.

NEW MATERIALS

In Japan every trend snowballs so rapidly that it soon turns into a 'boom'. This is what happened to the vague category of 'new materials'. To put together such an industry, targeters were rather eclectic in their choice. Anything that was new and anything that could be defined as a material went in. This included fine ceramics, rare metals, assorted plastics and glasses, carbon and boron fibre and, lately, gallium arsenide. It also subsumed optical fibres, which was a relatively separate item in certain ways.

While there may be some question as to the relationship among these various articles, there is no doubt that some of them were taking an almost revolutionary turn. Fine ceramics were much harder and more heat resistant than ordinary ceramics; carbon and boron fibre were much stronger and lighter than other fibres; new plastics had the strength of steel; gallium arsenide might replace silicon in computer chips. These resulted from promising technologies that were being developed in startling profusion and paved the way for potentially lucrative products of the future.

Once again, it was the private sector which saw the possibilities first. Admittedly, they were not in on the pioneering phase since American and European scientists and technicians had done all the spade work. But when products began emerging, Japanese companies were there. Kyocera quickly took the lead for fine ceramics, using it to package chips, while it and others developed a ceramic engine. Toray was the world's top maker of carbon fibre. Nippon Telegraph & Telephone fostered a group of local optical fibre producers. This was already in the 1970s.

Not until the 1980s did the Ministry of International Trade and Industry fully realise the potential. Late again, it went about diligently organising sectors which had grown up spontaneously and where new companies were flocking in droves. That meant inspiring trade associations, like the Optoelectronics Industry Promotion Association. More tellingly, it sponsored R&D cooperatives like the

Fine Ceramics Centre and New Glass Forum. In this case, it even entailed creating a 'science of new materials'.

For each one of the component sectors, MITI initiated, expanded or intensified its work, allocated more money and staff and extended more aid. Funds were especially pumped into R&D. Parts of this were a ten-year programme for high-performance ceramics costing ¥13 billion and a six-year programme for optoelectronics costing ¥18 billion. Lesser sums were devoted to other work on new plastics, glass, metal and so on. In cooperation with the Ministry of Post and Telecommunications, the Japan Key Technology Centre also began funding projects, expecting to invest ¥10 billion over ten years as of 1986.

None of MITI's operations were quite as effective as the promotion of fibre optics by NTT. Nippon Telegraph & Telephone early introduced research and helped its related suppliers develop adequate products. To do this, it was necessary to invent a new production method that escaped the patent rights of Bell and Corning Glass. To cover these expenses, it closed the domestic market to imports and bought from Sumitomo, Furukawa and others to cover the R&D costs and add a tidy profit. Even after privatisation, NTT continued to buy Japanese as much as possible so that the local suppliers might have a solid domestic base from which to launch the essential export sales needed to attain efficient scales.

This assistance, while helpful, was certainly not enough for Japanese companies to prevail over foreign competitors. They had to invest massive amounts as well. Indeed, the sums needed until the end of the century, as estimated by MITI, were astronomical: ¥3 trillion for new materials and ¥10 trillion for fibre optics. The only way such goals could be attained would be for leading companies, including some which had not initially been involved, to become major players. As the steel, chemical, electronics and telecommunications giants joined in it seemed that Japan could bring the necessary financial and human resources to bear.

What the ultimate result would be was extremely hard to predict at such an early stage. But this did not prevent the government and media from vaunting the merits of each new material. They were harder, lighter, stronger, more resistant and so on. They also had exceedingly great expectations. MITI forecast absolutely awesome growth. Sales of new materials were expected to expand from ¥300 billion in 1980 to ¥5.4 trillion in the year 2000. The optical fibre market would grow from ¥140 billion to ¥12 trillion during the same period. They would spawn related industries so that, by the twenty-first century, the sector would account for over 12 per cent of GNP.[1]

Of course, MITI and the media glossed over possible drawbacks. They forgot to mention that fine ceramics were still too brittle, that carbon fibre was hard to shape or that optical fibre was adversely affected by humidity. Above all, they failed to note that each of the new materials cost more than the old ones, sometimes ten or a hundred times more and could consequently only be used in special cases. Some day any defects or weaknesses might be overcome and production costs brought down significantly. But no one knew when that day would come. So, it was wisest to take MITI's figures and the media hype with the usual grain of salt.

ROBOTICS

For most of the early targeting exercises, Japan was initially far behind the leading contenders and needed substantial efforts to catch up. This was not the case for robotics, partially because the whole sector was so new. Robots were just a novelty or a costly and clumsy machine in the mid-1960s, when the first units were introduced by American makers like Unimation. With their concern for mechanisation and automation, Japanese tool makers saw the potential much faster than others.

Already in 1968, Kawasaki entered a licensing agreement with Unimation and was soon producing large numbers of robots. Other companies tied up with other American or European makers and some merely copied robots they bought. But the copying phase was amazingly swift since so much remained to be done to make robots a quality, priceworthy and viable product. This was accomplished largely through internal R&D and also by trying these new gadgets out on in-house manufacturing processes. As more and more companies joined in, there were ultimately several hundred, although the bulk of production was dominated by a smaller number of large firms.[2]

Since these firms had already proved their capabilities, possessed considerable staffs and ample financial resources and since, in addition, robotics was often just a sideline, they did not really need much help from the government. But MITI was not going to keep out of an attractive growth sector and it brought robotics under the 1971 Law for the Promotion of Specific Electronic and Machinery Industries and then the 1978 Law for the Promotion of Specific Machinery and Information Industries. It also undertook a number of activities whose importance, while secondary, should not be underestimated.

One was to create the trade association in 1971, even before there was a constituency. Two years later, this Japan Industrial Robot Association (JIRA) became an independent private association, including about a third of the robotics manufacturers, usually the larger ones, as well as domestic and foreign users. MITI also found a rather unconventional form of financing, funds generated by the minicar races.

Under the broader legislation, robot makers could benefit from assorted tax and financial assistance. Far more significant was the fact that purchasers of robots could benefit from even more facilities, especially small and medium-sized firms which might not have been able to acquire them otherwise. Favourable loans were provided by the Small Business Finance Corporation and People's Public Finance Corporation. Other loans came from special funds set up jointly by the central and regional governments. There was also a special depreciation allowance.

Of special note is the Japan Robot Leasing Company (JAROL), which was established in 1980 to lease robots to small and medium-sized firms. This was particularly helpful since, with rapidly evolving technologies, robots would preferably be leased and not bought, and then traded in as new models appeared. In addition, JAROL's conditions were particularly lenient. This was due to its sources of funding, mainly the Japan Development Bank, Long-Term Credit Bank and Industrial Bank of Japan. Not surprisingly, it leased only Japanese-made robots to Japanese clients.

While not large, there was some assistance in the form of research and development, usually on more fundamental or long-term projects than were undertaken by the makers. It included work on futuristic types of robots and the use of robots in flexible manufacturing systems and small-batch production. Some of the R&D was done by MITI's AIST and other projects by the Japan Small Car Promotion Association, also financed by the minicar races. But this was almost trivial compared to MITI's brainchild of a ten-year $1 billion international project to develop intelligent manufacturing systems (IMS), floated in the late 1980s, but which met with more suspicion than support abroad.

While it is harder to put one's finger on it, there is a further element which was probably more important than any financial or research assistance. This was the generally positive and supportive atmosphere surrounding everything related to robotisation, which was in sharp contrast to the more tempered and cautious mood in the West. MITI, and the government as a whole, insisted that robotisation was essential for Japan's economic and social well-being. It could improve the quality of working life by taking over dangerous and dirty tasks, and enhance productivity so that smaller firms could survive. Not a word was said about alienation or loss of jobs. . . .

This helps explain two interrelated phenomena. One is that Japanese companies quickly became the leading producers. They kept boosting output, from less than 2000 units a year in the early 1970s to over 30 000 in the late 1980s. But that was only possible because Japan absorbed the largest share. By 1990, Japan's industrial-robot population exceeded 275 000, more than twice the number in all other countries put together. This achievement, while impressive, still falls far short of the industry's grossly optimistic expectations in the late 1970s, when JIRA forecast levels more than twice as high for production, exports and total population.

BIOTECHNOLOGY

It is hard to grasp why the Japanese are credited with exceptional foresight in recognising emerging sectors before others. There was no sign of this with regard to biotechnology. American and European researchers were developing the essential processes, including recombinant DNA techniques, the basis for genetic engineering, back in the 1970s. Some initial products were even coming out. Yet, the sector was completely overlooked by the Ministry of International Trade and Industry in its earlier lists of growth industries. In fact, it was not until 1979 that MITI identified biotechnology as a potential area of growth. Then, in its 'Vision of the 1980s', it was formally targeted.[3]

It could not be said that the private sector was much more aware of the possibilities at first. Hardly any companies showed an interest in the 1970s, when pioneering venture-capital firms were sprouting up in the United States and Europe. Not until the early 1980s was there a movement, quickly degenerating into a mad dash, to get into the new sector, with many companies joining only because the others were there. Even then, the pull was not always as great as the push since relatively few of the participants grew naturally into biotechnology work, namely the pharmaceutical companies. The rest, including processed-food, chemical and textile makers only came because their main line of business was in trouble.

Nonetheless, it was clearly the private sector which was taking the lead. That was because the firms involved were not, as in the United States, small ventures but large and wealthy companies which could rapidly mobilise whatever funds and personnel were necessary. In short, they could engage in inter-company targeting while MITI backed them with broader industrial policy. Among the major players were Ajinomoto, Suntory and Meiji Seika (food processing), Mitsubishi, Takeda and Sumitomo (chemicals), Toray and Teijin (textiles) and Kyowa Hakko, Mochida, Green Cross and Hayashibara (pharmaceuticals). By the mid-1980s, over two hundred companies had joined the race and were carving some niche in the ebullient biotechnology industry.

With a 'biotechnology boom' on its hands, MITI could scarcely guide the companies in what it regarded as suitable directions. It was even hard-pressed to organise them in any rational order. Still, it did try to group them and establish appropriate machinery to avoid wasteful duplication and rivalry. It advised about a hundred companies to form a trade association, the Japanese Fermentation Industry Association, and then created an 'overlord' for biotechnology, the Bioindustry Development Centre (BIDEC). MITI also encouraged the formation of smaller, more specific groups to study various aspects of biotechnology. Meanwhile, it beefed up its own biotechnology operations in the Bioindustry Office and appointed an advisory Bioindustry Promotion Committee.

Given the critical position of research and development, and the possible risks involved, Japan finally adopted guidelines on genetic research in 1979. But they were much stricter than in other advanced countries. So, MITI promoted more liberal research guidelines. It took several years to achieve this modest goal. Meanwhile, it also began funding R&D, providing substantial grants to groups of firms working on key topics like recombinant DNA, bioreactor development and large-culture cell growth. It was intended to spend some ¥27 billion on these projects over a ten-year period as of 1981.

MITI, however, was not able to monopolise the field. The Ministry of Health and Welfare also promoted biotechnology research. As did the Science and Technology Agency. And the Ministry of Education. And the Ministry of Agriculture, Forestry and Fisheries which opened its laboratories and financed further projects in areas that interested it, like plant cell improvement, raising seed-growth efficiency and introducing bioreactors in the food industry. Between them, they probably sponsored as much research as MITI. As per usual, there was more rivalry than cooperation, let alone coordination.[4]

But the bulk of the resources was coming from private companies. R&D expenditures rose at a remarkable pace. By 1985, when MITI provided ¥4 billion and MHW, STA, MOE and MAFF about as much, private spending amounted to ¥95 billion. And this component was growing most rapidly. By then, leading companies were already devoting 10 per cent of sales to research, a level comparable to their overseas counterparts.

In this frontier sector, supporting research and development seemed to be about all the targeters could do. They could not close the market to biotech imports; these did not exist yet. They could not subsidise biotech exports; there were none of those either. However, they could protect and promote the leading biotech firms in their other activities, like pharmaceuticals, processed foods and chemicals. This, as we have seen, was undertaken extensively by MITI, MHW, MAFF, and so on. It permitted the companies to earn larger profits on their main lines of business which could then be tapped to subsidise work on biotechnology.

No sooner had they entered the field than, trying to make up for the great delay, Japanese companies sought to pull ahead of foreign rivals. It was hoped that this could be done because of their long experience with one of the key technologies, fermentation. While not as novel as gene splicing, it was crucial since fermentation was essential for cell proliferation needed to 'harvest' large quantities of desired substances. Indeed, they quickly made some notable contributions. But it was clear that the truly original work was being done abroad.

While many foreigners claimed Japan could not progress because of a lack of creativity, and the Japanese were afraid this would hurt them, it was not as vital as thought. Using the same techniques that had enabled them to come out on top in many other sectors, they turned the strengths of their opponents against them. Foreign companies applied for numerous patents which, if granted, would probably have made Japanese companies dependent on them for a long time. But the patents were simply not granted and Japanese companies could benefit from the knowhow displayed in the applications.

Japanese companies busily acquired foreign knowhow. This was done by licensing products and technologies. Going a step further, they also bought parts of more successful foreign companies like Genex, Genentech, Collaborative Research and others. They even did collaborative research with American universities or opened research centres in the United States. As one perspicacious observer noted, the tactics had not changed much. 'They'll spend 95 per cent of their resources on importing technology and 5 per cent on developing it. They've skipped the entire first stage of trial and error. Once Western companies have ties here, they'll lose everything, little by little, through the aggressive information-gathering campaigns by the Japanese.'[5]

The other basic tactic, also largely unchanged, was to make up for any weaknesses in scientific technologies with their proven excellence in production techniques. They could manufacture products discovered by others more cheaply and efficiently, a decisive advantage. This could be done for products licensed by them, or through joint ventures for the Japanese market, or by improving on existing products just enough to evade patent laws and sell wherever they wanted. Since fermentation knowhow was particularly useful in this aspect of the business, and they had ample funds, efficient facilities and trained personnel, the Japanese might do better with the products than the foreign originators.

According to a 1985 report of BIDEC, biotechnology should account for some 10 per cent of Japan's gross national product by the year 2000. This was just another one of those offhanded estimates an impressionable public relished. It was also claimed that by then Japan would be number one in the industry. That was equally open to question. But there is no question that what was once a laggard has been catching up at a breathtaking rate and will certainly give the Americans a run for their money.[6]

NUCLEAR ENERGY

No country can modernise and industrialise without a solid energy infrastructure, which is one of the more arduous and costly enterprises. It was tackled in Japan with a vengeance as more and more power stations went up, electric lines were strung across the country and electricity became readily available nationwide. This was one of the primary concerns of the Ministry of International Trade and Industry, which backed the development heavily. It also secured the largest loans, at the most lenient conditions, for the power companies.

But it did considerably more than that. Like many other countries, Japan could have left this task largely to private companies, allowing them to use the money in what they deemed to be the wisest manner. This, MITI was not willing to do. Its own bureaucrats busily studied the situation, determining how much total power, and from which energy sources, would be necessary over the years, and issued periodic forecasts. It got the utilities to adjust their plans to these targets so that supply would not fall behind demand.

What is more, MITI decided which should be the favoured sources of energy. Here, its decisions were frequently flawed. As we saw, it first tried to prop up the declining coal industry by keeping out petroleum. However, as the cost of coal continued rising and oil costs plummeted, it finally shifted to oil. It seemed not to realise that one day, simply as demand kept rising, oil costs might go up. It was even more oblivious to the political situation in the Middle East, so it was taken completely by surprise by the oil boycott and creation of OPEC. Thus, in the mid-1970s, MITI prepared for another shift to alternative sources, especially nuclear energy.[7]

As elsewhere, there was a choice between nuclear and other sources like wind, solar, biomass, geothermal and so on. MITI came down strongly for nuclear, which appealed to its bureaucratic thinking and could more readily be managed through industrial policy. Only with nuclear could huge quantities of power be cranked out, and this process could be expedited by a crash programme of the sort it was used to running. It did not entirely neglect the others, launching a Sunshine Project on alternative sources of energy and a Moonlight Project on energy conservation. Both were run by AIST within the New Technologies for the Future programme.

This massive nuclear programme, and the point seems to have eluded many observers, had two goals. One was to erect enough nuclear plants to generate whatever energy would be needed. The other goal was to produce as much as possible of this network on its own. It did not want other countries to provide the reactors and related equipment any longer than necessary. Japan was to cover as much of the domestic needs as possible with domestic production. That is why MITI's line was so enthusiastically endorsed by business circles.

Thus, anyone who thinks that targeting is a thing of the past has not taken a close look at Japan's nuclear programme. Stymied in the attempt to preserve coal mining, frustrated by the mounting cost and unreliable supply of oil, the economic authorities seized upon atomic energy as the solution to many of their problems. And they launched a broad campaign to progress in every aspect of the sector, power generation, production of plant and equipment, development of next-generation reactors and the fuel cycle.[8]

The standard explanations for this strategy are simple and compelling. Japan is a small island nation almost entirely dependent on imported fuels. It was vital to find an indigenous source, or one requiring less raw materials, which could generate power at a relatively low price. Nuclear energy supposedly had these characteristics. Yet, even assuming it did, this does not explain why Japan could not use imported technologies and equipment rather than developing its own. That derives from deeper urges which pervaded all its targeting exercises.

The highest government agency here is the Japan Atomic Energy Commission (JAEC) which is an advisory body to the Prime Minister. Chaired by the Minister of State for Science and Technology, it is serviced by the Science and Technology Agency, which actually outranks MITI in this sector. STA is directly concerned with the research and development programme, although the actual R&D is done by the Japan Atomic Energy Research Institute (JAERI) and the Power Reactor and Nuclear Fuel Corporation (PNC). MITI is less involved in research than commercial operations since it licenses and inspects plants and looks after safety and public acceptance.

The other partner is industry. This consists, on the one hand, of the nine power companies and, on the other, of the manufacturers of plant and equipment. The utilities clearly play the predominant role, since they participate actively in the research work of JAERI and PNC. They dominate the Japan Atomic Power Company (JAPCO), which imports or develops reactors, and Electric Power Development Company (EPDC), which has to provide stable electricity supplies, partially through alternative energy sources. The power companies coordinate their position through their own federation and deal formally with the vendors through the Japan Atomic Industrial Forum.

Like most other industrial activities, the politicians play a rather secondary role, whether from the ruling party, which promotes nuclear energy, or from those opposition parties which reject it. Most of the decisions are made by the technical bodies consisting of bureaucrats (and often industrialists) and are rarely reviewed or even debated in the Diet. The political dimension only arises when local groups oppose the installation of some specific plant or complain about malfunctions and accidents.

The government's role in promoting nuclear energy has several strands, none more important than finance in what is an exceptionally costly venture. Money is provided through multiple channels, so many that it is hard to keep track of the total. Some goes through the projects funded by STA and various research bodies, another portion is disbursed by MITI through its own research activities or as subsidies of one sort or another. It was estimated that some ¥510 billion was spent on nuclear generation and technology from 1966 to 1975 and another ¥3820 billion by 1985.[9]

Whatever the sum was, and the figures cited could be only a shadow of the total, even more money was generated in another manner. MITI was instrumental in determining the electricity rates charged by the utilities. Since it was so deeply involved in promoting nuclear energy with them it did not hesitate to grant the increases they sought, and which were high enough to cover any costs of introducing new technologies, building numerous power plants and establishing the related infrastructure. It was thus the consumers who paid, indirectly, bit by bit over the decades.

The government was also helpful in obtaining the essential technology. Naturally, as a latecomer, Japan had to import its first reactors from abroad. Most were American although some reactors and other equipment were supplied by Great Britain and France. With time, however, rather than importing reactors and equipment the Japanese built their own under the direction and with the aid of foreign firms, Hitachi and Toshiba cooperating with General Electric, and Mitsubishi with Westinghouse. Attempts to do otherwise were blocked, as when the Japan Atomic Energy Commission failed to import the CANDU reactor.

In this way, the equipment was bought at negotiated prices and the technology came along with it. By the mid-1960s, only a decade after the nuclear programme was formally launched in 1956, Japanese companies were building reactors under licence. Within another decade, they were improving on the technologies they had acquired and were able to design their own reactors aside from relatively few parts or specialised technical consulting. They had not only caught up, according to some authorities they had already surpassed their teachers.

But that was not enough. The Japanese wanted to move ahead to advanced technologies that still had to be created. From light water reactors, which were the mainstay of the industry, they wished to progress to more powerful thermal reactors and, early in the twenty-first century, the fast breeder reactor. Further down the road would come nuclear fusion. They also wanted to handle their own fuel cycle including reprocessing. This was the agenda of the various research institutes and they were soon turning out results. One of the first was a prototype advanced thermal reactor known as *Fugen*, which was unveiled in 1979. After testing the experimental fast breeder reactor *Joyo*, work began on a prototype called *Monju*. Then, in the 1990s, might come a demonstration reactor and, in another decade or so, commercial units.

While work was proceeding on new generations of reactors, more conventional nuclear power plants were being constructed around the nation in one of the most ambitious programmes in the world. Since it enjoyed such strong government backing, this programme did not get stalled like the American one and there was enough standardisation to keep costs in line. Moreover, the operating rate was among the highest in the world and accidents were relatively rare (or carefully hidden from public view).

In these various exercises, cooperation with the government in general, and MITI in particular, was fairly smooth. The interests of the public and private sectors coincided on the whole and any differences which arose were usually related to priorities. The companies were naturally more interested in nuclear, where large plants were the order of the day and considerable revenue could be generated in a reasonable time. They were much less interested in alternative energy sources, requiring costly research and long development periods while offering uncertain returns. Even within the nuclear sector, some projects were more tempting than others and businessmen clearly thought of their own interests first rather than the national goals pursued by the bureaucrats. This was reflected in Samuels' study of alternative energy.

Where commercial applications have been low in risk and immediately apparent, as in light water reactors, development has involved the initiative of private industry coordinated with the (often grudging) support of the state. Where risks have been high and applications distant, as in advanced thermal reactors, fast breeders and synfuels, the state has been enticed into accepting the bulk of financial responsibility without a commensurate degree of control.[10]

Still, it would be misleading to assume that things ran according to plan and without a hitch. As a matter of fact, there was deep concern among ordinary people about the safety of nuclear plants and several prominent accidents only increased the anxiety. In the absence of suitable public review, opponents engaged in demonstrations and violence to prevent the construction of certain plants. It became ever more difficult to find appropriate sites, the time and cost of construction rose and it was necessary to buy off the local population with subsidies, cheap electricity, schools and other social infrastructure, or even 'cooperation money'.[11]

Delays were so numerous that MITI's targets were never met and had to be revised downward from year to year. For example, in 1973 it projected a nuclear generating capacity of 60 million kilowatts by 1985. That was scaled down to 49 million kw some years later, and then 33 million kw in another few years, and still there were only 22 million kw in 1985. Nuclear energy was supposed to provide 20 per cent of total electricity by 1985, but it only attained 15 per cent. This, of course, did not keep MITI and the industry from coming up with more projections to the effect that nuclear plants would generate 45 million kw, or 33 per cent of total power, by 1994 and 90 million kw, or 58 per cent of total power, by 2030.[12]

Although they did not attain their production goals, the power companies insisted that nuclear energy was a great boon since it generated energy more cheaply than any alternative, being only half the cost of oil. These calculations, produced by the industry and not verified by independent sources, were subject to doubt. Even if the nuclear reactors were efficient and relatively cheap, this overlooked the related costs of research and development, subsidies and cooperation money that did not go into the industry's budget but were borne by the public. When the oil price fell even the restricted calculations may have been reversed and oil was cheaper than nuclear.

The situation among the vendors, the manufacturers of nuclear equipment, was not quite as good. They had overestimated the demand and were soon working at only a third or half of capacity. There was not much of an international market to fall back on. And, producing in small quantities, they could not attain economies of scale. They were neither low-cost producers nor very profitable entities. The suppliers could only get by because they enjoyed government aid, the power companies had to buy domestic products and this was just a sideline for them anyway.

This raised serious questions about the future. Japan was now engaging in complex and costly research on advanced thermal reactors, fast breeders and fuel reprocessing just to meet its own needs. It would be impossible ever to justify such an effort if it were not to gain a march on competitors in the international market. Yet, no one knew whether the research would result in practical commercial applications that were cheaper than existing methods. And, even if they did, no one knew whether Japan would have better processes and equipment than its rivals. Finally, even if it did, no one knew whether those rivals would buy Japan's products rather than protect their own industry.

Japan was playing for extremely high stakes. If it won, it might cash in. Or it might not. That depended on many things. If it lost, on the other hand, there was no question that it would sorely regret this particular act of targeting.

AIRCRAFT AND ENGINES

Having produced aircraft prior to the war, and done so even more energetically during the war, the Japanese have always nourished a nostalgia for the aeronautical industry. But there was nothing they could do about it during the first postwar decade when they remained under the eye of Occupation authorities that forbade any military production and were suspicious of aircraft even for peaceful purposes. Yet, every Japanese bureaucrat and businessman knew that the industry would reemerge one day.[13]

But most of them did not suspect that it was from the military – and not the civil – side that the initial progress would be made. The Japan Defence Agency, for reasons common to all defence ministries, felt a need to have much of its equipment and ordnance produced locally, by companies it knew and could trust, even if this involved more cost and some tension with its allies. It therefore gradually went over to local suppliers, forcing the earlier American suppliers to enter into joint production or licensing agreements. As of the Third Defence Program, in 1967, it engaged in what would have been regarded as targeting if it had come from MITI. By the late 1970s, some 90 per cent of its material was obtained locally.

This included aircraft. Over the years, it procured a number of different types of helicopters, trainers and fighters. Its mainstay was the F-15 fighters and P-3C anti-submarine planes. With some minor exceptions, all of these aircraft were developed abroad and yet most were produced locally under licence. Mitsubishi provided the F-15s and Kawasaki the P-3Cs. The engines for both were made by Ishikawajima-Harima. But there was always an urge to develop 'Japanese' aircraft. This was only whetted by the T-1, T-2, T-3 and T-4 trainers.

In the late 1980s the Defence Agency sought to give the aeronautics industry a big boost by developing a domestic fighter. This met with opposition in Washington, with the administration insisting that it would be cheaper for Japan to buy or license existing American aircraft, which would also be good for the worsening trade imbalance. But the proposal of joint production of the FSX jet stirred up a furore in Congress, where it was warned that an even greater danger would be for Japan to learn state-of-the-art technologies needed to foster domestic companies as potential rivals to their American partners. In the end, the FSX proposal was adopted, but not without misgivings on both sides.

The Defence Agency's exercise in industrial targeting proved extremely expensive. Because of the small runs, locally-built aircraft were much more expensive than imported ones, often by a factor of two or more. And the local manufacturers did not earn very big margins. But they were able to learn how to make modern aircraft. The necessary knowhow, production skills and even some of the latest technology were transferred almost by force. Although the production runs were small, they were large enough to train competent engineers and workers. From there, it was a small step to develop modest design capabilities with which to create their own models.

Without this military stimulus it would have been exceedingly difficult, if not impossible, for Japanese companies to get back into the swing of things.[14] But that could only take them so far. The defence budget was limited to 1 per cent of gross national product and grew slowly, only raising sales modestly from year to year. Moreover, with a ban on military exports, it was not possible to increase sales beyond what the DA procured. If the industry were ever to take off it would be necessary to build up the civil side.

That was a task primarily for the Ministry of International Trade and Industry.[15] It regularly extolled the advantages: more sales and exports, greater value added, new technologies and commercial spinoffs, to say nothing of national prestige. But it tended to underestimate the difficulties. Promotion required enormous financial support and only offered slow payoffs, something most private companies were not willing to wager alone, and which could exceed the government's abilities on occasion. Foreign competitors were more experienced, technologically advanced and commercially aggressive, and thus not willing to give up sales easily. In the face of this, MITI was remarkably inconsistent and irresolute.

True, it quickly established the standard machinery. It activated its Aircraft Division in the Machinery and Information Industries Bureau. There was an Aircraft Industry Committee on the Aircraft and Machinery Industry Council, the *shingikai*. And both the Industrial Structure Council and Industrial Technology Council remained vocal proponents of a forward policy.

Rather than wait for private companies to emerge and form a trade association, MITI precipitated the move by adopting an Aircraft Manufacturing Enterprise Law in 1954. It was to encourage an orderly development of the industry, not too many firms, not too few, which could attain scale and cooperate. Ultimately it had its way, since the sector was dominated by Mitsubishi Heavy Industries (MHI), Fuji Heavy Industries (FHI) and Kawasaki Heavy Industries (KHI) for airframes and Ishikawajima-Harima Heavy Industries (IHI), MHI and KHI for engines. These, and lesser suppliers, formed the Society of Japanese Aerospace Companies (SJAC).

But MITI went much further. It initiated a continuing series of special non-profit corporations to handle each one of the successive projects. The first, the Nihon Aeroplane Manufacturing Company (NAMCO) was a 50:50 joint venture between the government and the companies concerned. In the following cases, the government stood on the sidelines and merely encouraged the manufacturers to form a consortium. They established, among others, the Civil Transport Development Corporation (CTDC) and the Engineering Research Association for Aero-Jet Engines (ERAAE). They served as liaison groups and conduits for funds.

To make up for any lacks, the government – inspired by MITI – did its best to increase the funding. Most of this was formally limited to aid for research and development since actual subsidisation of production would have been objected to by foreign competitors. It therefore kept the bureaucratic machinery busy working on plans and projects, cost estimates and sales projections. Once a promising venture had been singled out, some of the many public R&D institutes began more specific work. This included MITI's Agency of Industrial Science and Technology and STA's National Aerospace Laboratory and National Research Institute for Metals and others.

SJAC also received grants for research by its Revolutionary Aircraft Development Centre.

Far more significant, once a project had been entrusted to one of the manufacturing consortia, it was possible to allocate substantial *hojokin* loans. These were supposedly only for development and not for actual production, but it was hard to tell where one left off and the other began. Moreover, since this cost was borne by the government, the manufacturers enjoyed better commercial prospects should the project succeed and little risk if it failed. While the loans had to be repaid in theory, many never were, so they turned out to be thinly disguised subsidies. And very fat subsidies at that, over ¥170 billion for the six major projects described below.[16]

It was impossible for the government to protect the whole market, or even smaller segments, for long since its action was monitored by trading partners and it was periodically pushed to buy more aircraft. It could, however, encourage domestic airlines to buy Japanese-made planes when they existed or, in the absence of domestic articles, they could be induced to acquire the products of joint ventures. This corner on the market was enough to tempt foreign manufacturers into joint ventures with the Japanese for purely commercial reasons.

Thus, while R&D was important in raising the technological level of the Japanese makers, it was not really as crucial as the need to transfer technology to Japanese partners. In one project after another, first military, then civil, fledgeling companies were painstakingly taught everything they had to know to construct, under licence, one part or assembly after the other. In some cases they were licensed to produce whole aircraft. Eventually, the foreign partner only maintained some few secrets, occasionally hidden in a 'black box'.

The tremendous head start of foreign producers, and the inability to make up for all the lacks, explain many of the twists and turns of official policy. MITI bureaucrats, at least those in the relevant industrial bureaux and divisions, wanted to go it alone and create all-Japanese planes. Those dealing with trade, on the other hand, were under ceaseless pressure to buy foreign aircraft or at least enter joint ventures. The Science and Technology Agency, and the National Aerospace Laboratory, naturally strove to create a distinctive Japanese presence. But they all had to contend with the Ministry of Finance, which found it hard to provide sufficient funds.

Japan's first project was the YS-11 transport, a 64-seat turboprop produced by the Nihon Aeroplane Manufacturing Company. The consortium, led by Mitsubishi, turned out 182 units between 1965 and 1974, when production ceased. The plane was good, but not exceptional. It was also costly and thus the bulk were bought by All Nippon Airways and Toa Domestic Airways. While a modest technical achievement, it was a commercial flop. NAMCO was not able to sell enough units to recover costs and ended up with a loss of ¥38 billion, a rather hefty sum for those days.

This put a damper on future projects. Discussed back in the late 1960s, it was not until 1972 that the government put up seed money for the YX programme. This was to be a small (90 passenger) commercial jet. The idea of going it alone had faded and much time was spent seeking a suitable foreign partner. Finally, in 1979, the venture boiled down to mere cooperation in production of the Boeing 767, along with American and Italian makers. The Japanese team of MHI, KHI and FHI, grouped in the Civil Transport Development Corporation, handled 15 per cent of the job.

The next-generation airframe project was dubbed YXX. It was to develop a somewhat larger commercial jet. This time the Japanese side played hard to get, negotiating with Boeing, Airbus Industries and McDonnell Douglas/Fokker on various competing models. The primary goal was to enhance Japan's participation, making it a 'full partner' in development, production and sales. Finally, after years of indecision, in 1984, Boeing was again chosen as the partner and the Japanese got 25 per cent of the total package.

Meanwhile, work was going ahead on the XJB programme to produce a 'new technology' fanjet engine with 8–10 ton thrust. The projected engine would be designed for the YXX aircraft. Here too the outcome was merely a joint venture with Rolls Royce which possessed the essential knowhow and wanted help with its own RJ-500 engine. This time, however, Japan was an equal partner with 50 per cent of cost and production. The work was carried out under the Engineering Research Association for Aero-Jet Engines, consisting of IHI, KHI and MHI.

But this did not keep the Japanese from doing some work on their own. This was sponsored by the Science and Technology Agency. One project, to design and build a short-take-off-and-landing (STOL) passenger plane, was undertaken by the National Aerospace Laboratory. It was hoped that the first units would be ready by the early 1990s. The other project was to develop an FJR-710 fanjet engine, one that was quite similar to the RJ-500 and which, to boot, was being developed by ERAAE. It could be used to power the STOL plane. These were 'national projects', for which the government provided the direction and financing and contracted out work to domestic manufacturers. Alas, Japan failed again. In 1989, the STOL project was abandoned and the sole prototype was put in a museum.

It is not as if the manufacturers only followed the government's lead. Several went into cooperation or licensing arrangements for helicopters and engines. Major companies like Mitsubishi and Kawasaki became subcontractors for Western firms including Boeing and British Aerospace. Mitsubishi also developed a small business jet, the MU-2, followed by the MU-300. But the bulk of their business still came from military procurement and national projects. Thus, they were on the lookout for more. Seeking a new project for the late 1990s, they hit upon the advanced turboprop (ATP). No sooner had MITI begun feasibility studies than the Society of Japanese Aerospace Companies set up its own committee and five leading manufacturers organised a joint venture. Their first acts, however, were to call for government funds and support, warning that otherwise the industry might lose out on another crucial breakthrough.

Despite a very spotty track record, MITI remained as ambitious as ever. It soon began pushing for a new project codenamed YS-X, a short-haul 75-seater. It was supposed to go into service by 1994. And, for the twenty-first century, MITI wanted a supersonic passenger plane that could fly from Tokyo to New York in three hours, its very own 'Orient Express'.

Considering that two sets of activities are running parallel, some in which Japan is a partner with a growing share of the action and others where it goes it alone, it is possible that the original goal of 'Japanese' aircraft has not been dropped. Indeed, any cooperation may only be tactical. Eventually, the national industry may possess the technological capability and financial strength to produce its own airframes and engines. It could then shed its foreign partners and enter the market alone. That is certainly the hope of more enthusiastic bureaucrats and businessmen. But a soberer assessment came from Eiichi Ono, STAC's president. 'We do not have a very confident future. . . . Conventional wisdom has it that we are 15 to 20 years behind in engines. In airframes, we have no experience, so we can't even assess how far behind we are.'[17]

Looking back, the results have not been very impressive. So far the only truly Japanese commercial projects have been failures: YS-11, MU-2 and MU-300. They sold small quantities and made little money. The 'national projects', although promising on paper, have not come through either. Licensing and subcontracting have been more lucrative, but not enough to make a big difference to the companies concerned. The only safe source of earnings was defence work, where prices were bloated and accountancy lax. And that was only possible because the Defence Agency was willing to pay so much to have its aircraft produced locally rather than importing. Even then, aircraft was not much of a profit centre and only accounted for 5–10 per cent of most companies' total sales.

This shows that Japan was far from infallible in targeting and promoting sectors. Indeed, it is almost laughable to reread the assorted projections of MITI and the trade associations. According to an early MITI 'vision', aircraft were to be 'one of the industrial monuments of the 1970s'. Civil production was supposed to quickly overtake military production, but it stabilised at a mere 15–20 per cent of the total. Aircraft and engine production was supposed to grow by double-digit figures, which rarely happened. Japan's industry was expected to claim an ever larger share of the world market, as much as 20 per cent by 1980. But it was still a minor player by 1990. In fact, it was only about half the size of the German industry, a third the size of the French and British industries and a twentieth the size of the American industry.

Failures to meet development schedules, failures to meet production and sales targets and just fair-to-middling technologies have not fazed MITI.[18] It still proclaims that, in the twenty-first century, aeronautics will be a significant factor in the national economy and Japan a major player in the world. It may be right. But it will cost the Japanese population much more than thus far and it may create so much trade friction as to be counterproductive. Moreover, if Japanese entry further heightens the existing competition, it may never bring any real commercial gains.

AEROSPACE

Despite the huge cost and mitigated benefits of targeting aircraft and engines, the Japanese government did not hesitate to grasp at the even more advanced and challenging end of aerospace, namely satellites and rockets. Over the years, the priority was raised and now Japan is doggedly trying to catch up with the few existing rivals: the United States, Europe and the Soviet Union. It seems to have little concern about the costs and hazards of such a race nor a very clear idea of what it stands to gain should it succeed.

Japan got off to a rather late start because the Occupation authorities banned any rocket work after the war and there were few visible commercial opportunities. Still, in 1955, the University of Tokyo began some research. Space activities were sharply upgraded in 1969, when the National Space Development Agency (NASDA) was founded. A year later, the first palpable results were seen when a small experimental satellite was launched. This big step for Japan, however, was quite a small one compared with the United States, which had already landed men on the moon.

While there was a considerable expansion of the space programme during the 1970s, the effort was not as focused as might have been expected. It was obvious that the government had to be the prime mover, given the substantial costs and lack of commercial returns. Yet, rather than one agency concentrating the authority, it was dispersed. NASDA had the principal role in developing commercial satellites and rockets. But there was some overlap with the Institute of Space and Astronautical Science (ISAS), which was more interested in scientific satellites. Each had its own budget, staff, projects and even launching centres. NASDA came under the Science and Technology Agency and ISAS under the Ministry of Education.

Duplication and conflicts were not entirely overcome by the Space Activities Commission, which depended on the Science and Technology Agency. Still, it did lay down Space Development Policy Principles in 1978 and 1983 which were to chart the essential path. Its first 'vision' was a bit fanciful, invoking the many great things Japan could achieve in the sector. The second was more realistic, outlining the strategy to the year 2000. But it was hard to reconcile its two foremost principles – development of national technologies and international cooperation.

STA's formal primacy did not keep the Ministry of International Trade and Industry from intervening increasingly. The space industry division of the Machinery and Information Industries Bureau dealt with the sector in practical terms. And its advisory body had clearly targeted aerospace as a likely winner. It stressed the potential, forecasting that this could become a ¥1 trillion industry by the mid-1990s. To this end, 'it is desirable for a group of Japanese companies to obtain the ability to enter the world market solely on its own'. MITI therefore selected, promoted and organised companies which might play this role.

There were other voices as well. The loudest were those of the users of satellites, especially Nippon Telegraph & Telephone. As the primary user of telecommunications satellites, it wanted to get the best material for the best price even if that meant buying abroad. It was usually backed by the Ministry of Post and Telecommunications. Keidanren, on the other hand, was more concerned about where the satellites and rockets were made, preferring it to be Japan as much as possible. This view was supported by the Liberal Democratic Party, some of whose elements also wanted to add a military dimension to what was still a programme dedicated solely to peaceful purposes.

Amidst the various divergencies, the most important was clearly whether Japan should opt for domestic design and production or cooperate with other countries. The proponents for autonomy included STA, NASDA and ISAS. They were backed by Keidanren and LDP sympathisers. MITI naturally promoted domestic makers. But it had to permit some liberalisation to placate foreign makers. NTT (and MPT) would only go along with the 'buy Japanese' approach if the costs were not too great. The consumers and taxpayers, who ultimately had to foot the bills, were largely ignored.

Fortunately the choice was not so crass in the early period, for the simple reason that Japan could not progress on its own. In fact, it was vital to sign a space treaty with the United States in 1969 in order to induce the essential transfer of technology. This came from leading firms like McDonnell Douglas, TRW, Hughes and so on. The real question was therefore how long the transfer would last and how rapidly production would be localised. Most Japanese preferred accelerating the process, invoking cost considerations, bothersome delays and the threat that one day the transfer might be cut off. Yet, the more they pushed for domestic independence, the more they appeared as competitors and worried the sources of technology flows.

Unlike most other industries, which are geared to some commercial demand, aerospace production has been a direct result of government programmes. The goals are set politically, although obviously taking into account imputed needs, and then the necessary sums are allocated. Most of the money has been channelled to NASDA, a smaller portion to ISAS, while MITI and NTT have their own resources. The national space budget grew quickly over the 1970s, reaching about ¥100 billion by the early 1980s. It stagnated thereafter, because of financial restraint, only attaining ¥155 billion in 1989. While this was a very large sum for Japan, it should be remembered how modest it remained compared with the United States. It was about a tenth of NASA's budget and a twentieth of the total space budget, which benefited from military expenditures as well.

Despite the late start and financial constraints, Japan has made noteworthy progress. The most successful component has been satellites. Japan became the third country to place a satellite into geostationary orbit as early as 1977. It launched about twenty satellites by 1985, many of them partly or wholly designed and made by Japanese. They included meteorological, television-broadcasting, telecommunications and earth-surveillance satellites. But they were smaller and more rudimentary than the best produced by American firms. So, in 1983, NASDA launched a special project to develop better satellites and also become independent of American technology by 1992.

Japanese technicians also enhanced the size and quality of the launching vehicles. They started with 'pencil rockets' in the mid-1950s, graduated into 'baby rockets' and developed several generations of sounding rockets in the 1960s. With the N-I, as of 1975, they could put a satellite in orbit. The N-II and H-I, introduced during the 1980s, carried a larger payload. But they were still much smaller than the European Space Agency's Ariane or the American Space Shuttle, both of which could carry payloads of 2000 kilograms while the H-I only took 550 kilograms.

This gap was extremely important since satellites had been getting bigger with the years. NTT was working on a major project that required satellites the Japanese rockets simply could not carry, and sought to have them put into orbit by the Space Shuttle. If this were not done, it could not complete its Information Network System. The desire to use cheaper foreign launchers only heightened after privatisation, when it faced competition from other firms that were less willing to tow the government line. It took very strong administrative guidance to keep users from buying foreign satellites and leasing foreign launchers more than they did.

To overcome any limitations and to help Japan catch up, the Space Activities Commission decided to upgrade the rocket programme in 1983. It was decided to complete a larger H-II rocket, able to carry a 2-ton payload, by 1990. This timetable could not be met and the initial launch was postponed until 1993. Meanwhile, NASDA introduced an even more spectacular programme to build a space shuttle that could be launched in 1997. Called 'Hope', this vehicle would carry Japanese scientists to the Japanese Experimental Module on the US-led 'Freedom' space station. While initially designed to weigh 10 tons, there were soon hopes of raising this to 20 tons. Alas, it had yet to be determined how the H-II vehicle with a 2-ton capacity could possibly carry a 10-ton, let alone a 20-ton, Hope shuttle.

Thus, by the 1990s, the space programme had a much higher profile. This was partly due to bureaucratic intervention. But Keidanren, through its space activities promotion council, lobbied hard to boost the nation's space budget. No wonder, the biggest winners would be aerospace and defence contractors like MHI, KHI and FHI and electronics companies like NEC, Mitsubishi Electric and Toshiba. Distinctly less pleased were users like NTT and other telecommunications companies, although they could not reverse the trend.

Obviously, the men who directed Japan's space programme were ambitious. Too ambitious, perhaps. They tended to underestimate the difficulties of developing domestic satellites and rockets. True, local companies and technicians devised unique solutions to certain problems and conceived novel design and production methods. They were particularly good at increasing precision and miniaturisation. But there was so incredibly much to do and it was not always possible to find other ways than what existed. Moreover, while they advanced, their rivals were not standing still; the Americans, Europeans and Soviets were also coming up with new ideas, sometimes better ones.

They were also a bit arrogant. They tended to discount the value of the assistance that had been received from others, especially the United States. Without the help of NASA and the aerospace companies which either made or licensed the rockets and satellites and transferred the essential technologies, Japan could never have made the progress it did. Yet, Japanese politicians and bureaucrats did not hesitate to complain about every failure or delay. They gloated over NASA's problems. Meanwhile, they forgot that they had also undergone delays, cost overruns, flawed launchings and satellite malfunctions. In addition, even into the 1980s, only about a quarter of each satellite and half of each rocket were actually made-in-Japan.

The worst drawback was the unwillingness to measure costs against benefits. Japanese satellites and rockets, such as they were, cost two and three times more than American or European ones. They were also smaller and thus had less capabilities. Carrying less fuel, the lifetime of a satellite might be cut in half. The insistence on a 'Japan first' policy could thus multiply the costs five or ten times over when one considered all the aspects. The total loss to the state and private sector, as well as to the individual consumers and taxpayers, was huge, probably more than the whole cost of the space programme.

This only highlighted the economic irrationality of targeting aerospace. If it had merely been a question of using satellites, it would have been just as well to buy foreign ones that were bigger and cheaper. Even if superior or more adapted local ones could have been designed, it would still have been wiser to have them launched by American or European vehicles. That would at least have made it possible to concentrate on the more promising satellite sector and avoid the riskier launcher aspect. Would the situation improve dramatically in the future? Given the modest domestic market, and the unlikelihood of attaining scale economies, costs would only come down moderately and the industry would still find it very hard to export. This would make it impossible to create a prosperous industry – or perhaps even recover the development costs – any time soon.

This does not mean that a domestic industry did not emerge. Over the years, companies did develop and sales gradually rose to ¥150 billion or so by the mid-1980s. Half of this can be attributed to the space programme. Here, it was largely a matter of channelling government funds, tied to government projects, to a number of prominent aerospace companies, each of which latched on to some aspect of the programme. Only eight were really significant: Mitsubishi Heavy Industries, Kawasaki Heavy Industries, Ishikawajima-Harima, Nissan Motors, NEC, Mitsubishi Electric, Toshiba and Hitachi. For none of them, however, was this business particularly important.

To find real success stories, one has to look elsewhere. They derive less from the spectacular leap into advanced technology than from a gradual progression upward from more conventional projects. When a specific product, like an antenna, transponder or even whole satellite ground station could be produced efficiently, the Japanese did quite well. In fact, half of the total sales of the sector were for ground stations. And Japanese companies, led by NEC, conquered half of the world market.

If true cooperation and specialisation had been sought, instead of national independence, it is likely that Japanese companies could have found dozens of excellent niches in which to display their ability. And they would have been welcomed by potential partners. They could thus have collaborated on joint design and production, as for aircraft and engines. That would have drastically diminished the huge initial investment and hastened the day when reasonable scales could be attained and acceptable profits assured. But this was not the chosen path.

Can Japan be criticised for putting national pride and prestige ahead of economic and financial rationale just like the others engaged in the space race? In this case, yes. For the United States, Europe and the Soviet Union had an overriding military concern which was strictly forbidden by Japan's constitution and unlikely to be reversed by the existing political leadership. Also, Japan had a smaller economic and population base to carry the load. Most crucial, however, is that it was not willing to accept the necessary commitment. Expenditures, while heavy enough to weigh on the national budget, were not really adequate to win. Why, then, compete?

8 Declining Sectors

Finally, although the Japanese do not like to think of it that way, there is another major phase that is not only unfolding at present but should continue extending indefinitely into the future. It is the attempt to save declining sectors. Judging by Japan's experience thus far and especially the experiences of the countries that preceded it, this may eventually become the most substantial dimension of industrial policy.

As Japan's comparative advantage shifted, some sectors which had been flourishing fell upon hard times and shrivelled. This was regarded less as a natural or inevitable phenomenon than as something the government had to counter because, among other things, it involved a drop in production, losses of employment, sometimes serious bankruptcies and, in general, a weakening of the economy. Since this occurred in certain sectors which the state had previously sponsored, the relevant divisions and bureaux felt even more called upon to act.

When the government stepped in, it made strenuous efforts to halt, or at least slow down, the decline so that the sector might be rehabilitated, or at least preserved on a reduced scale. Meanwhile, it tried to shift companies into other sectors and have workers relocated. This required considerable financial aid, tax relief and occasionally, to keep foreign imports from further disrupting the precarious situation, protection. It also involved mergers and cartels. This time the businessmen were more willing to cooperate in order to avoid worse.

While each sector differed, it is worthwhile taking a look at the general framework for declining sectors now. The initial legislation was the Temporary Measures for Stabilisation of Specific Depressed Industries, for the period 1978–83. However, it had to be extended and amplified by the Temporary Measures for the Structural Adjustment of Specific Industries which would run until 1988. There was another law of a similar nature called the Smaller Enterprise Business Switchover Act for the years 1976–86. This legislation still remains in force in one form or another.

These various laws covered a broad, and growing, range of sectors. The initial legislation included mineral processing (electric furnace steel, aluminium and ferrosilicon), synthetic fibres (nylon, polyacry-lonitrile and polyester), chemical fertiliser (ammonia, phosphoric acid and urea), textiles (cotton and wool), linerboard and shipbuild-ing. The Switchover Act dealt with a multitude of lesser areas like ship repair, canned foods, rubber and plastic footwear, metal dinner-ware, socks and stockings and embroidery lace. As must be obvious, most of these were very labour-intensive or strongly impacted by higher oil prices.

The techniques involved were standard, only this time oriented toward an orderly retreat. They included financial measures such as low-interest loans, tax credits and grants for retraining workers. There were provisions for the voluntary scrapping of equipment, although administrative guidance could be invoked. To expedite the process, special cartels could be formed or special 'business tie-ups' arranged to coordinate production, transportation and marketing. Most of these exercises were overseen by MITI, although MOT was in charge of shipbuilding.

The essential goal was not to support ailing sectors or prolong their agony but to phase them out or scale them down more gently and quickly. Thus, sectors had to be specifically designated, a process some observers called 'picking losers'.[1] These would be sectors facing extremely unstable economic conditions caused by external factors, and which could be aided by reducing excess capacity within a reasonably short time. That the process was more difficult and time-consuming than appeared is obvious from the need to extend the legislation and from the few sectors which 'graduated' and be-came viable again.

TEXTILES (2)

The textile industry was one of the first to reemerge after the war and it swiftly rose to prominence. In fact, by 1955 it contributed 19 per cent of all manufacturing production, which placed it at the head of the list. But it was also the first to peak and enter a decline. By 1965, its share of manufacturing had slipped to 12 per cent and, by 1975, it was only 8 per cent. This weakening has not yet ceased and now textiles are at the top of the list of ailing sectors.[2]

Naturally, the slippage differed from one branch to another of what is a rather variegated industry. The first to succumb was the downstream portion, consisting of innumerable small garment makers.

But it was not long before the spinners, weavers, dyers and others were hit. They were also quite numerous, relatively small and sometimes backward operations. Finally, the rot spread upstream to synthetic fibres dominated by large manufacturers.

There were a variety of reasons for this decline, most of which should have been perfectly evident to any country which based its industrial policy on dynamic comparative advantage, exporting and projections of future demand. Yet, both the manufacturers and the bureaucrats were repeatedly taken by surprise and, no matter how drastic any remedy appeared at the time, it eventually turned out to be inadequate.

The most obvious weakness, especially downstream and midstream, was that Japan was rapidly losing the inherent comparative advantage it had had shortly after the war. Its labour costs were rising implacably as the economy developed and other industries arose. Japanese labour could not possibly compete against the really cheap labour force in nearby Taiwan and Korea, let alone India or the People's Republic of China. While increased productivity slowed the process, there was always a point at which Japanese goods ceased being competitive.

The next factor, which the Japanese never seemed to grasp no matter how often they encountered it, was that there was a limit to how much they could export. Their textile companies took up exporting with a vengeance, shipping huge amounts abroad in a constantly rising crescendo. It could not be expected that the textile makers in older centres like the United States, Great Britain and the rest of Europe would accept this. And, given the importance to the national economy, the government could be talked into imposing restrictions.

There were already complaints of Japanese inroads in the early 1950s, and later on in the decade pressure was brought against Japan to restrain exports to the United States and Europe. By 1962, the gentleman's agreement had grown into the Long Term Arrangement Regarding International Trade in Cotton Textiles, which was directed primarily against Japanese exports. By the 1970s, the complaints and protectionism had spread to synthetic fibres and resulted in a much broader, and more restrictive, Multifibre Arrangement which included many developing countries.[3]

These trade impediments limited the scope of exports. But even more serious limitations arose from the emergence of competitors. Inevitably, numerous developing countries began promoting their own textile industry, giving it a very high priority. Since they had much lower labour costs, it was easy enough for them to take over the bottom end of the market from the Japanese. In fact, they were so successful in America and Europe that Japanese exporters were not even able to fill their quotas. The only safe market which remained was Japan itself. Yet, by the late 1970s, its growth was slackening.

One last blow was the oil crisis. This struck the healthiest part of the industry most severely: manufacture of synthetic fibres. Many of them were based on cheap petroleum which was no longer available. Moreover, most of the inputs had to be drawn from the Japanese petrochemical industry which was being promoted and protected. This made the cost of raw materials even greater and undermined the textile industry as a whole.

Faced with a steadily shrinking market, the textile industry was in serious difficulty. The most visible problem was chronic overcapacity which led to fierce competition (*kato kyoso*). While it could have been left to market forces to determine which companies survived and which went under – with the exit of companies adjusting supply to demand – this was not the path taken. The Ministry of International Trade and Industry, which had nurtured the industry, promptly intervened to bring about a more regulated downscaling. It started by encouraging spinners to cut back, and gradually spread its efforts to various other segments. This was done initially on an ad hoc basis and then through a series of special acts applying to small and medium enterprises, adopted in 1957, 1963, 1971 and 1976. By 1978, the textile industry was brought under the Depressed Industries Law, where cotton and wool figured prominently.

As early as 1956, MITI tried to control the installation of new spindles, fearing that there would again be excess capacity. But it encountered so little success that, by 1967, it was necessary to take more radical steps. It introduced a programme to scrap 262 000 spindles and 116 000 weaving machines. Ultimately, however, only 204 000 of the former and 26 000 of the latter were actually scrapped, while the rest were mothballed and put back into use later.[4]

It was therefore necessary to make another effort from 1978 to 1980. Between 10 and 20 per cent of the capacity of spinning, weaving, knitting, twisting and other facilities were to be scrapped. Reportedly, this was done. If it really was, it only happened because special funding had been provided through the Small Business Finance Corporation. It extended no-interest loans, many of which were put into interest-bearing accounts which financed much of the repayment. This sharply reduced the costs of an exercise that was inherently in the interest of the manufacturers to begin with.

Next came the turn of the upstream segment.[5] When synthetic fibres were designated a depressed industry, in 1978, the manufacturers were asked by MITI to scrap or mothball between 10 and 20 per cent of their total capacity for acrylics, nylon and polyester. This was done in cooperation with the Japan Chemical Fibres Association on the basis of quotas worked out as a function of the company's existing production capacity and share of the domestic and international markets.

Finally, in 1981, the garment sector admitted that it was plagued with overcapacity and decided to scrap industrial sewing machines. This time the initiative came from the manufacturers' associations which sold the idea to the Small Business Promotion Corporation. In return for hefty loans, some 50 400 machines, roughly 19 per cent of capacity, would be scrapped and, just to be sure, melted down into iron. The loss of machines, however, did not guarantee a real decrease in capacity since many makers proceeded to boost productivity with the remaining machines.

Despite these measures, capacity continued exceeding demand and the competition for sales led to sharply falling prices. MITI therefore intervened repeatedly to artificially limit production and bolster prices. In 1952, it issued its first administrative guidance to the spinners to reduce production by 40 per cent. Under subsequent legislation, which legalised 'recession cartels', it established them for midstream and then upstream producers in 1965–7, 1975, 1977–8 and 1981. While such operations were necessary to help the many spinners or weavers which could not agree among themselves, it was faintly superfluous for the big synthetics manufacturers. Their relations were so close that they had little trouble maintaining price stability most of the time.

MITI was initially spared the embarrassment of having to impose trade restrictions to protect the industry from imports. After all, Korea, Taiwan, Hong Kong, China and Pakistan were rapidly taking over foreign markets and obviously had low enough prices and high enough quality to sell to Japan as well. Yet, during the 1970s, their goods were hardly visible and, in the 1980s, when imports did rise, they remained at a rather modest level. Only in the 1990s did the encroachment become worrisome. This limited penetration can be explained by the fact that the textile manufacturers restricted market access through the textile traders and distributors.

The more positive measures included a rationalisation of the industry. The principal concern was to modernise facilities so that international competitiveness could be regained. The already efficient synthetic-fibre makers introduced yet more productive methods and machinery. The spinners installed water jet looms. And the apparel makers got huge sewing machines and presses. This dramatically reduced the number of workers in the industry and also the price of certain products.

Meanwhile, MITI was supporting research jointly with the industry to develop automatic sewing systems. Using laser and other high-tech methods for cutting, robots for handling and ultrarapid sewing machines, it was hoped that garments could be produced as cheaply as in the poorest developing country. The spinning industry was also working on an 'ideal spinning machine' that could raise efficiency 17-fold.

Equally promising were the attempts at upgrading the industry. Textiles makers strove to produce fabrics of such exceptional quality that they could be sold even in a sluggish market and, in addition, would bring enough value added to compensate for any decrease in quantity sold. Meanwhile, apparel makers had to move up-market, producing more fashionable goods in shorter runs, adapting to changing tastes. Both were accomplished to some extent. In particular, Japanese fashion designers gained an enviable reputation worldwide.

But none of this was adequate to restore the industry to its earlier form. Although some ¥40 billion were provided out of government funds alone from 1956 to 1978, production kept shrinking.[6] Many firms went out of business and there were periodic rashes of bankruptcies among the smaller spinners and weavers. The disappearance of garment makers was a regular event. Only the large and rich synthetic-fibre manufacturers accomplished a successful conversion, by going into pharmaceuticals, chemicals, new materials and other rising sectors. In fact, most of them were earning a third or more of total revenue from non-textile business by the late 1980s.

The holding operation had not worked and even an orderly retrenchment was not entirely successful. The makers simply refused to cut back as much as needed and cheated on their scrapping quotas. Or, more likely, they used the money to buy new machinery which was even more efficient and created new sources of overcapacity. In addition, they remained eternally hopeful and raised production as soon as the market turned up, with little thought as to whether it might not turn down soon after. Thus, while industrialists listened to MITI's advice with respect, they did not always act on it. So, it was eventually market forces which had the last word.

COAL, OIL AND PETROCHEMICALS (2)

Not surprisingly, some of the earlier sectors to burst into prominence were among the first to decline. For a few of them, however, it was not only a case of natural maturation or changing comparative advantage. It is permissible to ask whether the sectors should have been targeted to begin with. And, if there were mistakes, the subsidiary question has to be whether it was suitable to cushion their decline.

For coal, aside from a brief period after the war when the industry could flourish on its own merits, the whole history has been one of holding actions by MITI.[7] Admittedly, it did encourage rationalisation and other positive measures. But the only effective step was to block imports of competing fuels. Once oil was liberalised, coal was doomed. But the whole blame cannot be placed on cheap oil. Japanese coal was not competitive against coal from Australia, Canada or China. The seams were small, the pits deep and the mines remote. Labour costs were high and working conditions dangerous. Sooner or later the industry had to succumb.

MITI obviously preferred it to be later.[8] So did the mine owners, many related to major *keiretsu* it cooperated so closely with. There was also pressure from the workers, more aggressive and militant than most, who came out on strike against both poor pay and conditions, and any attempt to close the mines and deprive them of their jobs. In the end, it was necessary to adopt a decision at the highest level to break the logjam. This was done by Prime Minister Ikeda in 1962, on the basis of a report of the special Coal Survey Commission. It proposed letting coal production sink in keeping with market forces and maintaining just a core industry.

The suggested figure for production was 30 million tons a year, much lower than the 50 million tons recommended by MITI's Coal Industry Rationalisation Council in 1959. Yet, it was still too high and, by the late 1970s, the target was reduced to 20 million tons. Even that level could not be maintained into the late 1980s, at which point the target was dropped to 10 million tons. But this coal was still more expensive and the steelmakers refused to buy it. With that, the industry was finished.

Even this lacklustre performance was at a cost. The miners were poorly paid, worked extremely hard and the mines were not safe enough, to judge by repeated disasters in which hundreds lost their lives. The mining companies piled up losses and only survived because MITI allocated some ¥130 billion annually to the industry. In addition, it helped extract higher prices for domestic coal in negotiations with the electric power and steel industries. These costs were then passed on to the consumers.

While Ezra Vogel charitably describes this as a managed withdrawal,[9] a more extensive study concedes that the national plans were a 'dismal failure'.[10] Another study, by Richard J. Samuels, shows the futility of it all. No fewer than eight programmes were undertaken. 'None had any impact upon the structure of the coal industry other than to prop it up' until the targeters finally accepted the inevitable. But they should have realised much sooner.

> It seems clear that no government policy, no known technological innovation, no industry strategy could have produced a competitive Japanese coal industry in the late twentieth century. Mining firms seem to have appreciated the fact sooner and more clearly than the state planners did. These firms consistently shaped and used public policy to ease market transitions, and they did so in ways that frustrated the very state programs for which they had lobbied before circumstances changed.[11]

Coal was at least a domestic resource. Oil had to be imported from afar. Yet, it was promoted because, in addition to use for fuel, heating and power generation, it was a basic input for other industrial sectors. While refining was a necessary process, it was not certain how well petrochemicals would do under adverse conditions. That the conditions were very positive in the 1950s, when the targeting decisions were made, does not excuse the economic authorities for not considering alternative scenarios.

Oil refining was a problem for MITI. The sector was rather fragile as a result of considerable dispersion, with over thirty refiners and distributors. This meant that they were not very efficient nor strong enough financially. Just how serious this could be was only really noticed after the 1973 and 1979 oil shocks, when crude price shot up and consumption dropped. This provoked intense competition and cost-cutting which hurt the refiners and distributors. To overcome this, MITI urged companies to merge and tolerated collusion on prices. It also helped prevent imports and stockpiled surplus oil. Yet, even then, the industry frequently ran losses which could only be compensated for by keeping foreign exchange gains or refusing to pass on price decreases.[12]

Not all of MITI's efforts met with the approval of the Fair Trade Commission or the general public, no matter how welcome they were to the refiners. At the time of the first oil crisis it advised refiners to restrict production, but they went somewhat further in boosting prices as well. The Tokyo High Court ruled against the price hike although it refused to determine whether the 'administrative guidance' involved was legal. When oil prices finally fell, and the refiners tried to grab the gains, public opinion forced MITI to seek a compromise.

Although supposedly just a sideshow, an event occurred in 1984 which gave pause to those who thought that protecting the Japanese market was a thing of the past or that MITI's ability to wield administrative guidance had faded. The oil market was by then formally open, anyone could import oil who wanted to. Japan's oil prices were extremely high by international standards so there was an opportunity to profit. Thus, Taiji Sato of Lion's Oil, a small independent retailer, decided to import cheap refined oil from Singapore. While this was patently in the interest of the consumers, he was blocked by MITI, which defended the refiners' cosy cartel.

What was most disappointing was that the oil companies did not take the sort of action that could have recompensed MITI for its support and probably improved their own situation. In particular, they refused the mergers which would have permitted rationalisation and scale economies while creating stronger players. This was noted by Samuels in his study.

The activist Japanese state has failed at nearly every juncture – in peace and war, as early as 1902 and as recently as 1984 – to entice the private sector to consolidate on its terms and under its control. Economic bureaucrats (and in the prewar period, military planners) repeatedly aimed for a vertically integrated, nationally unified petroleum industry. What emerged instead was horizontally fragmented and vertically truncated.[13]

The petrochemical industry was in somewhat better shape. There were relatively fewer producers, although probably more than justified, and they possessed comparatively large, modern plants. Nonetheless, this sector, which looked so promising in the mid-1960s when MITI targeted it, was in deep trouble by the early 1970s. One reason, but only one, was the enormous rise in oil prices and then a worldwide recession which left companies with tremendous over-capacity. This was not just a question of bad timing. As Okimoto noted, 'Japanese industrial policy exacerbated the problem by pushing the installation of new plant facilities ahead at a faster pace than would have been sustained under a laissez-faire system.'[14]

There was another fatal flaw, one which MITI and the producers had foolishly ignored. Whatever the price of oil, Japan would always have to pay more than the oil producers and this alone would hurt competitiveness. Worse, Japanese companies used naphtha as a raw material and this was far more expensive than the natural gas tapped by competitors in places like Canada, the United States and, increasingly, the Middle East. Since the latter also built larger, more efficient installations, Japanese prices were hopelessly out of line and sales slumped.

By 1978, when the Depressed Industries Law came into effect, no less than half of the fourteen categories covered were related to the chemical and petrochemical industry. They included ammonia, urea, phosphoric acid and various synthetic fibres. The underlying problems were excess capacity and sluggish sales. These resulted in financial difficulties for numerous producers. Yet, they still insisted that there was no long-term decline and merely a temporary downturn. Even MITI's Industrial Structure Council knew things were worse.

MITI's main concern was to prevent 'excessive competition' which arose from excess capacity and the urgent need to keep producing at some reasonable scale. Stuck with growing surpluses, companies cut prices sharply and some were faced with bankruptcy. To reduce the *kato kyoso*, which it regarded as an ominous threat, MITI coaxed, urged or pushed makers to form groups or merge. With time, there was some consolidation of the industry, even if not quite to the extent desired. When mergers could not be brought about, joint marketing and increased specialisation by group members offered an acceptable alternative.

But there was simply too much excess capacity for such palliatives.

Thus, by 1982, it was decided that facilities would have to be scrapped and not merely mothballed, as had happened in the past. MITI sought a substantial cut of some 36 per cent for ethylene capacity and somewhat smaller reductions for various derivatives. Fertiliser capacity would also be reduced. Instead of a uniform scrapping throughout the sector, under a production consolidation plan it was possible for companies to 'swap' their obligations. A company with an efficient plant could pay another company to close down its less efficient facilities.

This programme managed to come close to its targets and the industry's capacity was shrunk, although the same downscaling would doubtlessly have taken place faster if left to market forces. While the more efficient companies still preferred fighting it out, even they accepted MITI's plan because it was sweetened with assorted financial incentives. They included, among other things, tax write-offs, rapid depreciation and low-cost loans. Processors were enabled to import naphtha without paying the standard tax. And various measures were adopted formally and informally to keep out imports that were increasingly competitive.

The trouble with this exercise, and most others as well, was that it was impossible to consider the petrochemical and oil-refining industries in isolation. They had crucial linkages, which is why they were promoted to begin with. Now the effect was negative. By allowing prices to remain high, and not switching to cheaper imports, there was a cost burden on the customers. These included producers and users of special chemicals, plastics and synthetic fibres; power companies; farmers who used fertilisers and pesticides; and ordinary citizens who paid more for gas and heating oil.

SHIPBUILDING AND TRANSPORTATION (2)

By the 1970s, the Japanese shipbuilding industry was on a roll. It was the largest and most efficient. It could even produce supertankers and other vessels which no other yards could and enjoyed a monopoly for the most lucrative end of the market. In addition to high quality, low costs and speedy delivery, it could offer exceptional credit terms. The shipbuilders thus had high hopes for the future. They knew a downturn had to come eventually, especially in such a cyclical industry. But they did not expect it soon.

Even the oil shock did not faze them. In mid-1974 the Japanese

Association of Shipbuilders forecast a lively demand for tankers which could keep them busy through 1980. They clearly misjudged the situation for, even then, demand was slackening, and slipped steadily until it bottomed out a first time in 1979. By then, Japan's production had fallen from 17.9 million tons to 4.3 million tons. The drop was sharper than the rise and more surprising.

This left Japan high and dry with huge, expensive shipyards with a total capacity of 9.8 million tons, a level that might not be attained for years . . . if ever. In such a situation the relative harmony in the industry was shattered and companies bid wildly against one another to fill their yards with anything at any price. Those which could not do so, and there were many, went deeply into debt with the banks or drew on related companies. Although they cut costs ruthlessly, dismissed workers and took on odd jobs outside of shipbuilding, most of them ran deficits and several dozen went bankrupt.

It is obvious that the Ministry of Transport did not act as effectively as it should have done. Indeed, it did little more than counsel discipline and hope that the situation would improve spontaneously. In 1976 it suggested reducing capacity, which was far too high. But it only tried to impose decisive measures as of 1978. It was then that the Shipping and Shipbuilding Rationalisation Council presented its recommendations. Soon after, shipbuilding was formally designated a structurally depressed industry under the Depressed Industries Law and a recession cartel was organised.[15]

The key to the plan was to reduce capacity by 3.4 million tons, or roughly 35 per cent. The Japanese Shipbuilders Association was to cooperate with the government to determine how much each yard should cut back. The decision was not easy. The smaller firms insisted that the larger ones could more readily bear the burden, while the larger ones wanted it shared equally. In the end, most of the reduction was incurred by the big seven. The government aided smaller firms by purchasing their shipyards, selling what equipment could be used and covering the difference with JDB loans.

To stimulate demand, MOT promoted a three-year shipbuilding programme, as of 1979, to construct 3 million tons of commercial shipping. Part of the construction and necessary loans would be subsidised by the government. The Maritime Safety Agency and Defence Agency were ordered to buy patrol boats and other vessels. The Shipbuilding Rationalisation Council seemed to think that would do the trick and reassuringly forecast an upturn from 1980 to 1985.

Like so many other predictions, this one failed to come through.

Sales remained sluggish, aside from a flurry of orders by Sanko Steamship in 1983. Shipyards continued working well-under capacity and more builders went out of business. In the mid-1980s, rather than turning upward, new orders slipped again. There were simply too many vessels around and until more could be scrapped or new customers found business would remain slow. Meanwhile, the companies were still saddled with 20–40 per cent excess capacity and masses of redundant workers, many of whom were ultimately laid off.

While the downturn hit all shipbuilding nations severely, Japan was hurt more than the others. Its erstwhile advantage, of having the world's biggest shipyards, turned against it as tankers, and especially supertankers, became less popular. Now they were filled with much smaller vessels that could just as well be built in smaller yards made for the purpose.

This second chapter in the recent history of Japan's shipbuilding industry was hardly as glorious as the first. In fact, it even cast doubts on the value of the earlier period. It was then that excessive capacity had been created which proved to be such a drag subsequently. In order to expand, most shipbuilders had accepted tight margins during the 1960s and early 1970s when they could have done better. Just after the oil crisis, they lost heavily on ship orders which were cancelled. Over the past decade or so, they repeatedly accepted to produce at cost or under cost and rarely made profits. Throughout, they benefited from financial and fiscal advantages. While becoming an extraordinarily productive industry, shipbuilding was never very profitable and constantly drew on public funds. Thus, although it was still the world's largest, this achievement brought few palpable gains to the companies or to Japan as a whole.

The fate of the shipping industry tended to follow, or rather precede, that of shipbuilding. It was the incredible glut of ships, especially tankers and supertankers after the oil crisis, that undermined both. Japanese shippers were also hurt by the high cost of Japanese labour and many switched to Liberian or Panamanian registers to get away from MOT guidance and the seamen's union. Since they could more readily pass on their increased costs to customers, they did not do as poorly in financial terms.

But shipping was an extremely competitive and risky business. This was conceded by the government which entered into various plans to support the shippers. One was to stockpile crude oil in tankers, helping both the oil refiners and shipping lines with excess vessels.

There were also financial assistance and fiscal relief. Still, the government could not save specific companies from the consequences of foolish decisions or global trends. The most disastrous case involved Sanko, which ordered several dozen new vessels at a time when shipbuilding costs were at their lowest and it thought shipping would pick up. It was wrong and went bankrupt in 1985. Others also got into financial trouble, including the illustrious Japan Line and Nissho Iwai. In the end, many of the shipping companies just went out of business.

ALUMINIUM (AND STEEL)

Although the proponents of targeting like to forget this, aluminium was also one of the strategic industries initially fostered by MITI, perhaps assuming that the success with steel could be replicated in similar sectors. Thus, tax deductions and cheap loans were forthcoming. The market was closed by tariffs and other barriers as well as collusion among the trading companies, closely linked to the aluminium companies established by major *keiretsu* like Mitsubishi, Mitsui and Sumitomo. With such support, by the early 1970s Japan had become the world's number three producer with an output of over a million tons.

But there were always intrinsic weaknesses in this industry. First of all, there were fourteen smelters belonging to six companies, which meant that the average unit size was relatively small. They did not have sufficient economies of scale. While the technological level was high, it was not that much better than newer plants opening abroad. So the producers could not really count on exports to justify such a large capacity.

Potentially more serious, Japan not only imported the bauxite or alumina for its smelters, it also imported the crude oil needed to fuel the plants. None too competitive to begin with, the industry's situation deteriorated markedly as oil prices shot up. Japanese smelters were eventually paying five times more for electricity than Canadian or American ones. And electricity accounted for over half of total costs. Ultimately, Japanese aluminium cost 60–90 per cent more than the going world price. It was patently absurd to continue production domestically rather than importing.

Although the writing was on the wall, it was not clearly perceived by the aluminium companies for some time. Expecting continued

Case Studies

growth, they continued expanding and raised total capacity to 1.6 million tons. But demand failed to keep pace and the smelters ran well under capacity. As the companies incurred considerable deficits, they turned to MITI for assistance.[16]

MITI gladly obliged. First it helped out informally and then more officially, once the aluminium industry was brought under the Depressed Industries Law in 1978. The aid took various forms. A tariff quota system limited imports and, when it was not effective enough, quotas were placed on duty-free imports. The tariff levels were set lower for the smelters which could then sell imported ingots and use the profits to finance their dwindling operations. Cheap loans were provided and the cost of electricity was subsidised. Aluminium was stockpiled by the state to cover some of the excess inventory.

In return, the companies were urged to reduce their capacity drastically. This would be accomplished through a MITI-sponsored recession cartel. Initially, the Industrial Structure Council recommended that capacity be decreased to 1.1 million tons, and, in 1981, proposed a mere 700 000 tons. The producers rejected such draconian measures, first arguing that this was only a temporary crisis and then pleading that a (rather high) minimum level be maintained for reasons of national security. By the time they grudgingly agreed to reduce capacity the sector was in complete disarray. Price differentials were so great that the trading companies and smelters themselves bought huge amounts of foreign ingots. As production plummeted, to 250 000 tons in 1983, smelters closed down and companies went bankrupt.

But MITI was not ready to concede defeat, at least not openly. In 1984, the Industrial Structure Council came out with new recommendations to reduce smelting capacity to 350 000 tons by 1988, raise tariffs on ingot imports to compensate for the cost of scrapping facilities and adjust supply and demand in the downstream sector to avoid excessive competition there. Meanwhile other measures, including differential tariffs and collaboration between the smelters and trading companies, were adopted to procure ingots, primarily from overseas ventures in which Japanese firms had invested. Finally, a crash programme was launched to invent new technologies that could make Japan's aluminium cheaper. R&D projects on aluminium salinisation electrolysis and an aluminium 'blast furnace' were supported by MITI and the industry.

In retrospect, MITI's attempt at rescuing the industry had failed. It had failed quite miserably. As Richard J. Samuels pointed out, when one looks closely at the political economy of this restructuring process, it seems rather clear that the unanticipated pace of industrial transformation is much more a response to the exigencies of the market than due to the foresightedness of MITI planners. Virtually every one of MITI's targets for collaborative reduction of onshore smelting capacity has been exceeded by magnitudes that belie any image of Japan's industrial policy machinery and its mechanism for administrative guidance as authoritatively prescient. Indeed, 'destructuring' may be a more apt description of the process.[17]

As intimated, it could validly be claimed that the aluminium industry should never have been targeted to begin with and that when economic forces asserted themselves it was bound to collapse. Before it did, however, it imposed heavy financial burdens on the country. For years, it was necessary to purchase more expensive domestic ingots rather than cheaper imported ones. The high price of aluminium raised the costs of local extruders and fabricators which were much less competitive and had to sell mainly at home, again at higher prices than imported goods. Yet, the smelters still ran up over ¥1 trillion in debts that had to be absorbed by themselves, other members of the groups and the commercial banks. And the government wasted precious tax revenue on subsidies.

It might be noted that what was happening to aluminium was soon being repeated on a smaller scale for copper, ferronickel and other metals. What if the rot spread to steel? That was not such an improbable hypothesis when one considers that it too is a processing industry drawing nearly all its raw materials from abroad. It is negatively affected by rising prices of coal, oil, iron ore and so on. Increased shipping rates, due to higher oil costs, have a similar effect. In addition, the once state-of-the-art plants have grown older and could be surpassed by newer ones in developing countries.

Indeed, by the late 1970s, some of the smaller, older and more inefficient producers were facing serious difficulties, especially the electric furnace and open-hearth steelmakers which represented almost a fifth of total capacity.[18] A cartel was formed for small steel bars and rods in 1977 and, in 1978, those sectors were brought under the Depressed Industries Law. This was supposed to be a temporary measure but the protection had to be extended and gradually spread to other branches of steel production. Indeed, the 1980s were a very trying period for the industry, as demand slipped and overcapacity in

Japan, and worldwide, triggered price wars and dumping.

In 1987, MITI was forced to intensify its efforts to reduce steel capacity, urging that production be reduced by 15–20 per cent by 1992. This involved closing down less efficient blast furnaces and laying off workers. Meanwhile, attempts were made at improving productivity and enhancing quality, with more makers turning out specialty steel. Many of them also entered other sectors, ranging widely from biotechnology to leisure. The expenses were carried mainly by the companies although weaker ones were assisted by MITI and a major bond issue helped reduce the debt burden. More decisive was a boost in public works expenditures, which absorbed more steel. While this recovery was welcome, there was no assurance that higher demand could be maintained.

Part III
Results and Reactions

9 Rating Success

On the basis of these case studies, it must be amply clear that industrial policy and targeting were – and still are – extremely widespread and played a significant role. They have been applied to a very broad range of sectors and products, not only in manufacturing but also in mining, agriculture and services. The exercises involved not only MITI but many other ministries and agencies as well as key politicians. The number of companies which participated in one project or another is legion. And the outcome affected every Japanese (and many foreigners).

It is therefore essential to answer two sorts of questions. The first has to do with the intrinsic merits of the techniques. Are they effective? Do they accomplish what they set out to do? Have there been failures as well as successes? And so on. The other, asked much less frequently, is whether targeting has been good or bad for Japan as a whole and also whether it has helped or hurt specific groups.

This analysis is not as easy as it appears. One cannot simply say, as so many do, that industrial targeting was a brilliant success or a dismal failure. It is necessary to consider it from various angles to see which aspects were more or less successful before concluding whether it was worthwhile as a whole. In addition, and this is often forgotten, it is necessary to look at industrial targeting from not only the economic but also the political, social and other viewpoints. Once that has been done, the final response may be very different from the initial reaction.

While the author has definite views on this subject, every observer should draw his or her own conclusion depending on which aspects and which effects are regarded as most important.

Still, before even starting, it should be obvious that the answer lies somewhere between the two extremes in the lively and sometimes ludicrous debate on industrial targeting. Some claim, without much evidence, that Japan has been unerring in its choice of sectors; that it has mounted a ruthlessly efficient machine which cannot be stopped. Others, with equally dubious reasoning, argue that this all had little effect, that things would have worked out much the same without any industrial targeting or, indeed, that industrial targeting was quite simply impossible given the overwhelming power of market forces.

Just to see the full range of possible responses, it does not hurt to quote Chalmers Johnson, who has become almost a guru on industrial policy. He credited MITI and friends with working an economic miracle. They 'single-mindedly turned the Japanese industrial structure from light, labour-intensive industries to steel, ships, and automobiles, of which Japan is today the world's leading producer'.[1] Steven Schlossstein writes in much the same vein.

The results of Japan's industrial policy, as analysts never cease telling us, not only have been impressive but outstrip any accomplishments in the West over a comparable period. . . . if we look at Japan's postwar economic achievements, we find they are telling indeed. The free world's leading steel maker. The number one producer of automobiles. Until recently displaced by Korea, the world's leading shipbuilder. Manufacturer *par excellence* of cameras and consumer electronics and office equipment. . . . Dominant in semiconductor technology, biotechnology, communications technology, the technology of miniaturization. On and on the list goes, seemingly endless, with achievement after unparalleled achievement in industry after advanced industry.[2]

At the opposite end of the spectrum you have, among others, Sadanori Yamanaka, the Minister of International Trade and Industry in the early 1980s. He implied that the bureaucrats were standing around with their hands in their pockets while the miracle occurred. 'In these policies, the role of the government is to provide forecasts of emerging industrial structure trends and, when necessary, to provide a modicum of support for industry's efforts to adapt and advance.'[3] This hands-off approach would certainly be applauded by Bruce Bartlett, a card-carrying Reaganaut, who claimed that historical record has proved 'that efforts to implement some sort of industrial policy, to target industries, or to impose protectionism as a means of accomplishing such goals are counterproductive and doomed to failure'.[4]

As intimated, the answer lies somewhere in between. But it can safely be assumed that it is closer to the concept of such intervention having a strong effect and deriving from rather close cooperation, if not actually a 'conspiracy' to crush everything under foot. By any standards, government support was a pretty big 'modicum'. And it hardly seems likely that the bureaucrats and businessmen would have worked so hard to protect markets, finance investments, acquire technologies, run research projects, rationalise operations and sell massively for nothing!

FASTER, FURTHER, MORE FORCEFULLY

Industrial targeting, as far as we are concerned, was a resounding success . . . in those ways sought by the targeters. The economy developed faster, further and more forcefully than it would otherwise have done. The result was a strong economy (if not actually a rich country) and Japan as number one in more and more sectors. Let us first consider these achievements.

Faster is easy enough to demonstrate.[5] What first attracted attention was the extraordinary growth rates achieved during the 1950s and 1960s, often exceeding 10 per cent. This slipped notably in the 1970s, averaging about 3 per cent, and was a bit higher in the 1980s, some 4 per cent. All in all, this was about three times as fast as ordinary developing countries, twice the rate of the United States and even considerably higher than the other superstar, Germany. In addition to the overall acceleration, Japan got into each sector it targeted much quicker than otherwise. It actually did speed up the evolution of comparative advantage and start producing steel, computers, chips, and so on much sooner than would normally have occurred.

Thanks to rapid growth, it went further. The economy achieved much larger dimensions at each point in time. By the 1990s it was more than twice as big as it would have been otherwise, because it was growing twice as fast all this time and the gains were compounded over time. Japan's per capita gross national product shot up from a tenth that of the United States in 1955 to 25 per cent larger in 1988, an incredible reversal. Only with regard to total GNP did it lag behind the United States, which after all has twice the population and vastly more land. But, given the trajectories of both, it could well be the biggest economy early in the twenty-first century.[6]

In this ascent, it should be noted, Japan achieved another prominent goal of targeting. It was able to foster sectors where it lagged behind, catch up and then press ahead. There are far too many to mention all. But even a partial listing is quite impressive. They range from automobiles to zippers, passing through cameras, computers, facsimile machines, machine tools, motorcycles, photocopiers, robots, semiconductors, ships, steel, televisions, VCRs and watches.

The country is much stronger than before, an even more primordial urge. It is less vulnerable to outside shocks than ever, actually recovering from the three oil crises and assorted currency appreciations better than others. Equally remarkable, it already possesses many of the world's largest and strongest companies. They are more than able to defend the home market while exporting to and investing in foreign markets. They are financially fit, well staffed and aggressive.

Japan's economy has thus fared better than anyone would have thought. By 1988, it had a gross national product of over $2867 billion, still lagging behind a much larger American economy, but per capita GNP was $23 382, ahead of every other country. Particularly significant is that a steadily growing share of this GNP consisted of high-tech products. According to JETRO, Japan's share rose from 13 per cent of the world total in 1980 to well over 25 per cent in 1990.[7]

That is the past. The future also looks promising. MITI recently released a survey on advanced technology indicating that Japan's products were as good as the best in 36 out of 40 categories.[8] This means it is now a front-runner. Whatever it does not have, it can develop. Whatever it cannot develop, it can buy. So, it should continue moving faster, further and more forcefully than the rest.

Another achievement, which should certainly not be overlooked, is that industrial targeting has itself evolved significantly. The state can now restrict its activities to some few sectors that are not commercially interesting. Otherwise, private companies have taken over the task. They can target whatever products are attractive and they can almost guarantee a smooth launch within the huge corporate groupings. By now, even if foreign competitors were to finally realise how crucial industrial targeting is, they could no longer stop it.

Of course, it can be argued that not all this success stems from industrial policy and targeting. There were other contributing factors. That is entirely true. Japan's defence burden was small, it was aided after the war by the United States, it could acquire technologies cheaply, and it was easy to penetrate the US and other markets. But many of these factors applied to other countries as well. Yet they did not create an economic 'miracle' and many remained or became an economic mess.

So part at least of these achievements must be attributed to something extra. The most evident 'extra' was industrial targeting. What part cannot be calculated with any accuracy. But it must have been a very large share because, as noted, Japan did not just outperform other economies marginally, it did so massively.

Under these circumstances, it is hard to comprehend comments to the effect that industrial targeting had no effect or did not even exist. That is nonsense and could only come from those who refuse to see the very palpable evidence. This does not mean that there were no drawbacks, no waste, no excesses. They did exist. And they will be referred to further on. But even they cannot deny Japan's accomplishments.

PICKING WINNERS . . . MOSTLY

What has just been described is the 'big' picture. It is still necessary to consider some details. One of the most pertinent is obviously how effectively policy was carried out. That is not an easy assignment. And it is impossible to make an exact assessment. It becomes more feasible when the task is approached from different directions. A good first approximation can be obtained by evaluating the ability to pick winners.

Did the targeters, as is often maintained, really pick the winners? After going through a list of sectors and products that were targeted and scrutinising the results, it is obvious that they did choose a large number of winners. Most of the sectors listed in the various case studies would be regarded as such: steel, shipping, semiconductors, satellites, etc., etc. These are just a sampling. There are literally hundreds more.

But, did they pick all the winners or did they miss some? This is a trickier question since it is harder to see what has not been done and oversights of this sort were often covered up. Still, it is obvious that the authorities initially mistook the potential of the automobile industry and left motorcyles, consumer electronics and numerous other sectors to their own devices . . . perhaps wisely so. More striking was the failure to recognise the value of the transistor, which might not have been developed if not for Sony's zeal, and also of computers at first.

Even for some that were targeted, Japan came in amazingly late, given the general knowledge of the sector and widespread views in the business community that these were, indeed, growth industries and perhaps also strategic ones. This occurred, as noted, for automobiles. But it also happened for biotechnology, new materials, robotics and aerospace. Thus, even if there was some foresight, the targeters were certainly not clairvoyant.

The more serious question is, of course, did the targeters also back losers? This is harder yet to answer since, by shoring up a sector, they could cloak the failure, and there has not been as much investigation of this aspect as one might wish. Still, it seems rather evident that it was foolish to target sectors which depended excessively on processing expensive imported raw materials, like aluminium, ferro-alloys and petrochemicals. It might be argued that commodity and energy prices were low when the decision was made. With some foresight, however, it should have been realised that ultimately Japan would not be well placed for such production.

There were relatively few outright failures. Aeronautics might be regarded as one. The Japanese only produced one purely domestic aircraft, which was a financial disaster, and never got another off the ground. Certain sectors that were targeted also failed to materialise. Undersea mining, alternative energies and aerospace are clearly lagging at present. A more obvious mistake was agriculture, where crops for which Japan was simply not suited were strongly promoted.

Without a doubt, there were vastly more successes – at least in the limited sense of sectors which emerged – than failures or omissions. Japan deserves definite credit for this. The only remaining query is: would the sectors or products have emerged anyway without being targeted?

Surely, in some cases they would. If ambitious companies could produce televisions, video cassette recorders and even personal computers on their own, it is possible – actually probable – that they could ultimately have graduated to larger, more complex computers. It is more evident still that pharmaceutical companies could have moved into biotechnology, machinery makers into robotics and basic material producers into 'new materials' whether or not the sectors were given official priority.

On the other hand, it is clear that the process was dramatically accelerated. It would have taken much longer for companies to develop sophisticated computers, just as it would have taken much longer for shipbuilders to make supertankers. The same applies to virtually every sector. Progress was expedited by market protection, ample funding and encouragement of technology.

In certain cases, the aid was decisive. There was a breakthrough, often coming at just the right time, which could not have been achieved otherwise. One of the most obvious was the upgrading of computer models, especially for the fourth-generation and supercomputers, without which the Japanese might have been hopelessly outdistanced by 1BM and other rivals. The VLSI project was also useful, this time in helping the Japanese chip makers take the lead. Other examples exist for specific machine tools, robot types or satellites.

Finally, there are certain sectors which might never have arisen without abundant government support. They simply demanded too much initial investment and had too long a gestation period for private companies to undertake the essential work alone. On occasion, they did not even offer chances of normal commercial returns. Chief among these are nuclear energy and aerospace.

All of the above refers to the more positive, more glorious part of industrial targeting, namely the creation and promotion of growth sectors. Japan's performance was not quite as good in the less constructive, messier business of aiding declining sectors. There, it did not always 'pick losers' well or, equally unfortunate, it refused to accept the logical consequences.

The basic principle was that these sectors should be phased out as quickly as possible so as to avoid undesirable waste. Alas, repeatedly, more capacity remained than was needed and the process of rationalisation would have been faster if left to market forces. Still, Japan was not quite as timid as European countries which created a wasteful life support system for hopeless cases. Nor did it allow sectors to disappear completely, as in the United States, if they might be revived later under different circumstances.[9]

On the basis of these considerations, one could give the Japanese authorities a rather positive rating. But it would have to be fair as opposed to excellent, as some avid admirers insist. As noted, they did fail to pick some sectors which were bound to be winners, they unwisely targeted some losers and they had trouble handling depressed sectors.

Another criticism is that the Japanese targeted so many sectors and products that they were bound to hit upon some successes. They did not narrow their focus as much as true experts might have done, only picking the sure winners and neglecting the rest. In so doing, they dispersed scarce resources and created unnecessary waste. That is partly true. There was an incredible number of targeting exercises. And both bureaucrats and businessmen were periodically guilty of latching on to each passing fad and clambering on the bandwagon just because American or European producers were already there.

But it must be remembered that, although many sectors and products were targeted, they were not all targeted at the same time.

In fact, there were definite phases during which specific categories were dealt with before moving on to the next. First came the basic industries, then mass-production manufactures, then high-tech and now futuristic projects. Even within sectors, certain products were taken care of so the machinery could shift to others, say, from simple to more complex computers, from rudimentary to more refined chips. So there was a greater concentration of efforts than might appear.

A more serious reservation is that targeting was 'easy' for the Japanese. After all, they were latecomers. They simply had to follow the path of those who went ahead, the pioneers, to see which industries they developed and in which order. In addition, one could check what their relative resource endowment was to know when specific sectors should come onstream. As Japan's own economy progressed, it was bound to pass through similar stages in comparative advantage and then it too would be prepared to tackle the coveted products.

If they wished to hasten the process, targeters could note that a given product was developed at a time when the forerunner had considerably more capital, or sophisticated technology, or better R&D than Japan possessed. They could then take the necessary steps to make up for any weaknesses by, for example, shifting capital to a given sector, acquiring advanced technology or launching special research projects. By following its predecessors, Japan could avoid many costly and time-consuming mistakes. It could compress the time and effort needed to accomplish as much.

This is entirely true. And it should somewhat deflate the egos of certain bureaucrats and subdue the applause of foreign admirers. But it is also irrelevant in certain ways. The Japanese could get ahead by copying and improving on the originals, and they have done so. It may not have been the noblest approach, but it worked. Moreover, they were not the only ones who could follow the leader. That option was open to dozens of other countries. The difference is that Japan, and not the others, pulled it off. That must show that even targeting from behind is not so easy.

But it is obviously simpler than targeting from ahead, which is the challenge Japan must master at present. This time the bureaucrats and businessmen will have to peer into a more impenetrable future and actually invent new products instead of borrowing from others. To date, it is hard to find anything truly novel in their plans and visions.

EASIER SAID THAN DONE

There is no doubt that, once having targeted products and established industrial policies to promote them, both the public and private sectors did what they could to achieve their goals. In most cases, the exercises proceeded roughly as planned. That does not mean that everything ran smoothly or worked out as intended. Still, on the whole, Japan was much better at this sort of operation than most other countries.

With regard to protection of the domestic market, which was such a crucial element, the authorities could hardly have done better. All possible barriers went up. There were exchange control, restrictions on investment, and tariffs, quotas and administrative regulations to block imports. This was maintained much longer than in comparable Western countries which threw their markets open to Japan, thereby adding the possibility of exports. Even when its OECD partners insisted that Japan get in step, it managed to do so slowly. The holding operation was usually sufficient for local producers to prepare for the onslaught.

What is most impressive is that, after formally opening the nation to investments and imports, they could still be inhibited informally. For one, by the time foreigners could invest in Japan it was extremely costly to set up wholly-owned ventures and existing companies were strong enough to resist takeovers. Simply the expense of renting premises, housing expatriates and recruiting local staff were exorbitant. Thus, the withdrawal of barriers at that late date brought little increase in investment.

The situation was even more satisfactory, in the view of the Japanese, with regard to imports. By the time the tariffs and quotas finally came down the market was well-nigh saturated and there were less sales for anyone to make. Naturally, entrenched Japanese manufacturers which had provided the first and perhaps second generation of products were preferred when replacement purchases were made. Only relatively exclusive, and rather costly, items were left to the foreigners and they offered only limited scope for sales.

Just to be sure that imports did not spread more widely, other impediments replaced the formal barriers. The various bureaucracies created countless nontariff barriers and, when forced to withdraw some, promptly inserted others. The private sector also pitched in. Through close relations with trading companies and importers they discouraged the introduction of competing products. In sectors where they dominated the distribution system, makers kept imports out of the retail stores, and thus unknown to potential consumers, while assemblers spurned foreign suppliers. Here too the supposed 'liberalisation' did little to facilitate import penetration. As Okimoto said, 'policies changed but outcomes did not'.[10]

Financial assistance was relatively well used in the sense that there were few outright abuses. Funds allocated to a given sector or project were used for the stated purpose. Loans were repaid although, in some instances, the 'matching grants' (*hojokin*) for R&D were not. Usually, the financial assistance was directed to companies that were properly suited for the effort and used it competently. The only drawback was that members of the corporate establishment got more than their share of the projects and funding.

There is somewhat more cause for concern where funds were sometimes provided too cheaply and too much of the risk was borne by the authorities that targeted a sector or sponsored a project rather than by the companies involved. This encouraged excessive spending. It was necessary to get the very latest machinery, the most sophisticated technology or the most automated plant. Companies strove for maximum scale. This was unduly expensive, especially if that scale were larger than necessary or managers decided to scrap the old plant and build an entirely new one.

The use of technology was very effective, although the targeters only deserve part of the credit. In the early years, bureaucrats occasionally put businessmen on the track of the right knowhow and helped them license it. Most of the subsequent effort, however, was undertaken by private companies. The same thing occurred with regard to research and development. The government's contribution was essential in the early phase, or for particularly complex or expensive projects, but companies quickly established internal R&D facilities and kept abreast on their own.

With regard to research, there is no doubt that the various projects sponsored by MITI, NTT, STA, MOE and others made definite contributions to economic progress. But, it must be recalled, most of these projects involved more applied than basic research and, often enough, it was merely a question of finding other ways of accomplishing what had been done by foreign companies already. The closer the projects came to the frontiers of knowledge, the harder it was to proceed. There were few notable innovations in biotechnology, despite Japan's supposed predisposition for this. Aerospace research not only lagged behind, the gap continued growing. More embarrassing was the inability of ICOT to produce the long-awaited 'fifth generation computer'.

This means that one should question the validity of claims by Japan's more enthusiastic admirers that its research projects generated 'world-beating new technologies' or gave participants a 'great leap forward'.[11] A more balanced and serious assessment was provided by Martin Fransman, who studied Japan's research efforts in *The Market and Beyond, Cooperation and Competition in Information Technology in the Japanese System*.

There is no evidence that the Japanese programs have produced world-beating new technologies (according to any reasonable interpretation of this phrase). There is no evidence that the VLSI program gave the Japanese electronics companies a great leap forward. . . .[12] Competition between the participating Japanese companies limited the sharing of knowledge. The greater part of most of these programs involved co-ordinated research rather than the fuller sharing of knowledge attainable under joint research in joint research facilities. The main aim of the Japanese programs was to extend existing knowledge in key areas in an incremental and practical way, that is to undertake oriented basic research, rather than to produce world-beating new technologies.

There is evidence that they have succeeded in this aim. There is evidence that the Japanese companies allocated significant additional resources to the selected research areas as a result of these programs, compared to what they otherwise would have allocated.[13]

Anyone who thinks that Japan's research efforts were so admirably structured or promising that private companies were sorely tempted to join in might reflect on these comments by Daniel I. ᐧkimoto. 'Quite apart from having to divert research personnel, Japanese corporations often have the same reservations about *itakuhi* as US companies do about federal contract research: reams of paperwork, minute and irritating regulations, rigid accounting procedures, constant government monitoring, strict technical specifications, no guaranteed markets for commercializable products, and so forth. Sometimes it does not seem worth the hassle.'[14] As for the widespread idea that 'harmony' prevails, one might consider the distrust and friction that arose in many projects, including the highly touted VLSI Project. There, it 'took several years of administrative massaging by the project's executive director before it could get on with the business of joint research'.[15]

When it comes to market restructuring, another basic thrust of industrial policy, the results are rather ambivalent. MITI and other ministries repeatedly urged companies to merge or at least consolidate production, but they were rarely heeded. Only in steel was a noteworthy merger engineered. Most others occurred in depressed industries, where companies faced the alternative of going under. But, in vibrant, growing sectors, this solution was rejected outright, as it was for automobiles.[16] And no company willingly halted an old production line or failed to enter a hot, new line if it could. According to a study on the machine tool industry, 'makers fragmented the market: new entrants flooded high-tech equipment sectors, existing firms flatly refused to coordinate or consolidate production'.[17]

Nonetheless, there was a definite reduction in the number of players in most sectors and some few usually emerged as clear leaders. That was more because of corporate dynamics and the competitive urge than anything else, although MITI's muzzling of the FTC helped. Mergers were not popular because it was hard to combine personnel. Internal expansion, creation of subsidiaries, control of suppliers and occasional acquisitions, on the other hand, were more compatible with the system. Moreover, the constant striving for market share regularly tightened the circle of contenders as weaker ones dropped out.

In the end, although it was not really their achievement, the targeters did get large, solid companies that were competitive internationally. In fact, they probably exceeded their original expectations. By the 1990s, Japan had some of the biggest automobile, electronics, steel, shipbuilding and other companies. It also boasted top banks, securities and insurance companies. If one considers that many were parts of even larger horizontal and vertical groupings, then these were among the foremost players in the world.[18]

However, for Japanese companies to be this big by international standards, they had to be gigantic by Japanese standards. They had to dominate their sectors domestically. The result was an increasing number of oligopolies and monopolies, sectors controlled by the top three, two or just one producer. The effect of this could be decidedly less beneficial. In fact, it was one of the worst drawbacks because the oligopolists then proceeded to collude on their own, raising domestic prices and keeping out new entrants.

That was not accidental or coincidental, it was a direct result of industrial policy. So much was pointed out by Kozo Yamamura, one of the few scholars to study this aspect.

Despite its claims to the contrary, when MITI aided large firms in the major industries during Japan's rapid growth period, the following occurred: as the industries matured, competition in their markets became significantly compromised, as attested by considerable evidence of various forms of collusive conduct by the large firms in the steel, home electronics, chemical and other industries in the 1960s. To believe that similar anticompetitive behavior will not be repeated by the large firms in the high technology industries as they mature is to ignore the lessons of postwar Japanese antitrust history.[19]

In reading about the 'targets' set by bureaucrats in their various reports and visions, we are led to believe, by the popular press and indulgent academics, that they were amazingly accurate. Closer study shows that, to the contrary, they were frequently not only off, but far off. That could hardly be avoided given the propensity to indicate targets for nearly everything, capacity, investment, scale, sales, exports, etc. To make things worse, the targeters broke any objectives down by product line, year, specific market and so on rather than sticking to global figures. Usually, they were unduly optimistic. Sometimes, however, they underestimated the prospects.

We have seen that in many of the case studies in this book and similar discrepancies were noted in more extensive industry studies. For example, the targets were repeatedly underfulfilled for solar energy, nuclear energy, aircraft production etc., and overfulfilled for steel, ships, semiconductors, etc. In the machine tool industry, this was clearly shown by David Friedman. MITI's targets were missed for production volume, unit costs, investment, exports and product technology. In fact, 'there is not a single instance in which the objective set forth in the first two five-year plans of the Machinery Promotion Law came close to being realized. As these planning documents were the basis for bureaucratic regulation between 1956 and 1965, it is difficult to claim that MITI effectively managed the machine tool industry.'[20]

The results were even worse with regard to declining sectors where capacity had to be scrapped. Repeatedly, the authorities sought to maintain a level that was still too high and they never seemed to realise just how far sales could fall. This occurred for aluminium,

other metals, textiles and especially coal. According to Richard J.
Samuels, 'in 1969 the MITI program had projected 3.9 million tons of
scrapped capacity; actual totals came to more than twice that
amount. Government targets and forecasts were obsolete as soon as
they were developed.'[21]

In one sense, that was not the fault of the targeters. It is impossible
for anybody to forecast accurately things which are strongly influenced by constantly changing circumstances. But it was patently
presumptuous of MITI, MOF, MOT, etc. even to try. And it was
foolish of them to continue setting new numerical targets after they
had guessed wrong so often that few insiders took their figures
seriously any more (although they always generated enthusiasm
when first published).

Worse, it must be conceded that the bureaucrats simply did not
know how to make forecasts. They were far too mechanical about it,
picking some fixed rate of growth and then just drawing a straight line
into the future showing how things should be. Such linear projections
are never useful in sectors which are known more for ups and downs.
Like so many others, they were also hopeless optimists, assuming
that they really could give a decisive impulse whenever they wanted.

If forecasting was weak, supervision was even more lacklustre. The
bureaucrats sat in their offices, chatted with businessmen, occasionally visited factories, but their writ did not reach very far. They never
knew whether companies were, indeed, investing as much as recommended, building to the optimum scale, refining quality, improving
technologies, doing useful research, or anything else. In most cases
the companies were, because it was in their own best interest. But, if
they were not, there wasn't terribly much the targeters could do to
force them to comply.

Under these circumstances, it is not surprising that implementation
was also spotty. Most attempts at forming teams of companies to
make better use of available resources and avoid unnecessary competition, whether for automobiles, computers or semiconductors,
failed. Goals laid down elaborately in formal programmes were quite
often not achieved, as we have seen with the annoying inability to
reach numerical targets. Even broader objectives, such as coming up
with a fifth-generation computer or a commercial aircraft, stalled. And
much of the alternative energy programme never got off the ground.

Nonetheless, considering the huge number of exercises that were
launched over almost five decades, the results were rather good. The
setbacks were relatively few and many were actually made up for

later on. Even in sectors which are still not responding well, it would be shortsighted to predict that the situation will not improve. While the targeters were not omniscient or omnipotent, they certainly deserve much credit for Japan's spectacular economic resurgence.

HOW RATIONAL?

So far, we have been considering the 'effectiveness' of Japanese industrial policy and targeting. This is because most observers want to know whether it worked or not, whether the goals were achieved or not. But that may not be the best criterion. After all, these practices involve artificial interventions that distort the market situation by blocking competing products, providing cheaper funding, carrying some of the normal development costs, and so on. In fact, they are a direct attempt at altering comparative advantage by providing what is lacking. That means it is extremely difficult to tell whether a project or sector succeeded on its own merits or only through external help.

In short, with enough assistance, almost anything can succeed. Even products which are made poorly and inefficiently can be sold if the market is closed to better or cheaper ones. If loans are supplied at low cost and, in the eventuality that they are not well used, just written off as grants, one can produce almost anything. This has been done quite extravagantly in some developing countries or within the Soviet bloc. It does not mean that the exercise was a success and, as regards other places, this is often recognised.

But Japan also had some questionable cases. Petrochemicals were never really competitive and foodstuffs, more subsidised and protected than anything, could only prosper in an artificial context. Attempts were made at rescuing the aluminium smelters by charging less for electricity, and at saving the coal mines by charging users more. Many incidental costs of nuclear energy, especially those relating to infrastructure and keeping the local population sweet, were borne by the state. As for aerospace, it could only progress because the government did the essential R&D and also bought most of the products.

While the situation was not as crass as elsewhere, there is no doubt that cheap financing facilitated the rise of every sector that was targeted. If it had not been provided, then production costs would have been higher and the companies would have been less competitive.

Underwriting of research also lightened their burden. When it came to exports, they attained a further competitive edge because that could be subsidised by domestic sales.

For such reasons, there are some quibbles about the true success of certain sectors targeted and then heavily supported by the government. This applies less to commercial products, which were chosen more spontaneously on the basis of existing comparative advantage and benefited from less artificial intervention and backing. But, given internal company targeting, the doubts are not entirely dissipated.

Even if the exercises were 'effective', in the sense that companies were ultimately able to manufacture fine products that were popular at home and competitive abroad, there is still the question of whether they were cost-effective. The amount of money that was channelled into some projects, especially those enjoying high priorities, was enormous. And that is when you consider just specific government allocations. To get a true idea of total cost, it is necessary to include the cost to the consumer of higher power and telephone rates, higher medical expenses, higher insurance fees and lower interest on savings accounts, to say nothing of higher prices for imports and some locally-made products in a closed market. Last, but not least, there is the cost of the whole targeting machinery of thousands of bureaucrats, hundreds of committees, and assorted politicians.

It is out of the question to add up all the costs since they were so dispersed, deliberately so in order to make it impossible to know the total. But there is no doubt that it was tremendous. If they were to be calculated into the expense of creating certain industries, it is not certain that they were worth it. For some will never pay the investment back, such as coal, light metals, shipbuilding, nuclear energy, aerospace and agriculture.

There is a final concern, one which is too often overlooked but is probably the most worrisome. It is possible to be overeffective. There is such a thing as industrial overkill. Once a sector is targeted, and companies rush in to develop it, and the government stands by with assorted protection and assistance, there is reason to fear that the industry will grow too much. This danger is only enhanced in Japan where companies strive for larger scale, bigger market share and a higher ranking than their peers, and the government also likes bigness.

This can result in overcapacity such as has constantly plagued Japan. In fact, there has been trouble with overcapacity in virtually every sector. This not only happened where sales shrank for normal causes or when foreign rivals captured part of the market, as in some of the declining sectors. Even in their prime there was too much capacity as industries exceeded any reasonable bounds. This clearly applied to shipbuilding, it also affected steel, and it occurred periodically for computers and semiconductors. Even for more commercial articles there were innumerable excesses, as in production of VCRs or motorcycles.

Overcapacity is obviously wasteful. It means that much of the capacity is not being used. It would thus have been better if that capacity had never been created since it absorbed precious financial and human resources. Worse, working under capacity in too large a plant is less efficient in most cases than working at capacity in a smaller plant. Any economies of scale are lost when that capacity cannot be filled.

This is only one side of the problem. The other is actually more damaging. When companies work under capacity, they face greater pressure to increase sales. If that cannot be achieved in any other way, they will do so by cutting prices. This kind of competition can become endemic in sectors which have massive overcapacity they cannot shed. It brings about perennial losses which must be borne by other parts of the company or group or by the government. If less acute, there may simply be slim profits, profits which are not commensurate with the huge investments.

This sort of difficulty has cropped up in one sector after another. It has been typical of shipbuilding and shipping for decades and now applies to steelmaking. In certain declining industries it has been necessary to shed a quarter, half, three-quarters of existing capacity. Even in commercially-based operations there is some question as to whether any company is making much money, certainly the kind of profits one would expect from such popular items as VCRs or semiconductors.

The root of this particular evil was that both bureaucrats and businessmen seemed blissfully unaware of what every student learns in Economics 101, namely the law of supply and demand. When supply increases beyond demand, prices have to come down in order to sell the lot. Yet, companies repeatedly expanded supply, not moderately but massively and rapidly, and each time they did this prices plummeted. Worse, often a small increase in supply elicited a large fall in prices, so much so that profits were sharply reduced or disappeared. That would have worried Americans, Europeans and most others, but not Japanese bureaucrats, who measured success in terms of total output, or businessmen who were obsessed with market share. By overshooting, they frequently ended up with less, not more.

Admittedly, it was not only because most bureaucrats and many businessmen never studied economics that they pushed so hard for market share. That was a conscious and almost unavoidable practice because they were following a different logic, one not compatible with classic economics. They sought to dominate sectors which would permit them to raise prices freely and boost profits through collusion rather than competition. This stage has actually been reached for many articles domestically, but it has been much harder to create worldwide oligopolies because of resistance from Western companies, the rise of Korean and other Asian companies and stricter antitrust laws elsewhere. So, the Japanese are not really earning very much money on exports yet.

The most distressing aspect of this phenomenon, however, is that by trying to solve the problem of overcapacity and tight profits (or mounting losses), the government only compounded it. The answer, in the view not only of MITI, but of MOT, MOF and others, was cartelisation. Whether for a growing industry just passing through a temporary recession or for an older industry that was finally winding down, cartels were established so that capacity could be reduced. Alas, the amount retained was a function not of sales but of rated capacity. Rather than encourage cautious expansion this incited reckless expansion since the larger the capacity, the larger the ultimate market share. This was clearly shown by Kozo Yamamura two decades ago.

> In addition to the desires of firms to out-rationalise their competitors, hopefully to increase or at least maintain their market share and to enjoy a larger share of export markets, there was an assurance that more elaborate and effective cartels would come to rescue their collective and planned overinvestment. Those who lagged in overinvestment – for reasons of sound financing (not depending on loans too heavily) or conservatism in estimating the future – would be punished. This punishment would come in the form of a reduced relative share as MITI and cartels chose to restrict output by an equal percentage of respective rated capacity. Cartels in effect were used to reward those firms that overinvested and punish those that failed to do so.[22]

These various observations bring us back to the idea that the Japanese system is highly rational. This refrain is constantly repeated by an Abegglen ('Japan's [industrial policy] is more economically rational, more internally consistent . . . than most') or a Johnson ('one of the most rational and productive industrial policies ever devised by any government').[23] Yet, while the Japanese showed tremendous determination, could work marvels of technological proficiency and, yes, be astonishingly productive, they most assuredly were not rational. They were moved by many economic theories and cultural hangups that exalted the competitive urge. And time after time they gave in to the temptation to press ahead as rapidly and vigorously as possible and worry about problems later. A more reasoned and circumspect approach would have generated fewer problems to begin with and could certainly have enhanced any gains.

That profit was not uppermost in the minds of Japanese bureaucrats and businessmen is clear. That this was a serious mistake is equally clear. Unlike market share, the profit motive serves a precious economic function in transmitting market signals that inform bureaucrats and businessmen alike as to whether they are in the right sector, using the right factor endowment, producing at the right level, selling at the right price and, in short, behaving rationally.

So, it is necessary to reconsider one of the most popular, and erroneous, conclusions that have surfaced in the literature. Chalmers Johnson offers a choice between having an economy that is 'plan-rational' or 'market-rational', crediting Japan with possessing the former.[24] No matter how appealing that alternative may be to some, there really is no choice. The only true rationality is that of the market. Only economic forces and market signals can determine whether a country should be in a given sector or companies make given products. Plans, or in the case of Japan, industrial policy and targeting, only make sense to the extent that they successfully approximate or anticipate the direction that will be taken more spontaneously by fundamental economic forces.

If the authorities guess right, then plan-rational will nearly coincide with market-rational. They will need considerably less effort and any interventions can be quite modest. If they guess wrong or get carried away by ambition, then they can only achieve their aims by reinforcing the effort with more funds, greater R&D support, markets that are closed more firmly, and so on. They will require interventions that more drastically distort the existing comparative advantage in order to attain the desired results. And this will cause more inefficiency and more waste. Under such conditions, being plan-rational becomes irrational and the more plan-rational one is the bigger the blunders.

BUREAUCRATS V. BUSINESSMEN (SECOND ROUND)

Having burst some of the prevailing illusions about the effectiveness of industrial targeting, it is appropriate to return to two particularly tenacious myths. Both have already been dealt with in theory in the chapter on institutions. The earlier, tentative conclusions have now been confirmed by practice.

The first, which can safely be discarded, is the notion expressed by its foreign friends that MITI was not only the primary practitioner of industrial targeting but also somehow stage-managed the whole process. Reading their words, one is left with the impression that the MITIocrats were the mastermind behind everything and that all other actors were secondary. This idea is conveyed in a key paragraph of Johnson's seminal work.

> Using FILP, the Development Bank, the Industrial Rationalization Council, and several other powerful institutions, [MITI's] Enterprises Bureau singlemindedly turned the Japanese industrial structure from light, labor-intensive industries to steel, ships, and automobiles, of which Japan is today the world's leading producer. . . . Although it is obvious that MITI could not have accomplished what it did without a mobilized people, without innovation and competition in the private sector, nor without the supplementary programs of other agencies of the government, it is equally true that the developmental effort itself required management. This is what MITI supplied.[25]

(Un)fortunately, the case studies prove this bit of MITIfication to be quite incorrect. For starters, and it is hard to understand how a supposed expert could make such mistakes, shipbuilding was promoted by MOT, and not MITI, and MITI only played a marginal role for automobiles. There are also any number of other sectors where it was either not involved or only shared the honours. They include, along with shipbuilding: shipping, pharmaceuticals, biotechnology, telecommunications, parts of computers and aerospace etc. Then there were literally thousands of products which derived all or most of their impetus from entrepreneurs, such as motorcycles, televisions, photocopiers, sewing machines, zippers, etc., etc.

As we have seen, many other ministries and agencies intervened, not at MITI's behest but on their own, to protect and promote the sectors under their jurisdiction. They included MOF, MOT, MHF,

MAFF, MPT and others. While none sponsored as many projects, collectively their contribution was about as large and perhaps even larger than MITI's. They were exceptionally important because, as is not often enough stressed, they also fostered sectors beyond manufacturing such as agriculture, construction and financial services.

What is even clearer is that MITI most assuredly did not manipulate the other bureaucracies. They definitely did not take orders from the MITIocrats and usually went their own way. In periodic conflicts, they stood their ground and rarely compromised, holding the interests of their own agency and clientele uppermost. We have already seen this with regard to biotechnology, computers, telecommunications and space research, among others. As for research and development, it was actually the Science and Technology Agency and Ministry of Education that had the biggest budgets and did most of the work.

The result was some cooperation and coordination of an ad hoc nature, and very few formal joint projects, since rival bureaucracies found it hard to work together. There was also an abundance of overlapping and duplication which generated inefficiency and waste. However, while the competition was inherently negative, it must be admitted that it generated more industrial targeting than otherwise.

The second misconception, perpetrated by the same sources, is that the bureaucracy was in charge. In the earlier quote, the private sector only got a small pat on the back from Johnson, and other commentators ignored it entirely. That does not reflect the realities. Companies did a lot of targeting on their own and businessmen participated very actively in the state-run programmes. They did so at all levels, from inception to implementation. While the bureaucrats usually took the initiative and picked the sectors to be supported, this was not always done without business involvement, as the following example given by Malcolm V. Brock shows.

Despite the identification of biotechnology by MITI as early as 1979 as an important area of future economic growth, and the subsequent publication in March 1980 of *MITI's Vision of the 1980s*, it was not until the autumn of that year that MITI really began a feverish campaign to boost this technology in Japan. This was a direct result of provocation from the domestic private sector after the explosive sale of biotechnology equity in the U.S. Large Japanese private enterprises, communicating mainly as a collective through the business federation, Keidanren, pressed MITI to

develop fully its half-baked policy initiatives toward biotechnology
or witness Japanese industry fall technologically years behind the
Americans.[26]

Businessmen were even more active in shaping the various support
programmes and research projects. They had a seat in all the consultative bodies and they chaired some of them. Privately, through
contacts with the bureaucrats most directly concerned, they pressed
their views and saw to it that they were incorporated in those
measures which interested them. Through connections with the politicians, they managed to obtain more funding for programmes that
would benefit them most. So they were usually satisfied with most of
the industrial targeting that took place. On the other hand, if they
disliked some aspect they would try to suppress it before formal
adoption, or, when faced with a fait accompli, ignore or resist it.

This has been seen in many specific cases, some of which have
already been reported. It has also been endorsed by most of the
industry studies. Here is the conclusion of Friedman in his very
revealing analysis.

Though the bureaucratic regulation thesis contends that Japanese
industry was guided by a 'strong state,' the machine tool industry
exhibits an unbroken record of failures dating from the late 1920s.
From the Depression to the present there is not one example of the
adoption let alone success, of a MITI or an MCI initiative. If we
think of a strong state as one that sets goals and then manipulates
financial and other incentives to achieve them, Japan appears to be
extremely *weak*: the government was forced to provide resources
but could not insist that its goals be met in exchange.[27]

This supports the opposing view, as expressed in the earlier sections on the business community, that businessmen ended up playing
a more decisive role than the bureaucrats. But it does help to provide
two nuances.

First of all, there were sectors in which the bureaucracy prevailed
because these sectors were more readily dominated or easier to
manipulate. They included some which were more concentrated due
to their inherent characteristics, like modern shipbuilding and especially steel. Others were more cartelised, with fewer players, and thus
easier to supervise, like computers or finance. Yet others needed

state support more urgently, and were more willing to submit to control, such as agriculture and the various declining industries. Companies in younger, more dispersed or more dynamic sectors paid less heed, for example, consumer electronics, motorcycles or machine tools.

Secondly, the situation evolved over time. There is no doubt that the bureaucrats could impose more readily on businessmen shortly after the war when companies were weak and desperately needed finance, technologies and, above all, protection and support. This happens to have been the most effective and 'glorious' period of industrial targeting. Later on, however, companies developed their own sources of funding, created R&D departments and became efficient enough to compete at home and abroad. They no longer needed help from the state and only cooperated when it was in their clear interest to do so. Thus, later exercises were often more modest, or in the few remaining sectors where backing was needed . . . or in depressed sectors.

Parallel to this transition there has been another one, from largely public to largely private targeting. More and more it is the companies which are picking the winners, financing them internally, undertaking the necessary R&D, creating markets within the corporate family and, when possible, subsidising exports. The only role the bureaucrats play here is to smooth over trade conflicts with trading partners that are upset by having yet another domestic industry maimed or destroyed.

Far from lamenting the relative rise of the business community and decline of the bureaucracy, as some may do, this should be seen in a positive light. The active participation of businessmen increased the sources of information, experience and expertise, which was to the good. Even more essential, it injected some much-needed commercial sense into the various exercises. While costs, profits and other aspects were sometimes downplayed, they were not entirely ignored. And this increased the odds of entering sectors that could ultimately fend for themselves and generate the wherewithal to launch further exercises.

If things had been the other way around, if the bureaucrats had been able to order businessmen around, as many of them wanted and some academics would have gladly granted, industrial targeting would have been much less successful. More flashy, monumental, show-window projects would have been launched and more resources would have been lavished on them to create the appearance of 'success'. In short, Japanese performance would have tended toward that of countries which foolishly let government run business.

PEOPLE'S COSTS AND BENEFITS

So far, imperceptibly and almost inevitably, we have been evaluating industrial policy and targeting from the viewpoint of the government and business community. The concerns have been whether strong industries emerged, whether improved technologies were introduced, whether factories were rationalised and better goods manufactured and whether Japanese companies could compete abroad. We have focused largely on output and judged results in terms of production gains and increased exports.

Certainly, these are relevant yardsticks for measuring the value of the efforts undertaken. But they cannot be the sole criteria. Industrial targeting must be seen in a broader context as well. Manufacturing is not the only economic activity and production is not the only goal in any country. Moreover, influential politicians, senior bureaucrats and company executives are not the only ones who have to be pleased. There is also the population at large.

Although the Japanese people rarely intruded in the decision-making process and accepted economic policies almost as a given, they were essential participants. Theoretically at least, most of this was done for them. So it is necessary to see what they won or lost.

There is no question that ordinary people gained from the progress. By opening new industries, the economy was strengthened and enlarged. Domestic products ultimately cost less and exports brought the wherewithal to buy imports. More factories meant more jobs and eventually better jobs. This raised per-capita income and contributed to an improved standard of living. More abstractly, the shame of wartime defeat was replaced by a new pride in the nation's economic prowess. To deny this would be absurd.

But it would be no less foolish to overlook the costs and drawbacks. Ordinary people contributed tremendous amounts of time and money to this cause. Even after four decades, Japanese employees were still putting in considerably more hours and accepting working conditions that had long since disappeared in other countries of a comparable economic level. They were also paying for the targeting exercises in countless other ways.

Only the more obvious ones are usually dealt with in books on Japanese industrial policy, and sometimes they are glossed over. After all, the enormous sums that go into subsidising production, supporting R&D and bailing out declining sectors must come from somewhere. Where they come from is primarily tax revenue, much of this collected from ordinary people. If they got something in return for promoting the rise of new industries, they got much less from easing the demise of older ones. In neither case were they asked. But surely the bigger waste was the latter, especially when this was only a holding operation for a sector that had to disappear.

That the bureaucrats were more concerned with running their projects and the politicians with helping their constituency was particularly blatant for coal mining. According to Samuels, 'the political benefits of providing unlimited state subsidies to coal producers seemed always to outweigh the staggering economic costs'. He indicated more graphically that, even when it was decided to let the industry die, 'the final shaft had been sunk long before – and, as usual, directly through the heart of the Japanese taxpayer'.[28] But subsidies did not only go to helpless cases like coal, they also accumulated for aluminium, other light minerals, shipbuilding and, above all, agriculture.

This is only part of the story. Further costs were borne by ordinary people as consumers.[29] These seem to be overlooked by most observers but are actually far greater than any subsidies. Japanese had to spend considerably more on imports because of protection during the many long years when the market was firmly closed. In many cases they had to go without superior products until local companies could supply them. Yet, even then, there was no guarantee they would be as cheap because local makers frequently kept prices high enough to subsidise exports. The undervalued yen, another tool of industrial policy, continued making imports more expensive than they would otherwise have been, without actually lowering the cost of domestic products. Market manipulation by cartels, oligopolies and monopolies, either promoted or tolerated by the authorities, only pushed prices higher. On top of this, the government granted higher rates for electricity, telephone, transport, insurance and so on while permitting banks to pay lower interest rates.

Japan's high cost of living can be traced partly to industrial targeting in another way. Companies strove to build the largest and most advanced factories, which were certainly more productive, but also more costly than merely expanding or refurbishing older facilities.

Worse, they frequently went too far and created overcapacity. Just how much is hard to estimate but it was massive for shipbuilding, aluminium and steel and considerable even for semiconductors. The urge for market share rather than profits, not instilled by the targeters but certainly aggravated by their practices, kept companies from earning bigger profits. This meant that they paid less in taxes and offered workers lower wages than otherwise.

Even less attention was paid to the external dis-economies. There were many of these. The obsession with economic growth and indifference to broader interests led to multiple abuses. One of the more visible was the mounting concentration of population in major cities and industrial zones concurrent with a depopulation of outlying regions. The result was crowding, long commuting times and exorbitant housing costs. To make way for industry, nature was defiled. Then, because inadequate precautions were taken, there was an alarming degree of pollution and environmental destruction, only some forms of which have abated. The stress on rationalisation within targeted industries increased efficiency but decreased the need for workers, so that unemployment arose even in Japan.

Another crucial aspect, one that is hardly ever mentioned, is that any rewards were unevenly distributed and therefore industrial targeting had far-reaching economic, social and political implications. After all, by helping some sectors it could not be avoided that others would be hurt. There was only so much time, energy and money to go around. The essence of targeting is to back certain sectors and neglect others. Not only were those others left to their own devices, they were deprived because they had to pay more for loans, were subject to taxes from which others were exempted, could not attract as capable managers and workers, and so on.

Among the sectors that were passed over were several basic pillars of the economy. Relatively few services were aided aside from finance, some types of transportation and lately software. Wholesale and retail distribution, which were notoriously inefficient, were not upgraded adequately. The same applied to construction, making housing, amenities and infrastructure unduly expensive. Even some branches of manufacturing were passed over, especially those turning out older, more labour-intensive articles, those producing goods primarily for domestic consumption, and traditional crafts.[30]

Moreover, within the sectors that were targeted and that benefited from assistance, it was not every company which gained. Only select companies, those with the ability to become national champions (and strong political connections), were given a boost. Scant attention was paid to second and third-rate firms, including emerging ones with the potential to grow. More generally, small and medium enterprises had to get by on their own. Any assistance that was provided was minor compared to what the big companies got and sometimes just a sop to avoid complaints. The odd thing about this is that the big companies could do quite nicely alone while smaller ones really needed the help.

This was particularly serious because the economy was being significantly skewed by industrial policy. Most of the effort was going into a relatively small core of key sectors while ignoring the rest. If they had been large enough, it might not have mattered. Alas, the targeted sectors did not represent more than a fifth of the overall economy while the neglected portion was the bulk. Likewise, most of the government support was channelled into a small circle of companies, most of them large. They accounted for about 1 per cent of the total, with perhaps 20 per cent of the workforce.

This differential stress left a strong imprint on society. Most notable was that the dual economy which had characterised Japan ever since Meiji days was further accentuated. There were highly advanced sectors and more backward sectors. There were strong, dynamic companies and weaker, struggling ones. Insidiously, the weaker firms were coming under the control of the stronger ones, which dominated one sector after the other.

The social hierarchy was also polarised. The elite consisted of the influential politicians, senior bureaucrats and top company executives who so manifestly shaped policy in their mutual interest. Those who worked in the ruling party, in key bureaucracies and in leading companies, were closer to the summit. Naturally, more educated employees, the white-collar class, were a rung above the factory workers, the blue-collar types. Beneath them were the staff of smaller firms, especially those in the services or older industries. Then came part-time workers, temporary workers, home workers and the like, many of them women.[31]

Here too it is clear that a small privileged elite was doing much better than the broad masses. This was especially unfortunate not just because they represented a minority. More shocking was that the haves were gaining disproportionately more than the have-nots, which went against the formal goals of equality and social justice.

Spreading the perspective further, there was a definite tendency to encourage only production and neglect everything else that goes into forming a balanced existence. With so much government funding tied up in economic development and infrastructure, it was not possible to scrape together adequate sums for housing, amenities, social security and welfare. In addition, people worked too much to engage freely in hobbies, sports or other leisure. Family life, community life, the inner life of religion or philosophy, intellectual and cultural activities suffered. These lacks were repeatedly condemned by the media and public opinion polls. They were even conceded by an erstwhile MITI targeter, Yasuhisa Tashiro.

> Japan may have a coherent industrial policy. But its fruits are not fully utilized for the benefit of the Japanese people because Japan lacks a coherent economic policy for improving its standard of living. . . . If Japan is unfair, it is because Japan is now sacrificing its own affluence. If Japan has succeeded in getting consensus in the area of industrial policy, why cannot Japan do the same thing in the more important field of social policy?[32]

Finally, industrial targeting affected the political system adversely. Most of the exercises were undertaken with little feedback from the electorate, and even LDP politicians did not have much say. This lay largely within the realm of the bureaucrats, bureaucrats who adjusted the budget to finance their pet projects and who implemented them with very little government oversight, often on the basis of informal (and illegal) administrative guidance. As noted, most foreign (and Japanese) proponents of industrial targeting stressed that the lack of political 'meddling' was to the good.[33] Perhaps so. Perhaps not. This last section casts some doubt on that assertion. But it is perfectly clear that it was not good for democracy.

It was claimed that rather little corruption resulted. That is not quite true, since there were major scandals involving shipbuilding and airlines. And there was doubtlessly a lot of favouritism by specific bureaucrats, repaid if not in cash then through gifts and entertainment while they were in office and then a post-retirement job. That, however, is petty compared with the gross distortion which ultimately came about. By the 1980s, the *zaikai* were clearly manipulating not only the bureaucrats but the politicians, who had become terribly dependent for campaign funds. Much of that money came from the very companies which benefited from industrial policy of one sort or another.

None of this denies the validity of industrial policy and targeting as *economic tools*. It does, however, show significant limitations and abuses that should not be lost sight of even amidst the impressive successes Japan could boast.

10 Foreign Repercussions

Japan's swift, inexorable rise after the war inevitably created strains in the world economy. While economic growth was only a few per cent a year in most other countries, Japan averaged nearly 9 per cent in the 1950s and 1960s and still 3–4 per cent in the 1970s and 1980s. It was therefore expanding more rapidly than other countries, which had to make way for it. Those most directly affected were the advanced industrial economies of Europe and America, none more so than the United States.

During this period, Japan progressed from a relatively minor 2 per cent share of world gross national product to the point where it proudly boasts 10 per cent. For certain specific sectors and products, it moved from the position of a rank newcomer to that of a top contender and, in some cases, the world leader. This meant that other countries fell back and sometimes were driven out of product lines they had invented and developed. Meanwhile, more backward countries sometimes found it harder to advance because Japan was just too effective for them even to try competing.

The situation was aggravated by Japan's dynamic outward-looking strategies. If it had limited itself basically to import substitution, like most other countries which expanded in the Third World, it would not have had much of an impact. True, it would have closed off its market. But it would not have exported massive quantities of goods which had to be absorbed elsewhere. And it would not have upset existing trade circuits so dramatically, adding an element of fierce and deadly competition.

Japan's resurgence therefore caused much more disruption than that of others which caught up, even one as similar as Germany. In trying to discover why, industrial policy and targeting have often been regarded as the principal culprits. While admired for their efficiency, they were increasingly feared. In addition to being disruptive, they were repeatedly branded unfair and dangerous.

WHAT TARGETING WROUGHT

Foreign countries were irritated by both Japan's import and export policies. Their first grief was the difficulty of selling to Japan because of the many barriers erected to protect the domestic market. It was hard to get through the tariffs and quotas, the foreign exchange regulations and limitations on investment and technology transfer. Products which had once sold there, and were still competitive, were blocked. And it could not but be noticed that this protection closely followed the shifts in industrial policy. Each time a new sector or product was targeted, the barriers became more impenetrable.

If, after having created the desired sector, the market had been truly opened to imports, the frustrations might have dissipated. But it gradually became obvious that the formal liberalisation was not sufficient. There was a thick tangle of nontariff barriers and the distribution network was still complicated and impervious. It was not always realised that this was due to private enterprise replacing state industrial policy, but it was perfectly clear that, despite claims of an 'open' market, that was hardly the case.

Potential exporters were thus aggrieved on two accounts. They were disturbed that, more than four decades after the war, and two decades after other advanced countries had opened their markets to Japan, it was still impossible to expect much reciprocity. And the situation was not likely to change significantly because, in the interim, Japanese companies had become sufficiently productive and competitive to hold off most foreign rivals. So, for one reason or another, access to the world's second largest market remained tantalisingly out of reach.

Japan's trading partners were even more annoyed by the attempt to pin the blame on them. The standard explanation, that Japan did not import much because foreign products were of inadequate quality, or did not meet consumers' expectations, or were too costly, only embittered them. For, when foreign manufacturers possessed the right goods, of the right quality, at the right price, they were not allowed to sell them. Indeed, it was only when they had become uncompetitive against the Japanese that they were let into the market. While they could agree with the need to 'try harder', and many did try harder, this was never enough.[1]

Whatever the reason, and whoever was at fault, the result was the same. It was uncommonly difficult to export manufactured goods to Japan. All it imported in quantity were raw materials, crude oil and foodstuffs. Countries unable to provide these, and even some which could, quickly found that they were running trade deficits. If they could not come up with something to sell to Japan they would be in serious trouble.

Japanese exports to its trading partners were sometimes seen as an even more worrisome problem. This was not only because of the great quantities, which kept rising implacably, but also because of the intensity of the throughput and, on occasion, the prices.

It was out of the question for any country to absorb a steadily growing amount of Japanese goods over an extended time, especially if its own sales were not growing at about the same pace. Yet, Japan continued expanding exports by 10, 20, even 30 per cent a year during the whole postwar period. The unavoidable outcome was a notable worsening of the trade balance which was felt most acutely in the United States, Europe and parts of Asia. Since the trends for both exports and imports held steady and certainly did not indicate any reversal, this would obviously be not a short-term but a perennial problem.

Even this was less disturbing than certain peculiarities of Japanese export strategy. One was the narrow focus. Exports did not cover a broad range of products, only moderate amounts of each arriving at any given time. To the contrary, even in the 1980s, Japan was selling a fairly small array of goods and each of the items in very large quantities. The exact composition varied over the years, with steel, ships and textiles predominating earlier and consumer electronics and automobiles later on. These leading exports could account for two-thirds of the total.

But they were not even fed into the export stream smoothly, only growing gradually over time. To the contrary, once a new product was developed, production scale and exports rose sharply and sales in a given market could increase by 20, 30, 40 per cent and more a year. There have been cases where key products, like TVs, VCRs, certain chips doubled or tripled from one year to the next. Such surges were commonplace and they made Japanese imports far harder to absorb. They also aroused complaints of 'torrential' exports and a 'laser beam' approach.

During the initial stage, moreover, there was a manifest tendency to sell on low price in order to expand market share more rapidly. This led at least to predatory pricing, with Japanese goods deliberately sold for less than local ones.[2] This might be done because Japanese costs were lower. It was equally likely to result from subsidisation by the state or through the company. Charges of dumping were incessantly raised and quite often substantiated.

It is obvious that domestic manufacturers could not resist such massive, concentrated attacks on a specific sector, product or model. In some cases they were pushed back by the Japanese manufacturers and had to limit their sales to more sophisticated or expensive models, as with automobiles, motorcycles and watches. In other cases they were simply wiped out, as with sewing machines, televisions and, increasingly, machine tools.

That was considerably more dangerous than trade deficits since it was destroying the economic machinery needed to produce manufactured goods that might be exported or compete with imports. It not only undermined the sectors concerned but dragged down related ones, steel weakening because automobile production had fallen off or semiconductor sales sinking as computer and electronics production went offshore. In short, the same linkages that reinforced Japan's economy were eroding foreign ones. Ultimately, this could reduce an industrial country to the status of a service economy, at least until Japanese services began encroaching.

So, in addition to trade and eventually payments imbalances, countries were faced with a loss of assets as factories were closed and companies went bankrupt. More and more workers were laid off and unemployment became a major headache. With companies and workers paying less in taxes (since they earned less), it was harder to cover the costs of infrastructure, education, welfare and so on. The ripple effects could create an unmitigated disaster.

Here too there was a clear correlation between this phenomenon and industrial targeting. As each new sector or product was targeted, production swelled in Japan and soon spilled over into exports. Foreign producers were pushed back in that sector and unemployment spread. The circle of distressed sectors expanded as the list of targeted sectors grew. In fact, by studying Japan's plans and visions, foreign governments and companies had a pretty good idea of what was going to happen to them.

THE VICTIMS

All of this is a bit abstract when one speaks of casualties and injuries without looking at the 'victims'. This is necessary not just to show who lost out in these competitive battles. It puts targeting in the proper perspective for, unlike mere industrial policy or economic development in general, it was directed specifically against foreign industries and companies. Whether the actual intent was to destroy them or merely to catch up, the outcome was often the same.

No country was hurt more than the United States.[3] It was the one Japan was most familiar with, whose market was most wide open and whose companies were in the forefront of the most sectors. It made perfectly good sense to target those sectors and pump Japanese exports into the vast and receptive American market. This happened not once or· twice for assorted articles but over and over for a never-ending list of products. Indeed, it became almost routine to visit the United States, see what was being developed, find out if it could be copied and improved upon and then sell pretty much the same thing for less.

The first efforts were for ordinary labour-intensive products like textiles and garments, later upgraded to synthetic fibres and more fashionable clothing. Cheap consumer electronics followed, including transistor radios and black-and-white televisions. Then came colour televisions, so massively that most American firms were driven under.[4] This left the field open for VCRs and the rest. With heavy industrialisation, Japanese steel gained a foothold. Then came automobiles, construction equipment and machine tools. Soon the Japanese were nibbling at the market for computers and swallowed yet more for semiconductors. But there was no end in sight, for now the companies were working on robots, biotechnology, even satellites.

As Japanese sales advanced, American production receded; as Japanese companies pushed ahead, American ones pulled back or went into other sectors. By the 1980s, it was evident that the retreat was turning into a rout. Imports met a growing share of demand. The penetration rate was dangerously high, and still mounting, for textiles, garments, steel, ships, machine tools, automobiles, computers, semiconductors, and so on, and so forth. For motorcycles, many household appliances, consumer electronics, VCRs, and so on, there was hardly any genuine American presence.

Much the same thing was happening in Europe. Only, it was somewhat slower. Japan paid less attention to European markets because they were smaller, less affluent and more closed. The Europeans were also more suspicious of Japanese inroads and more willing to defend their own producers. Through the European Community, they engaged in counter-targeting. Japanese companies were promptly fined for dumping, forced to produce locally, then obliged to boost local content and kept out of sectors reserved for European companies by bureaucratic rules and regulations.

Nonetheless, Japan also targeted some key industries and pushed back the European competitors. It rivalled Great Britain for ships and eventually ruined the shipbuilding industry not only in Britain but throughout the continent. It drove the Germans out of the camera business and then began working on machine tools. It displaced Switzerland for watches, grabbing the lion's share of the world market. Japanese automobiles increased market share aside from France and Italy, where it was limited, and Germany which remained competitive enough not to succumb until later. Never tiring, it even took on France for haute couture and Holland for tulip bulbs.

The same sort of events were occurring in the Third World, although they were much less noticeable. The reason was that developing countries had relatively few strong industries or significant companies. So they were not undermined or destroyed by Japanese exports. What happened was that they were prevented from arising or growing as Japanese companies preempted one sector after the other. When they were prevented from exporting, by government regulations, they created local subsidiaries that expanded more vigorously than indigenous companies. For readers tired of American and European griping, it may be enlightening to see that even Koreans said much the same thing.

Japanese manufacturers have come out with a dumping offensive to dominate the world semiconductor market from the beginning. They come out with a dumping offensive that does not even recover production costs in order to overturn their competitors. . . . Japan's dumping offensive is striking a major blow at our country's semiconductor industry in particular. Our semiconductor industry has only now acquired systems for mass production of the 64K DRAM and is going on the final stages in development of the 256K DRAM and cannot escape bitter struggle as it is disrupted by Japan's bud-nipping tactics.[5]

In the erstwhile Soviet bloc, among the centrally-planned economies, there were no such problems. They had closed markets, traded article by article, maintaining an acceptable trade and payments balance. They did not import anything that competed with what was made locally but, rather, imported machinery to make it better. Now that they are going 'capitalist', Japan may teach them that it is not so easy, as it did to the People's Republic of China, which was so quickly and thoroughly inundated with Japanese products that it had to reverse its policy.

In short, the more a country traded with Japan, the more it was hurt by industrial policy and targeting. The less it had to do with Japan, the smaller the impact, if any. The advanced, industrial economies, the United States first and foremost, were most intimately linked with Japan and suffered the worst damage by far. In East and Southeast Asia, while benefiting from Japanese investment, it is becoming harder to repay any loans and the trade imbalance is often even more grotesque than in the West. Some of these countries may be in for trouble.

In fact, when you consider the tremendous number of sectors which are already dominated by Japan, it is hard to figure out just what will sustain certain economies. If they are lucky, countries may produce raw materials and perhaps also process them. They can sell agricultural produce to Japan, if it opens the market more. For manufactured goods, however, there is not much left after you subtract those listed from A to Z in the section on Japan's success. True, there are aircraft and engines, rockets and especially military hardware. But some of those are not really interesting commercially. As for the services, which were supposed to support advanced countries in their old age, many of them are slipping into Japanese hands as well.

This is particularly distressing. For it was Japan's close trading partners, those it dealt with most regularly and substantially, which were weakened most. They were importing more and exporting comparatively less. Gradually, as one product after another flags, they are running out of things to trade. This is not only sad for them, it is unfortunate for Japan. Any gains in present sales are being offset by losses of future sales. One day they simply might not have the money to buy more. Then Japan would be in an extraordinary predicament because there are no other markets that offer the same potential.

More serious, these were not only commercial partners, they were friends and allies. The trade and payments imbalances are upsetting not only economic relations but political ones as well. Since this could be seen as unfair, in that Japan did not import even while it exported, trade conflicts could quickly degenerate into broader ones or at least tarnish Japan's reputation. Declining economies might also be unable to afford to spend as much on military preparedness. Washington might question the 'free ride' and insist that Japan pay more. It might even rethink the 'alliance'.

Finally, this is a threat to Japan's future growth in a more unusual sense. Ever since the war, indeed, ever since the country was opened over a century ago, it has developed on the basis of absorbing new products, assimilating new technologies and leaving the creative activity to others. True, it has proved innovative, and it has improved on much of what it borrowed, but it was not in a position to take the lead. If the Western economies were undermined, and companies lost their preeminence, they would not or could not pave the way. Japan would have nothing more to target.

MIXED REACTIONS

Given the relentless pressure on their own markets and a hollowing of their economies, as well as continued difficulties in exporting to Japan, its trade partners have had to react. The reactions have taken various forms, at various times, in various countries. Some have been dynamic and positive, others more defensive and negative.[6]

The most constructive solution was for companies under attack from Japanese competitors to rise to the occasion by upgrading their own operations. They too could buy new machinery, improve production processes, use the workforce more efficiently, cut costs and engage in other forms of rationalisation. Since, initially at least, Japan had a comparative advantage for labour, they would basically have to increase the capital and knowledge content of their products and production.

This, however, was not so easy given the circumstances. The effect of Japanese industrial policy was specifically to make up for any comparative advantage through government assistance. Funds were provided more cheaply, technologies were acquired more readily, sales were guaranteed more effectively, and so on. This meant that Japanese companies would artificially be on a par with foreign ones and at the same time maintain a competitive edge for labour costs. With this backing, they could still defeat foreign rivals unless an exceptional effort were made.

Alone, most foreign companies could not make such an effort. They could not outspend a Japanese enterprise which received cheap loans from the government or commercial banks, got substantial tax write-offs for being in the right sector, and above all showed little concern for profits until it had attained a satisfactory market share. They had to use their more costly funds more sparingly and, if they did not turn a profit, even internal financing might disappear. In addition, they were not producing for a 'captive' domestic market and perhaps also the broad, internal one of a corporate group, so they could not thereby attain large enough minimal sales to remain viable.

The only way foreign companies could really fight back on equal terms was to enjoy the support of their own governments commensurate with whatever the Japanese government was providing. Even then, without violating antitrust laws, they could not muster the corporate backing. Yet, even if both these conditions were satisfied, it would still be necessary for the whole population to regard the economic endeavour as a patriotic – or at least desperate – struggle that required working longer hours for less pay, sacrificing family and personal life for the company, and putting exports ahead of domestic needs.

Only on such a basis could one speak of competition between equals. That is why few sectors have resisted. They needed national champions of exceptional size and ability to sustain them, an IBM, General Motors or Philips. Or they had to be specially promoted, most likely on national security or scientific grounds like aeronautics, aerospace or semiconductors.

Another positive solution was to adjust by moving into new sectors. Managers did this at first. But each time they moved up a rung, the Japanese followed. Eventually, there was no place to go but the frontier industries. And these still had to be developed and might not provide much of a return for years. Foreign firms trying this did not even know whether they would reap the benefits. Perhaps Japan would cut in again.

That's the rub. There is no point to developing new sectors and products without the assurance of making at least enough financial gains to cover the costs. Alas, the Japanese have already targeted not only some but all high-tech sectors. They are doing considerable research on their own. And they are busily monitoring the research of others. They can probably buy up the technologies, or replicate them, and take over the nascent sectors faster than their competitors. Under such conditions, most foreign companies are fazed, and moving up does not appear to be a feasible solution for any but the best.

Indeed, in a growing number of areas, foreign companies could not develop new products even if they wanted to. Most innovations grow out of existing lines and many of these have been abandoned to the Japanese. You cannot develop high-definition television without a television industry; you cannot make video cameras after you have stopped making movie cameras; you cannot produce the latest chips if you missed out on their predecessors and you cannot design robots once you give up on machine tools. It would be hard to get back into motorcycles, or ships or microwave ovens, because the existing producers would quickly undercut interlopers.

This goes even further. Once you have lost certain assets, the very process of manufacturing becomes difficult. You lose trained managers and skilled workers. You lose the essential resources and the knowhow to put them where they can do the most good. You don't have suitable R&D. The very infrastructure collapses as suppliers and distributors disappear. Once countries have lost the basic foundation, it is futile to dream of taking the lead again and the idea of a 'comeback' is just wishful thinking.[7]

What should one do? Should companies simply admit that ultimately they will be driven out by Japanese competitors? Should they stop investing in more machinery? Should they stop engaging in costly R&D? Should they passively accept their fate and just hang on as long as they can?

This happens to be a solution as well. Many companies have given up on hopes either of outdoing the Japanese or of finding new products. They are happy if they can cling to some niche and eke out a living. If not, they try to maintain modest operations as long as they can and let the company gradually sink into nothingness. Others actually sell out to the Japanese. The more ambitious lead a shell existence by having products manufactured offshore, perhaps in Japan, but market them under their own label. This is a particularly widespread reaction which only accelerates the hollowing of the economy.

The final alternative is protectionism. The government intervenes not to strengthen production or shift into other sectors but to rescue threatened companies and sectors by restricting competition. Exports are limited in quantity by quotas or 'voluntary restraint' or the prices are raised through tariffs, taxes and other techniques. This way the domestic industry can hold its own, companies can survive and jobs can be saved.

To the economic theoreticians, this is a very negative solution since it preserves inefficient producers and boosts the cost to consumers.

What is gained by the former is lost by the latter. But these decisions are not taken by economists, they are taken by politicians for political reasons, and saving companies and jobs are among the most popular. Moreover, if the alternative is letting yet another sector collapse, they are not certain that they like economic theory.

While protectionism is not a praiseworthy reaction, and few openly claim that it is, it must be remembered that it is particularly attractive since that is what the Japanese are doing. The Japanese have always protected weak sectors, both infant industries and depressed ones, so they can hardly object if others do the same. Despite statements to the effect that 'protectionism does not work', it seems to have paid off handsomely for Japan.[8]

Thus, some politicians engage in protectionism to help local industries and the national economy. Others put a different face on it by insisting that such measures are only taken to convince Japan to practise 'fair' trade. They are mere levers to pry open the market and obtain such laudable goals as a 'level playing field' and 'reciprocity'. Since Japan actually seems to prefer export restraint to truly opening the market, it acquiesces to most of the protectionist demands with little fuss and officials warn companies in advance to ease up on exports.[9]

At present, all these solutions coexist. In some countries, in some sectors, in some phases of the trade conflict, they are all used. But there are clear trends which indicate a shift from the more positive to the more negative. There are fewer, apparently futile, attempts to compete actively, at least not without government backing. While new products are sought, they are not easy to find and the Japanese are already competing for them. Meanwhile, more sectors are succumbing, many without a fight. And it is protectionism in one form or another that is emerging as the predominant reaction.[10]

WAS THERE A CONSPIRACY?

It is not really proper to conclude this chapter without taking a further look at the non-economic aspects of the issue. No matter what one may think of the opposing views, it is necessary to consider the question of *why* Japan engaged in industrial policy and especially targeting. Was it a natural reaction growing out of Japanese cultural and economic practices or was there a deliberate attempt to crush competitors? Was the goal merely to improve economic conditions or actually to dominate the world economy? Was it a spontaneous economic phenomenon or an insidious 'conspiracy', perhaps even a quasi-military effort to win an economic war over those who humbled it in the past?

These questions have frequently been glossed over and any accusations treated as ridiculous. But it would be incorrect not to consider them since they are so widespread and form an integral part of the subject. This aspect was dealt with most bluntly in Marvin Wolf's *The Japanese Conspiracy*, subtitled 'the plot to dominate industry worldwide'. He wrote, among other things,

> Japan has 'borrowed' or copied foreign technology, or acquired it through joint-venture agreements which it has later disavowed. When this has failed they have resorted to bribery, industrial espionage and outright theft. Its industries often act in concert, as did the prewar Japanese cartels, the *zaibatsu*, targeting their competitors in other nations and dumping their products at a temporary loss in order to win larger and larger shares of the world's markets and eventually achieve monopoly positions. The Japanese educate their scientists and engineers in American and European universities; they then return home to use their new skills in a trade war against those who educated them. Japan, it is now becoming clear, is winning the trade war because it refuses to play by the rules.[11]

Naturally, there is no conclusive evidence to prove an effort to dominate industry worldwide, destroy the competition or create an economic empire. But the Japanese have engaged in enough loose talk to make it seem that way by quoting them. They frequently use military terminology such as trade offensives, attacking competitors, conquering market share and so on. We have already quoted a MITI Vice-Minister on the need to concentrate fighting power in strategic industries, like Clausewitz and Napoleon. Fiery sales managers use even more of this jargon. Such comments are trotted out by the critics and, if nothing else, betray a strange state of mind.

There is also a fair amount of circumstantial evidence. One can say what one wants, there is no doubt that Japan's expansion has left much economic trouble and damage in its wake, more so than that of other rising economies. Not only have companies collapsed or been driven out but, in an appreciable number of industries, Japanese firms do possess a worldwide oligopoly or monopoly. Also, no matter

what one may say, there are very close relations between the government and business. By placing itself at the centre of these activities,
MITI could not help becoming a prime suspect. As for questionable
commercial practices, pirating knowhow, turning on former partners,
dumping and predatory pricing, they are common occurrences.

There is more than enough of this for those who distrust Japan to
make a case. And the more the Japanese, their paid publicists and
lobbyists, friendly groupies and Japanapologists try to confuse the
issue, the more any suspicion grows. Certainly, the recent tack of
claiming that Japan never engaged in industrial policy or targeting, or
at least that it stopped long ago and, to boot, others now engage in
the same practices more, makes one believe that they do have
something to hide.

But there are weaknesses to the arguments. The expansion has
been too incremental, erratic and uncontrolled to show much deliberate intent or a master plan. There is no one control post. In fact,
the action is too diffuse and oblique to deduce the existence of a
carefully organised campaign. Moreover, much of it was seen as
defensive: protecting the Japanese market, warding off invasive
foreign capital, facing up to international competition, holding on to
market share (often against other Japanese companies), maintaining
exports and so on. There is much less concern with what one is doing
to others than with what would happen to one's own economy or
company if one did not act decisively.

It also overlooks the crucial fact that much of what Japanese
companies did occurred not because they wanted it but because they
had no other choice. They were forced by the system to take strong,
often drastic, action. We have already given numerous examples of
this. Companies were pushed to export by large scale, they had to
dump because it was not possible to unload the goods otherwise, it
was out of the question not to build larger factories to begin with
because then they would have been passed by competitors. The
cruellest taskmaster was market share. Every company had to fight
for every last sale because, if that went to a rival, it would gradually
lose its position in the market. And the final culmination might be to
disappear entirely.

Unless one realises how fiercely Japanese companies compete with
one another, it is impossible to grasp why they were so ruthless in
dealing with outsiders. But this was not done in anger. It sprang from
a cold calculation made so often that it had become second nature.

The logic was already expressed years ago by Dan Fenno Henderson, who observed it up close.

> when overcapacity results from a corporation's investing to protect its 'market share' instead of profit potential, the excess produce is sold abroad (even dumped) by the ubiquitous trading sibling as long as the variable costs are recovered, since high fixed costs for debt (interest) and wages (life employment) cannot be avoided anyway. This is 'market penetration' by forcing other world producers to move over and make room for the new Japanese position 'in the sun.' Still, there is probably no other way. . . .[12]

Of course, ambitious bureaucrats must have known that by expanding Japanese production to the extent they did there was bound to be overcapacity. This would create a glut and somebody else would have to give way. In the ensuing competition, in which Japanese companies were supported by their government and consumers, foreign firms would be more likely to callapse while Japanese ones expanded. But that did not seem to disturb them. They felt that Japan had to expand, to grow, and, if others could not hold on, that was their problem. As MITI said, it was export or perish![13]

Similarly, aggressive managers regularly targeted bigger market share, knowing that the only way to attain it was to take some away from competitors. In many cases, this was seen more specifically as eating into the share of foreign firms. Once again, there were no qualms. Japanese managers owed it to their staff, their company and their own career to push ahead no matter what happened to others. Indeed, they had to expand even if it put their own company under pressure. The collapse of others was not disturbing, it was part of the game. After all, competition was healthy and those who could not survive were obviously not sufficiently fit to worry about.

The key point is probably less that Japan launched a campaign to conquer certain foreign industries and destroy certain foreign companies than that it had an irrepressible urge to grow and did not care much what happened to others or, indeed, to itself. Yet, this dispersed action, this defensiveness, this need to succeed at all costs, this disconcern about what happened to others, are very reminiscent of how Japan got into and behaved during the Second World War. Obviously, the malicious intent was lacking this time. But, does that really matter? As Karel van Wolferen said, 'although there is no convincing reason to suspect that the administrators have worked out a grand master-plan for industrial domination of the world, what they are doing has the same effect as if there were such a plan'.[14]

While such behaviour seems to make sense in the senseless matter of war, it is perplexing during a period of peace, and especially when the worst victims are the closest partners, friends and allies. In an increasingly interrelated world community, one in which cooperation and mutual benefit are constantly praised, it would be assumed that Japan might behave differently. When one considers how often Japanese leaders have reaffirmed their nation's desire to contribute positively, it would be assumed that they realise this need. But the frantic sparring goes on and the casualties mount.

11 What Now?

By now it must be obvious that, while industrial targeting was a domestic policy option of Japan, it had tremendous external repercussions. It affected virtually every country the Japanese dealt with, some of them quite severely. It was consequently necessary for those countries to decide whether, and how, to react.

Before doing so, it was first essential to discard the comforting idea that industrial policy was being phased out or had actually ceased. That is what many Japanese officials and friendly academics claimed. A look at the situation will show that the practice is continuing, perhaps toned down in some respects, but intensifying in others. There are many more frontier sectors and declining ones to promote or defend. And new prospects are opening with the rise of managed trade.

How to react is still an open question. In the last chapter, various possible reactions were considered, with some stress on what has become the predominant response, namely protectionism. But there is one last alternative which should not be forgotten. It is to copy Japan. After all, there may be aspects of industrial targeting which could help other countries develop their own economies or at least resist Japan's advance. To do that, of course, it would be helpful to have a somewhat clearer understanding of industrial targeting than at present.

NO END TO TARGETING

As noted in the first chapter, there have recently been statements to the effect that industrial targeting has been greatly reduced, no longer exists or never existed to begin with. Since these emanate largely from the Japanese establishment and foreign apologists, they are naturally suspect and should be taken with several grains of salt. Having reviewed the situation, it is perfectly clear that the rumours of targeting's demise were greatly exaggerated. It is still there and is unlikely to disappear soon.[1]

As a matter of fact, industrial policy and targeting presently flourish at both ends of the spectrum, although there is a gradual shift in emphasis from rising to declining sectors.

What is most impressive is how many futuristic projects are still being promoted. They include new materials (carbon composite, intermetallic compounds, nonlinear photonics material, high-performance ceramics), energy (nuclear, solar cells, fuel-cells), HDTV, protein engineering, advanced robots, excimer laser and ion beam processing, superconductors, super and hypersonic transport, unmanned space-experiment systems, artificial intelligence, three-dimensional ICs, 'neuro-computers', a sixth-generation computer, etc., etc.

In the meanwhile, more and more sectors are 'ailing' and feel that government aid would be more than welcome. Admittedly, now and then a few are taken off the sick list once they have been rationalised enough or business picks up, like shipbuilding and steel. But they may be back later. And there are still dozens of recession cartels even in a time of relative bouyancy, so one can only guess how long the list would be in really bad times.

Aside from that, bit by bit, it is possible to see a third category emerging. These are sectors or products which are subject to government supervision under tacit or formal agreements to limit exports or regulate prices. This is done to restrain exports enough so that foreign countries do not have to resort to cruder protectionism. We have mentioned automobiles, steel, semiconductors and textiles in the case studies. But there are others, and this is clearly regarded as a growing activity by MITI, one in which it can restore its authority, that was somewhat diminished by inability to do more for rising industries.[2]

There are only three things that have changed significantly. The first, relatively superficial, is that it has become much harder to find out about targeting. The various ministries, MITI and the rest, no longer publicise their efforts, of which they are still very proud but which would only provoke negative reactions abroad. They have become more secretive. That is why there was no list in MITI's *Vision for the 1990s*. Japan's foreign friends, closely following the party line, have also stopped congratulating it on its wonderful achievements. Still, if you observe the economic realities carefully, it becomes sufficiently evident which sectors are being helped and how. The telltale sign is usually which ones are benefiting from government sponsored R&D projects.

The second major change is that somewhat different methods are being used. Those which are most visible to the naked eye, and could most readily be denounced as violations of GATT rules or free trade, are less prevalent. But other techniques have been developed to do much the same thing, or other things that can be equally helpful. Here one might interject, in reference to the claims of targeting's demise, 'Targeting is dead! Long live targeting!'

Through the various liberalisation exercises conducted under GATT or imposed by the United States, Japan has actually gone rather far in dismantling the formal barriers. Its tariffs have dropped beneath the levels of other advanced countries and the number of quotas is similar. But it has not made as good a job of removing the nontariff barriers. In that respect, it still ranks as one of the worst offenders, with new ones cropping up as old ones cease.

Other methods of keeping the market closed are more refined, less visible and also not ordinarily subject to international regulation. These include the numerous complexities of the distribution system, often explained away as cultural ticks of the Japanese, but nonetheless impediments. As indicated, much of this was caused by close relations between domestic manufacturers and distributors which allowed them to control the market and keep newcomers out. The most effective instruments were the links within the various *keiretsu*.

In this connection, it should be mentioned that the 'buy Japanese' policy is being toned down by the government. Indeed, it has almost gone into reverse with 'promote imports' campaigns which, alas, are less effective than the former. Still, government procurement is clearly declining. The same does not apply to the 'buy group' policy that exists in most *keiretsu*. Banks, insurers, manufacturers and so on still do a lot of business together in the horizontal groupings. In the vertical groupings, parent companies almost systematically buy from the 'family' of suppliers.

Given Japan's enormous export prowess and increasingly negative sentiment abroad, it is obvious that the government is unlikely to subsidise exports formally or even provide much tax relief for exporters, as in the old days. But it will continue offering cheap loans for major export projects and guaranteeing payment through the Ex–Im Bank and its loan schemes. And it will continue supporting research and development, either through its own laboratories and projects or by subsidising private sector efforts. The state's share, however, is bound to shrink further as private companies pour ever more money into R&D.

Restructuring industry, as opposed to merely promoting it, will also be harder. Foreign countries are already wary of the vast number of formal and informal cartels and, with time, they have figured out that there are negative implications for their own companies. Still, it is unlikely that many cartels will be disbanded and, even if they are, part of the goals can be achieved through more discreet administrative guidance. Meanwhile, new cartels may emerge as MITI tries to regulate exports and, since this is done at the request of foreign governments, there should be no complaints. As for the Fair Trade Commission, its bark will remain worse than its bite and neither are enough to prevent mischief.

We have gone through most of the old tactics and found a general tendency toward reduction which could lead one to believe that there has been, and will continue to be, progress. But we skipped one last technique, the one that is most often missed or glossed over by observers, but which we held for last because it is becoming the most serious impediment, namely exchange rates. This is often overlooked because it is not a formal barrier that one can pin down. It is rather hard to prove conclusively that rates were out of line; it is also hard to measure the impact. Nevertheless, there is no doubt that yen rates have repeatedly been too low, making foreign goods more expensive and harder to sell to Japan and making Japanese goods cheaper and easier to export. Unlike tariffs, quotas, etc. this weapon has never disappeared from the Japanese arsenal. As late as 1985–6, there was a major appreciation in which the yen's value doubled against the dollar. Later, in 1990, while the German mark and other currencies remained stable or strengthened, the yen began to weaken against them inexplicably, once again making Japanese exports cheaper.

Such large realignments, which occurred repeatedly, are sufficient indication that there has been some manipulation of the currency.[3] In addition, due to the distributors' control of the market, even such appreciation as there was did not help as much as it should have done. American goods, which, under the 1985–6 adjustment, should have cost half as much as before, did not. Importers, traders, wholesalers and retailers simply expanded their margins and kept prices about where they were. This meant that the articles were still expensive when they should have been much cheaper. By the way, this market manipulation was noticed by the public, condemned in the media, and even conceded by the government and MITI which tried to bring prices down . . . to little avail. That made the Japanese situation quite different from those of Germany and other European countries where much the same appreciation led to cheaper American goods, cheaper not only in theory but in practice for consumers, and then to rapid improvement in US sales.

What is particularly troublesome about this form of protection is that there are no GATT rules or other mechanisms that govern exchange rates. They are supposedly set spontaneously by market forces. But everyone knows they can be manipulated by governments. In fact, all governments do this at one time or another. But few have done it more actively and regularly than Japan. And few have the means of doing it more effectively through MOF working with a rather small number of major banks, brokers, insurance companies and traders and the Bank of Japan.

The third noteworthy change involved a reversal in the status of the main actors. It is perfectly obvious that the role of the government waned while that of the private sector waxed. The real barriers are now created by manufacturers and distributors, internal buying occurs through the groups, most of the R&D will be funded by private companies and so on. Even what the state does, and this will remain substantial, is increasingly being done at the behest of business circles. Businessmen, not bureaucrats, let alone politicians, are deciding which sectors should be promoted, how they should be helped, what to do to placate irate trading partners and so on. If they seemingly give in to MITI on certain issues, such as restraint in exports, it is not because they fear the bureaucrats but because they know it is best to pacify Washington and Brussels.

There is just an outside chance that the bureaucrats may recover some of their power. With managed trade expanding and more sectors coming under restraint and similar agreements, MITI can intervene and give orders to company executives. It is also angling for legislation that would permit it more broadly to regulate exports in order to prevent excessive sales even before they create conflicts. If this should come to pass, then it would be possible to think of a new era as suggested by Leon Hollerman. After the 'Japan, Incorporated' of the early postwar decades, and the 'Japan, Disincorporated', when the bureaucracy's authority dwindled, there could be a 'Japan, Reincorporated'.[4]

Alas, for foreign countries, it is not at all certain that any of these changes will better their lot. It is amazing how one measure after the other, each introduced under foreign pressure and with high hopes of solving external problems, has failed to improve the situation much and sometimes actually made it worse. As noted, the Japanese market is still closed, only in different ways. Exports are still strong, but for other reasons. And even the latest phase of managed trade may not do the trick.

With luck, this will keep Japanese companies from exporting so aggressively that foreign companies go under and whole sectors shrivel. But managers have found a way around this restraint, namely to invest and produce locally through 'transplants'. That does bring in funds and create production and jobs, which is to the good. On the other hand, it increases the sums that will eventually be taken out in profits. And, by competing locally, as many or more factories and jobs may be lost by genuine national companies. These latter would then have such small scales that they could not possibly defend their position, let alone export more. This has already happened to American television makers, and automakers may be next.

No, industrial policy and targeting have not vanished, nor are they likely to. That is because they are not merely techniques adopted by the ruling elite but an emanation of that elite. In every sphere, politicians, bureaucrats and businessmen cooperate. Since the economy is still the top priority, it is only natural that cooperation there should be most intense. Moreover, this sort of jointly manipulated economy is the only kind anybody knows, including the businessmen. Genuine free enterprise is as alien to them as it is to the targeters, and they still get enough benefits to leave the system intact.

So, industrial policy and targeting will be around for a long time to come. How long? Nobody knows. Certainly for another decade or two and probably well into the twenty-first century. Beyond that, it is hard to see clearly. But it would not be surprising if they were to last forever, even if they are periodically reborn in new manifestations.

LEARNING FROM JAPAN

If Japanese industrial targeting is here to stay, and is going to continue affecting the rest of the world, other countries might as well come to terms with it. This phenomenon can be studied and perhaps emulated; it can be ignored (although that is no longer so easy); or, as at present, it can merely generate confusion. We would opt for the first alternative, namely to understand how the process works and to adopt any aspects that appear useful. But not much can be done until the other two are discarded.

First, it is necessary to do away with the puerile, but fairly widespread, notion that it does not exist. That is the view of many American and some European economists, who believe firmly in free trade and free enterprise and see no other conceivable alternative.

They cling to theory and go by the textbooks and, since there is no provision for targeting, they claim it does not exist. If Japan succeeded, it must have been because it was pursuing the same sort of policies as everybody else, only better.

We quoted several of those 'experts' in the section on the great industrial policy debate. As noted, some tow the Japanese line, and it is presently argued by Japanese officialdom that there is no such thing as industrial policy and targeting. As shown in sector after sector, their insistence that the practice has disappeared is premature, to say the least. But that will not keep them from doing their best to lead gullible foreigners astray.

Obviously, the Japanapologists cannot be trusted to take an objective stance. But they actually confuse the debate less than the ideologues who do not seem in the least bit interested in facts. As noted, many claim there was no industrial targeting. Others insist that, even if there were, it could not have accomplished anything. Such a conclusion seems a bit silly given the emergence of Japan's steel, shipbuilding, computer, telecommunications, pharmaceutical and other industries. True, other sectors grew on their own, but that does not deny the impact of industrial policy on those that were targeted.

No sooner are you finished with arguments that question the existence of industrial policy, than you are inundated with complaints that there is too much. These come from the inveterate enemies who admit the practice exists but wish it did not. Many of these are also free-enterprise types who insist that such gross violations of classical theory will have baneful consequences for the Japanese one day. Meanwhile, they are already aggrieved by what targeting has done to their own country's economy. They therefore argue that the Japanese must be stopped. That might have been possible two or three decades ago. Now that Japan is the world's second biggest economic power, it is just wishful thinking.

The other main source of confusion is the misconception that under industrial targeting the economy is run by the bureaucrats. That is not surprising. The idea was propagated by many of the supposed authorities on the subject. As has been repeatedly demonstrated, it is incorrect. Businessmen always played at least a supporting role and gradually took the lead. But many Western and other businessmen do not realise this. Until they do, they will be wary of adopting policies that might conceivably give government the upper hand.

Results and Reactions

Naturally, individuals holding the various views just mentioned will not want to discuss industrial targeting seriously, let alone adopt it. But even its supporters, including some who advocate it for their own country, hurt its cause by adding to the confusion. They do this in various ways. The most noticeable is to praise industrial targeting too highly and awaken expectations that cannot be met.

Many of the more popular books, including those which aroused attention in the United States, gave the impression that Japan's experience was a resounding success. They played up the many triumphs and played down – or simply forgot to mention – the assorted failures. Most were written by bureaucratophiles who also stressed the decisive role of MITI. Citing a few failures might have enhanced the credibility of their position. It might also have warned readers of potential dangers.

Some backers of industrial targeting, for ideological or political reasons, also present an expurgated version. They accentuate the positive: finance, research, productivity and so on, and eliminate the negative. This negative is protectionism. Even Chalmers Johnson, leading the campaign, proposed a rather strange hybrid, one which does not protect domestic markets, an indispensable part of every Japanese exercise. After all, that may have been good enough for the Japanese, but we Americans have to play by stricter rules.

> Americans should avoid protectionism, in the sense of import substitution, at all costs. . . . Protectionism does not work. Industrial policy is the specific antidote for it – the only way to maintain both competitive domestic industries and free trade.[5]

Of course, this is only a variation on a free-trade gospel that can occasionally be even more rigorous. Many ideologues insist that the United States, and others, should not even defend themselves from predatory pricing or dumping of targeted goods. Cheaper prices, they argue, are fine for the consumer. And, in a just world, it is Japan which will ultimately suffer more because its consumers have to pay higher prices. That, in the meanwhile, American companies go bankrupt and American workers lose their jobs (and the wherewithal to consume) does not disturb them in the least.

This lack of realism and simple-minded faith in pure doctrine is touching but dangerous. Industrial targeting is a tougher, more muscular form of economic development. And that must be conceded by those who would copy it. It should also be grasped by those who want to defend themselves. For this, pragmatism is considerably more useful than noble principles and lofty thoughts which get so mixed up in the American debate that it becomes an exercise in futility.

Elsewhere there have also been debates on industrial targeting, in most cases in smaller circles and on more rational terms. The subject has exercised government and business leaders in many developing countries, especially in Asia. It has been much discussed in Europe, both in the individual countries and within the European Community. In none of these places were the participants so squeamish as to rule out protectionist measures, most assuredly not against Japan's own mercantilist practices.

But even these debates were less concrete than they might have been. And, given the amount of misinformation masquerading as information, they often failed to note both the strengths and weaknesses. That is a pity. Industrial policy certainly deserves a fair hearing so that it can be adopted or rejected on the basis of its real merits and demerits. A garbled, confusing debate does not help anyone. Above all, it does not help those who could learn useful things from it.

From this study, it must be obvious that industrial targeting had definite beneficial effects on Japan's economic development. It could do the same for others. One might even go so far as to argue that many countries would do well to adopt one technique or another, and perhaps the whole system in certain cases. This idea of learning from Japan is hardly original, it has been expressed quite frequently not only in developing countries but in the United States.[6] So, let us see what can be learned.

The nobler side of targeting is to promote new sectors. This is apparently less useful for advanced countries because they already have, to some extent at least, most existing sectors. But some are now falling behind and may need to catch up. Catching up is far more critical for latecomers and they are the ones who could benefit most. This group includes over a hundred developing countries and it would not be surprising if former East-bloc states were to regard this as a tempting alternative to both communism and pure capitalism.

These apprentices might pick more suitable products, support them more effectively, increase cooperation between the public and private sector and, especially, supplement (and correct) import substitution with export promotion. If they are fans of planning, they might do this more pragmatically; if they eschew planning, they might at least structure their efforts more efficiently. As for protecting their markets, that is almost a reflex action and hardly needs to be encouraged. But they might be urged to protect a bit less and lower the barriers gradually so that companies are forced to upgrade enough to get by on their own.

The subsequent task is considerably less admirable, but no less essential, namely to rescue, shore up and hopefully turn around declining sectors. The Japanese have been fairly good at that although, occasionally, they might have been wiser just to let the sector disappear. They provided both direction and support, which others do, but also imposed certain ground rules so that the beneficiaries did not just profit but made a genuine effort themselves. In this area, while not flawless, Japan could certainly teach other advanced countries a thing or two.

Despite the present vogue for Japanese research projects, it is not certain that there is much to be learned as far as the techniques are concerned. The United States and Europe have often put together not only multi-company but multinational teams that worked more harmoniously. The best advice would be to alter the proportions of basic and applied research. The former is more sophisticated and wins Nobel Prizes. But it is the latter which keeps the economy humming and brings in the money needed to finance the former.

These features are not only useful, some have been adopted by others and more will certainly follow. Export promotion has become a hot export to the Third World. Malaysia targeted various industries including steel and automobiles. Taiwan also picked winners like shipbuilding, steel and electronics and engaged in crucial research and development. Hong Kong, a staunch free trader, still had a very handy Trade Development Council. Even the United States adopted legislation for general trading companies and set up some research consortia.

In most cases, imitators just adopted one or another technique and inserted them in the existing framework. This might lead one to believe that the system is hard to transfer as a whole, which is true. But it is not impossible. Korea's recent, dramatic take-off can be traced to a system that not only wielded virtually every tool that Japan used, but did so more intelligently and more effectively. If there is any ideal model for industrial targeting, then it is probably Korea and not Japan.[7]

Other countries did not copy Japan as such. Rather, they evolved rather similar methods to meet their own specific needs but, since they were in roughly the same position, the differences are not very great. In Europe, France and others fostered national champions to resist American encroachment. This included companies in electronics, computers and telecommunications. The steel and automobile industries were also buttressed. By the way, France and Canada did a better job of promoting nuclear energy and France and Germany are ahead for high-speed trains. Even more impressive were the multinational joint ventures which resulted in the Airbus and Ariane rocket.

In the European Community, which is run by its own bureaucracy, there has been a bit of industrial policy. There is no doubt the Europeans felt that the expanded single market was theirs and that outsiders should only participate on acceptable terms. Thus, they did not hesitate to impose dumping duties or oblige foreign manufacturers to use a rather large local content for their products to qualify as European. They also picked certain industries they wished to preserve, or promote, and took measures to that end, including a limitation on Japanese auto exports. Finally, they launched a whole series of research projects from Esprit to Eureka.

Of course, the doubters will object that targeting cannot be transferred for cultural reasons. 'Our society is too different. We worship individuality and other things that are totally different from the Japanese way,' protests an American journalist.[8] That doesn't wash. True, Japanese culture is different. But many individual techniques have been borrowed by countries with equally different societies, like Malaysia and France. In addition, Japan's own culture was different in the late 1940s, when targeting was initially imposed, from what it is now. It was then more disorganised and almost anarchic . . . and that is the very reason why industrial policy was so badly needed.

Anyway, these are just economic techniques. They can be applied in any culture if given a chance. It is hard to see why export subsidies, research grants, tax relief, export promotion bodies, tariffs and quotas, even some modest picking of winners, should be wholly dependent on culture. These techniques can be adopted and, if necessary, adapted and adjusted.[9]

Moreover, as noted, some of the techniques mentioned in this book are important not only for what they do specifically but as correctives. Industrial targeting, even in a very rudimentary form, is useful for individualistic societies that cannot get their act together, because it imposes more cooperation. It forces the various economic actors to consider what is in the nation's interest as opposed to solely their own. It makes them think more of the future and creates a longer time horizon. This is just what is missing in places like the United States and Europe.

However, since there are risks, imitators might consider some basic guidelines.[10] First, remember which economic stage you are in and adopt policies used by Japan in that stage. This means developing countries emulating the early period and advanced ones focusing on its more recent strategy. You don't promote basic industries in the same way as high-tech or declining sectors. Every country can find some useful measures. Only adopt full-fledged targeting if your own circumstances allow that, otherwise pick and choose. Don't overdo things. Limit intervention and support so as not to completely mask market signals. And limit the period of support so companies don't get lazy. Lastly, don't become so obsessed with economic growth and 'effectiveness' that all other goals (environmental, social, equity, quality of life, etc.) are sacrificed.

Finally, if all else fails to convince, it should be added that there is another reason for even those who disapprove of industrial targeting to take it more seriously. That is for defensive purposes. The Japanese will continue targeting. And they will be joined by imitators who adopt at least some of these practices. So, it is essential for others to at least know what the targeters are doing, why they are doing it and what the possible side effects may be.

Only on this basis can those on the receiving end devise policies to counteract targeting. This can be for the purpose of competing against Japanese rivals at home or abroad, or of avoiding the unpleasant consequences of their strategies. More passively, a better understanding will make it possible to argue more cogently for the suppression of certain measures that hurt others or to find better antidotes. This is certainly more intelligent and constructive than just grumbling about closed markets and griping about exporters that play dirty tricks to gain an unfair advantage.

Notes

Background

1. Ira C. Magaziner and Thomas M. Hout, *Japanese Industrial Policy*, p. 7.
2. Thomas Pepper et al., *The Competition*, p. 70.
3. US International Trade Commission, *Foreign Industrial Targeting*, p. 17.
4. See Michael R. Czinkota and Jon Woronoff, *Unlocking Japan's Market*.
5. *Japan Times*, 12 June 1981.
6. Marvin J. Wolf, *The Japanese Conspiracy*.
7. See Ardath W. Burks (ed.), *The Modernizers*.
8. See William W. Lockwood, *The Economic Development of Japan*; and William D. Wray (ed.), *Managing Industrial Enterprise*.
9. On this period, see Chalmers Johnson, *MITI and the Japanese Miracle*, pp. 82–197.
10. Karel van Wolferen, *The Enigma of Japanese Power*, pp. 384–93.
11. Hugh Patrick (ed.), *Japan's High Technology Industries*, p. 9.
12. Myohei Shinohara, *Industrial Growth, Trade and Dynamic Patterns in the Japanese Economy*, pp. 23–9.
13. Ibid., p. 24.
14. OECD, *The Industrial Policy of Japan*, p. 16.
15. Johnson, op. cit.
16. James Abegglen, *The Strategy of Japanese Business*, p. 101.
17. For further analysis of the debate on whether targeting does/does not exist and always/never existed, see David Friedman, *The Misunderstood Miracle*, pp. 1–36; Johnson (ed.), *The Industrial Policy Debate*; and Program on US–Japan Relations, *US–Japan Relations: Learning from Competition*, pp. 1–37.
18. *The Economist*, 27 May 1967.
19. *Far Eastern Economic Review*, 21 August 1981, p. 53.
20. Wolf, op. cit., p. 16.
21. Philip H. Trezise, 'Industrial Policy is not the Major Reason for Japan's Success', *Brookings Review*, Fall 1983, p. 18.
22. Katsuro Sakoh, *Industrial Policy* (Washington, DC: The Heritage Foundation, 13 July 1983).
23. *Daily Yomiuri*, 30 April 1986.
24. OECD, op. cit., p. 7.
25. Saburo Okita, *The Developing Countries and Japan*, pp. 96–7.
26. MITI, *Background Information on Japan's Industrial Policy*, May 1983, p. 11.
27. Ibid. pp. 13–15.
28. See Gary Saxonhouse, 'Tampering with Comparative Advantage in Japan', Statement before the USITC, June 1983.
29. See Bradley M. Richardson, 'Industrial "Targeting" in Japan', Statement before the USITC, June 1983.
30. One of the best descriptions of industrial policy is by a team of Japanese

specialists who have no doubt that targeting existed and will continue. See Ryutaro Komiya, Masahiro Okuno, and Kotaro Suzumura (eds), *Industrial Policy of Japan*.

Institutions

1. See van Wolferen, op. cit.; and Jon Woronoff, *Politics, The Japanese Way*.
2. See Woronoff, *The Japan Syndrome*, pp. 120–5.
3. See Shinohara, op. cit.; and Woronoff, op. cit., pp. 104–33.
4. See Lockwood (ed.), *The State and Enterprise in Japan*, p. 503.
5. Johnson, *MITI and the Japanese Miracle*, p. 249.
6. For details of the slow and painful process of 'liberalisation', see Dan Fenno Henderson, *Foreign Enterprise in Japan*, pp. 236–90.
7. See Morton Peck and Shuji Tamamura, 'Technology', in Patrick and Rosovsky (eds), *Asia's new Giant*, pp. 44–58.
8. The most blatant case was making Texas Instruments wait until 1990 to get a patent on integrated circuits invented by its scientists 34 years earlier.
9. On this epic battle, see Johnson, op. cit., pp. 255–65.
10. See Michael K. Young, 'Structurally Depressed and Declining Industries in Japan', in *Japan's Economy and Trade with the United States*, (Joint Economic Council, US Congress, 1986) pp. 133–49.
11. On the effect of cartels, see Kozo Yamamura, *Economic Policy in Postwar Japan*.
12. For more details on how MITI operates, see Johnson, op. cit.
13. For a discussion of administrative guidance, see Johnson, op. cit., pp. 265–74 and 296–302; and Pepper, op. cit., pp. 129–35.
14. Henderson, op. cit., p. 157.
15. Abegglen, 'The Economic Growth of Japan', *Scientific American*, March 1970.
16. See Pepper, op. cit., pp. 233–40; and Ezra Vogel, *Comeback*, pp. 127–39.
17. See Pepper, op. cit., pp. 108–22.
18. Yamamura, op. cit., p. 36.
19. On *amakudari*, see Daniel K. Okimoto, *Between MITI and the Market*, pp. 161–5; and Woronoff, *Politics, The Japanese Way*.
20. Woronoff, op. cit., pp. 158–66.
21. Ibid., pp. 150–8.
22. Dodwell Marketing Consultants, *Industrial Groupings in Japan*, pp. 36–8.
23. For more on groups and *keiretsu*, see Czinkota and Woronoff.
24. For details of the membership, structure and financial situation of the various groups, see Dodwell, op. cit.
25. Ibid., pp. 26–31.
26. A good example is *A Vision of the 21st Century – The Quest for Industrial Restructuring*.
27. Johnson, op. cit., p. 24.
28. Friedman, op. cit., p. 4.

29. Richard J. Samuels, *The Business of the Japanese State*, p. x.
30. Johnson, op. cit., p. 21.
31. *The Economist*, 27 May 1967.
32. Lockwood, op. cit., p. 509.
33. Friedman, op. cit., p. 85.
34. Johnson, op. cit., p. 247.
35. Okimoto, op. cit., p. 23.
36. Abegglen, op. cit.
37. Wolf, op. cit., p. 15.
38. van Wolferen, op. cit., pp. 159–80; and Woronoff, op. cit., pp. 181–94.
39. Shinohara and Yanagihara, *Japanese and Korean Experiences in Managing Development*, World Bank Staff Working Paper, no. 574 (1983) p. 22.

Techniques

1. For more on export orientation, see Woronoff, *Asia's 'Miracle' Economies*, pp. 228–44.
2. See Pepper, op. cit., pp. 85–108.
3. See USITC, op. cit., pp. 73–80.
4. John B. Shoven and Toshiaki Tachibanaki conclude that, 'overall, the tax wedge on new corporate investments is significantly lower in Japan than in the United States', in Shoven (ed.), *Government policy toward industry in the United States and Japan*, pp. 51–96.
5. OECD, *OECD Economic Studies: The Role of the Private Sector*, p. 29.
6. *Financial Times*, 3 December 1990.
7. This ranged from nearly 30 per cent of total capital available to industry in the early 1950s to under 10 per cent (of a much larger amount) in the 1980s. See Okimoto, op. cit., p. 77.
8. Ronald Dore, *Japan Economic Survey*, May 1986, p. 6.
9. One should not be misled by government figures for basic research which are inflated by including many unrelated expenses.
10. Okimoto, op. cit., pp. 83–6.
11. At the same time that Japan's governmental share of R&D was 20 per cent, in the mid-1980s, it was nearly 50 per cent in the United States, 45 per cent in France, and 40 per cent in Germany and Great Britain.
12. Okimoto, op. cit., p. 78.
13. STA, *White Paper on Science and Technology* (Tokyo, 1981).
14. Quoted in Yamamura, op. cit., p. 79.
15. Henry Rosovsky, 'What are the Lessons of Japanese Economic History', in A. J. Youngson (ed.), *Economic Development in the Long Run* (London: Allen and Unwin, 1972) p. 244.
16. For a comparison of the Japanese and American approaches to antitrust policy and their economic implications, see Yamamura, 'Joint Research and Antitrust: Japanese vs American Strategies', in Patrick (ed.), *Japan's High Technology Industries*, pp. 171–209.
17. Frank K. Upham, in *Law and Social Change in Postwar Japan*, provides useful insight into the legal system and social background in general, as well as industrial policy and certain cases related thereto (pp. 166–204).

18. The best expression of this viewpoint is in Vogel, *Japan as Number One*, pp. 53–96.
19. See William R. Nestor, *Japanese Industrial Targeting*.
20. See Czinkota and Woronoff, *Unlocking Japan's Markets*, pp. 31–64.
21. On the role of *keiretsu* in industrial policy, see Okimoto, op. cit., pp. 132–42.
22. On the role of *keiretsu* in financing companies, see Robert Zielinski and Nigel Holloway, *Unequal Equities*.
23. On market share maximisation, see Okimoto, op. cit., pp. 41–5.

Risen Sectors

1. For a study of the priority production system, see Laura E. Heim, *Fueling Growth*, pp. 107–28.
2. For more on the rise of the oil industry, see Heim, op. cit., pp. 285–310; and Nester, op. cit., pp. 137–53.
3. For more on the rise of the steel industry, see Nester, op. cit., pp. 79–89.
4. Ibid., p. 81.
5. USITC, op. cit., p. 139.
6. To see how Japanese steelmakers overcame their American mentors, see Michael Borrus, 'The Politics of Competitive Erosion in the US Steel Industry', in John Zysman and Laura Tyson (eds), *American Industry in International Competition*, pp. 60–105.
7. Magaziner and Hout, op. cit., pp. 53–4.
8. *Japan Steel Bulletin* (Tokyo: JISF, September 1980) p. 1.
9. For more on the rise of shipbuilding, see Vogel, *Comeback*, pp. 27–49.
10. USGAO, *Industrial Policy: Japan's Flexible Approach*, p. 32.
11. Vogel, op. cit., pp. 41–3.
12. See Yoshikazu Kano, 'Prospects for an Agricultural Revolution', *Economic Eye*, March 1981, pp. 8–13.
13. *Japan Economic Journal*, 29 November 1983.

Rising Sectors – Public

1. For more on the rise of the computer industry, see Pepper, op. cit., pp. 200–31; USGAO, *Industrial Policy: Case Studies in the Japanese Experience*, pp. 11–81; USITA, *Japanese Industrial Policies and the Development of High-Technology Industries*; USITC, *Foreign Industrial Targeting and its Effect on US Industries: Japan*, pp. 131–8; and Vogel, op. cit., pp. 125–67.
2. Ken-ichi Imai, 'Japan's Industrial Policy for High Technology Industry', in Patrick, op. cit., p. 143.
3. Pepper, op. cit., p. 214.
4. According to Okimoto, 'staving off domination by IBM, even eventually overtaking IBM if possible, may be the overriding objective for Japan's computer industry', in Okimoto, op. cit., p. 29. See Marie Anchordoguy, *Computers Inc., Japan's Challenge to IBM*; and Robert Sobel, *IBM v. Japan*.
5. For further details, see Vogel, op. cit., pp. 133–63.

6. Okimoto, op. cit., p. 71.
7. See Feigenbaum and McCorduck, *The Fifth Generation*.
8. Robert S. Ozaki, 'How Japanese Industrial Policy Works', in Johnson, *The Industrial Policy Debate*, p. 63.
9. See Pepper, op. cit., pp. 207–20.
10. For a comparison of the American and Japanese industries, see Okimoto, Sugano and Weinstein (eds), *Competitive Edge*.
11. For a detailed study of the rise of Japan's semiconductor industry, see Thomas R. Howell, et. al., *The Microelectronics Race*, pp. 35–144.
12. Vogel, op. cit., pp. 143–5.
13. Okimoto, *Between MITI and the Market*, p. 71.
14. Howell, op. cit., pp. 60–88.
15. See Michael Borrus, James E. Millstein, and John Zysman, 'Trade and Development in the Semiconductor Industry', in Zysman and Tyson, op. cit., pp. 142–248.
16. As Clyde Prestowitz pointed out, 'with everyone losing money, the winner is not the most efficient producer but the one with the deepest pockets'. *Wall Street Journal*, 26 September 1986.
17. See Semiconductor Industry Association, *The Effect of Government Targeting on World Semiconductor Competition*; and Clyde Prestowitz, *Trading Places*.
18. *JTECH Panel Report on Telecommunications* (Turin, 1986) pp. 6–25.
19. Magaziner and Hout, op. cit., p. 87.
20. Pepper, op. cit., pp. 237–40.
21. Vogel, op. cit., pp. 159–66.
22. For more detailed studies of the machine tool industry, see Friedman, op. cit.; and Vogel, op. cit., pp. 58–95.
23. Vogel, op. cit., p. 67.
24. Magaziner and Hout, op. cit., p. 80.
25. See Friedman, op. cit.
26. Friedman, op. cit., p. 119; and Vogel, op. cit., pp. 70–1.
27. See Carla Norton, 'The Pharmaceutical Trade Talks: Cure or Bitter Pill?', *The ACCJ Journal*, May 1985, pp. 15–22.

Rising Sectors – Private

1. This story is best told by Michael A. Cusumano, *The Japanese Automobile Industry*. See also C. S. Chang, *The Japanese Auto Industry and the US Market*.
2. For more on government support of the automobile industry, see Chang, op. cit.; Cusumano, op. cit.; and Nester, op. cit., pp. 99–118.
3. Cusumano, op. cit., p. 1.
4. Ibid., p. xix.
5. Ibid., pp. 4–8 and 23–5.
6. See Woronoff, *World Trade War*, pp. 148–84.
7. See Woronoff, *Japan's Commercial Empire*.
8. See Shigeo Suzuki, 'Long Struggle Preceded Motorcycle Success', *Business Japan*, April 1983, pp. 92–3.
9. *Japan Times*, 30 April, 1 July, and 16 September 1983.

10. See Jack Baranson, *The Japanese Challenge to US Industry*, pp. 53–71.
11. According to Baranson, 'in many cases, the US electronic products, both consumer and non consumer, which accompanied the US servicemen stationed in Japan, were reverse engineered by the Japanese firms for reproducible copies. In this way initial technological capabilities were developed by the Japanese consumer electronics industry. With the introduction of television broadcasting, this reverse engineering was performed on RCA and Zenith sets by Japanese firms.' Baranson, op. cit., p. 54.
12. Baranson, op. cit., pp. 73–121.
13. See Wolf, op. cit., pp. 22–60; and Woronoff, *World Trade War*, pp. 15–22.
14. See James E. Millstein, 'Decline in an Expanding Industry: Japanese Competition in Color Television', in Zysman and Tyson, op. cit., pp. 106–41.
15. For more on the composition and size of the electronics industry, see Dodwell, *Key Players in the Japanese Electronics Industry*.
16. *Financial Times*, 3 December 1990, p. VIII.
17. *Japan Economic Journal*, 5 August 1980, and 9 March 1982.
18. Dodwell, op. cit., pp. 308–16.

Sectors Slated To Rise

1. *Japan Economic Journal*, 26 October 1983, and 8 May 1984.
2. See Kuni Sudamoto (ed.), *Robots in the Japanese Economy* (Tokyo: Survey Japan, 1981).
3. For more on the government's role, see Malcolm V. Brock, *Biotechnology in Japan*; and Gary Saxonhouse, 'Industrial Policy and Factor Markets: Biotechnology in Japan and the United States', in Patrick, op. cit., pp. 97–136.
4. See Brock, op. cit., pp. 66–88.
5. Terril Jones, 'Biotechnology: Will Japan Overtake the US?', *ACCJ Journal*, March 1985, pp. 35–42.
6. On the threat to US industry, see USOTA, *Commercial Biotechnology: An International Analysis* (Washington, DC, 1984).
7. On the rise of nuclear energy, see Samuels, op. cit., pp. 135–67.
8. See Michael W. Donnelly, *Japan's Nuclear Power Strategy*.
9. *Petroleum News*, December 1978, p. 22.
10. Samuels, op. cit., p. 255.
11. For example, the 1990 budget included ¥255 billion to obtain 'public acceptance' of nuclear projects.
12. MITI, *A Vision of Nuclear Power*, July 1986.
13. On the rise of the aeronautical industry, see David C. Mowery and Nathan Rosenburg, *The Japanese Commercial Aircraft Industry since 1945*; and Richard J. Samuels and Benjamin C. Whipple, *Defense Production and Industrial Development: The Case of Japanese Aircraft*.
14. USGAO, 'US Military Co-Production Programs Assist Japan in Developing its Civil Aircraft Industry', 18 March 1982.

15. For further details, see USGAO, *Industrial Policy: Case Studies*, pp. 32–43; and USITA, op. cit., pp. 28–40.
16. USITA, op. cit., pp. 33–9.
17. *Financial Times*, 3 December 1990, p. IX.
18. Yes, even the technological side was lacking. The flawed YS-11, the stalled STOL and even the F-1 fighters. 'It was put into production with so many faults that, to this day, the F-1 is virtually unflyable at night, and has a blind spot which ensures that few F-1 pilots will come out of any dog fight alive.' *The Economist*, 8 April 1989, p. 72.

Declining Sectors

1. For more on the declining industries, see Merton J. Peck, Richard C. Levin, and Akira Goto, 'Picking losers: public policy toward declining industries in Japan', in Shoven, op. cit., pp. 195–240; and Robert M. Urui, *Troubled Industrial Sectors in Japan*.
2. See USGAO, op. cit., pp. 44–57.
3. See Woronoff, *World Trade War*, pp. 108–15.
4. See Yoshio Yonezawa, *Analysis and Evaluation of the Adjustment Process and Policies of the Japanese Textile Industry* (Tokyo: Japan Economic Research Centre, 1981).
5. On the restructuring of the synthetic fibre industry, see Urui, op. cit.
6. See Yonezawa, op. cit.
7. See Samuels, op. cit., pp. 68–134.
8. For background on the decision to support coal over oil, and its eventual reversal, see Heim, op. cit., pp. 288–310.
9. Vogel, op. cit., pp. 96–108.
10. Heim, op. cit., p. 315.
11. Samuels, op. cit., p. 134.
12. For more on the oil sector, see Samuels, op. cit., pp. 168–227.
13. Samuels, op. cit., p. 225.
14. Okimoto, op. cit., p. 6.
15. For further details on the restructuring, see Magaziner and Hout, op. cit., pp. 67–71; USGAO, op. cit., pp. 58–67; and Vogel, op. cit., pp. 49–57.
16. On this less than glorious exercise, see Samuels, 'The Industrial Destructuring of the Japanese Aluminum Industry'.
17. Samuels, op. cit., pp. 497–8.
18. On the restructuring of the electric furnace steel sector, see Urui, op. cit.

Rating Success

1. Johnson, *MITI and the Japanese Miracle*, p. 240.
2. Steven Schlossstein, *The End of the American Century*, p. 27.
3. *Japan Economic Journal*, 26 April 1983, p. 4.
4. Bruce Bartlett, 'Trade Policy and the Dangers of Protectionism', in Johnson (ed.), *The Industrial Policy Debate*, p. 172.
5. We agree with George C. Eads and Kozo Yamamura that 'the clearest

measure of success would be a demonstration that, but for the industrial policy, the real economic growth of an economy would have been lower', in Yamamura (ed.), *The Political Economy of Japan*, p. 425.

6. According to Professor Iwao Nakatani, this would occur in the year 2001, 'if Japan's economy grows at a rate of 2–3 per cent higher than that of the US, and the yen climbs about 5 per cent annually against the dollar'. *Japan Economic Journal*, 1 December 1990.

7. *Financial Times*, 3 December 1990, p. i.

8. *Tokyo Business Today*, November 1990, p. 18.

9. To see how the United States dealt with some of its declining sectors, see Zysman and Tyson, op. cit.

10. Okimoto, op. cit., p. 25.

11. Guy de Jonquière, 'Shortcomings of Joint Research', *Financial Times*, 16 October 1990.

12. This view was endorsed by Okimoto, op. cit., p. 70. 'None of the national research projects have yet achieved momentous breakthroughs in state-of-the-art technology. Some have failed to reach even modest objectives.'

13. *Financial Times*, 31 October 1990.

14. A similar sentiment was expressed by a senior managing director of Canon, Hajime Mitarai, who complained: 'if you can do something yourself, it is better not to do it with the government, there are too many restrictions on government projects'. *Financial Times*, 3 December 1990, p. v.

15. Okimoto, op. cit., pp. 81 and 71.

16. On the failure to consolidate the automobile, banking and oil sectors, see Friedman, op. cit., pp. 203–8.

17. Friedman, op. cit., p. 33.

18. See Dodwell, *Industrial Groupings in Japan*.

19. Yamamura, 'Joint Research and Antitrust: Japanese vs American Strategies', in Patrick, op. cit., p. 202.

20. Friedman, op. cit., p. 83.

21. Samuels, op. cit., p. 130.

22. Yamamura, *Economic Policy in Postwar Japan*, p. 85.

23. Abegglen, *The Strategy of Japanese Business*, p. 113; Johnson, *MITI and the Japanese Miracle*, p. 199.

24. Johnson, op. cit., pp. 18–23.

25. Ibid., pp. 240–1.

26. Brock, op. cit., p. 130

27. Friedman, op. cit., p. 125.

28. Samuels, op. cit., pp. 134 and 132.

29. Even Okimoto, who is on the whole favourable to industrial policy, conceded that producer and consumer interests did not always converge and that consumer interests regularly took second place to producer interests. Okimoto, op. cit., pp. 35–6.

30. For more on Japan's failure in farming, distribution and construction, see Nester, op. cit., pp. 43–77; and Woronoff, *Politics, The Japanese Way*, pp. 247–54 and 305–14.

31. See Woronoff, *The Japanese Management Mystique*.

32. Yasuhisa Tashiro, 'America's Industrial Policy Debate', in Program on US–Japan Relations, *US–Japan Relations*, p. 14.
33. According to Okimoto, 'being able to keep industrial policy from falling into the hands of politicians, for example, is a rare feat'. Okimoto, op. cit., p. 111. Vogel was even more ecstatic about the idea that, because political leaders 'rarely interfere with the main trends of ministerial policy, the continuity of policy is unimpaired by elections, cabinet reshuffles, or short-range political pressures'. Vogel, *Japan as Number One*, p. 67.

Foreign Repercussions

1. As van Wolferen explained, 'even those who have tried extremely hard in Japan have mostly failed as dismally as those who have taken it easy'. van Wolferen, op. cit., p. 406.
2. The most notorious example is the 1985 memo of Hitachi America instructing its salesmen to underbid US competitors by 10 per cent as many times as was needed to win an order.
3. See Prestowitz, op. cit.; Schlossstein, *Trade War*; and Zysman and Tyson, op. cit.
4. See Baranson, op. cit.; and Wolf, op. cit.
5. *Hanguk Ilbo*, 1 March 1985, p. 4.
6. For American reactions to Japanese competition, see Johnson (ed.), *The Industrial Policy Debate*, pp. 159–72; and Zysman and Tyson, op. cit.
7. As Zysman and Tyson note, 'the costs of recapturing a lost market share will go up if the infrastructure, in the form of suppliers and distribution networks, is undermined. The collapse of suppliers may affect the industry's collective ability to sustain its technological position.' Zysman and Tyson, op. cit., p. 29.
8. Johnson, op. cit., p. 23.
9. Naoki Atsumi, 'Voluntary Restraint Agreements, The Case of Automobiles and Steel', Program on US–Japan Relations, op. cit., pp. 39–50.
10. Woronoff, *World Trade War*.
11. Wolf, op. cit., p. 16.
12. Henderson, op. cit., p. 157.
13. OECD, op. cit., p. 16.
14. van Wolferen, op. cit., p. 405.

What Now?

1. For several scenarios of how industrial policy may evolve in the future, see Eads and Yamamura, 'The Future of Industrial Policy', in Yamamura, *The Political Economy of Japan*, pp. 423–68.
2. See Atsumi, op. cit.
3. Previous major revaluations occurred in 1971 and 1973, also under strong foreign pressure. For more on the benefits of an undervalued yen, see Nester, op. cit., pp. 239–45.
4. See Leon Hollerman, *Japan, Disincorporated*.
5. See Johnson, op. cit., p. 22.

6. See Johnson, op. cit.; George C. Eads and Richard R. Nelson, 'Japanese High Technology Policy: What Lessons for the US?', in Patrick, op. cit., pp. 243–69; Lester Thurow, *The Case for Industrial Policies*; and Vogel, *Comeback*, pp. 269–85.
7. See Woronoff, *Asia's 'Miracle' Economies*.
8. Carla Rapaport, 'Covering Japan', *The JAMA Forum*, August 1990, p. 21.
9. Okimoto provides an interesting list of policies which have been applied by other countries in 'Regime Characteristics of Japanese Industrial Policy', in Patrick, op. cit., pp. 86–8.
10. For another list of mistakes to avoid when learning from Japan, see Patrick, in Patrick, op. cit., pp. xix–xx.

Bibliography

Industrial Policy

ADAMS, F. Gerard, and Lawrence R. Klein, *Industrial Policies for Growth and Competitiveness: An Economic Perspective* (Lexington, DC: Heath, 1982).

BARANSON, Jack, *The Japanese Challenge to US Industry* (Lexington, DC: Heath, 1981).

JOHNSON, Chalmers, *MITI and the Japanese Miracle, The Growth of Industrial Policy 1925–1975* (Stanford: Stanford University Press, 1982).

——, (ed.), *The Industrial Policy Debate* (San Francisco: ICS Press, 1984).

KEIZAI, Doyukai, *A Vision of the 21st Century – The Quest for Industrial Restructuring* (Tokyo, 1984).

KOMIYA, Ryutaro, Masahiro Okuno, and Kotaro Suzumura (eds), *Industrial Policy of Japan* (Tokyo: Academic Press, 1988).

MAGAZINER, Ira C., and Thomas H. Hout, *Japanese Industrial Policy* (Berkeley: Institute of International Studies, 1980).

Ministry of International Trade and Industry, *Basic Plan for an Industrial Society in the 21st Century* (Tokyo, 1986).

——, *Features of the Industrial Policy of Japan* (Tokyo, 1983).

——, *Japan's Industrial Structure – A Long Range Vision* (Tokyo, 1975).

——, *Industrial Policy in Japan: A Question-And-Answer Overview* (New York: Japan Trade Center, 1983).

——, *Industrial Structure of Japan in the 1980s – Future Outlook and Tasks* (Tokyo, 1981).

——, *Vision of Trade and Industrial Policy for the 1980s* (Tokyo, 1980).

NESTER, William R., *Japanese Industrial Targeting, The Neomercantilist Path to Economic Superpower* (London: Macmillan, 1991).

OKIMOTO, Daniel I., *Between MITI and the Market, Japanese Industrial Policy for High Technology* (Stanford: Stanford University Press, 1989).

Organisation of Economic Cooperation and Development, *The Industrial Policy of Japan* (Paris, 1972).

PEPPER, Thomas, Merit E. Janow, and Jimmy W. Wheeler, *The Competition, Dealing with Japan* (New York: Praeger, 1985).

SHOVEN, John B. (ed.), *Government Policy Towards Industry in the United States and Japan* (Cambridge: Cambridge University Press, 1988).

THUROW, Lester C., *The Case for Industrial Policies* (Washington, DC: Center for National Policy, 1984).

US Department of Commerce, *Study of Foreign Government Targeting Practices* (Washington, DC, July 1985).

US Department of Labor, *Trade and Employment Effects of Foreign Industrial Targeting* (Washington, DC, 1985).

US General Accounting Office, *Industrial Policy: Japan's Flexible Approach* (Washington, DC, 1982).

US International Trade Commission, *Foreign Industrial Targeting and its Effect on US Industries: Japan* (Washington, DC, October 1983).

US Trade Representative, *Report on Foreign Industrial Targeting* (Washington, DC, July 1985).

WHEELER, James, et. al., *Japanese Industrial Policy in the 1980s* (Croton on Hudson: Hudson Institute, 1982).

WOLF, Marvin J., *The Japanese Conspiracy* (New York: Empire Books, 1983).

ZYSMAN, John, and Laura Tyson, *American Industry in International Competition, Government Policies and Corporate Strategies* (Ithaca: Cornell University Press, 1983).

——, et. al., *US and Japanese Trade and Industrial Policy* (Washington, DC: US–Japan Advisory Commissions, 1984).

Case Studies

ANCHORDOGUY, Marie, *Computers Inc., Japan's Challenge to IBM* (Cambridge: Council of East Asian Studies, 1989).

BROCK, Malcolm V., *Biotechnology in Japan* (London: Routledge, 1990).

CHANG, C. S., *The Japanese Auto Industry and the US Market* (New York: Praeger, 1981).

CUSUMANO, Michael, *Japan's Software Factories: A Challenge to US Management* (Oxford: Oxford University Press, 1990).

——, *The Japanese Automobile Industry* (Cambridge: Harvard University Press, 1985).

DONNELLY, Michael W., *Japan's Nuclear Power Strategy* (Toronto: University of Toronto Press, 1985).

FEIGENBAUM, Edward A., and Pamela McCorduck, *The Fifth Generation: Artificial Intelligence and Japan's Computer Challenge to the World* (Reading: Addison-Wesley, 1983).

FRANSMAN, Martin, *The Market and Beyond, Cooperation and Competition in Information Technology in the Japanese System* (Cambridge: Cambridge University Press, 1990).

FRIEDMAN, David, *The Misunderstood Miracle, Industrial Development and Political Change in Japan* (Ithaca: Cornell University Press, 1988).

HEIN, Laura E., *Fueling Growth, The Energy Revolution and Economic Policy in Postwar Japan* (Cambridge: Harvard University Press, 1990).

HOWELL, Thomas R., et. al., *The Microelectronics Race, The Impact of Government Policy in International Competition* (Boulder: Westview, 1988).

KIKUCHI, Makoto, *Japanese Electronics, A Worm's-Eye View of Its Evolution* (Tokyo: Simul Press, 1983).

MOWERY, David C., and Nathan Rosenburg, *The Japanese Commercial Aircraft Industry since 1945: Government Policy, Technical Development and Industrial Structure* (Stanford: Stanford University Press, 1985).

OKIMOTO, Daniel I., Takuo Sugano, and Franklin Weinstein (eds), *Competitive Edge, The Semiconductor Industry in The US and Japan* (Stanford: Stanford University Press, 1984).

PATRICK, Hugh (ed.), *Japan's High Technology Industries, Lessons and*

Limitations of Industrial Policy (Seattle: University of Washington Press, 1986).

SAMUELS, Richard J., *The Business of the Japanese State: Energy Markets in Comparative and Historical Perspective* (Ithaca: Cornell University Press, 1987).

——, 'The Industrial Destructuring of the Japanese Aluminum Industry', *Pacific Affairs*, Fall 1983, pp. 495–509.

——, and Benjamin C. Whipple, *Defense Production and Industrial Development: The Case of Japanese Aircraft* (Cambridge: MIT, 1988).

Semiconductor Industry Association, *The Effect of Government Targeting on World Semiconductor Competition* (Cupertino, 1983).

SOBEL, Robert, *IBM v. Japan: The Struggle for the Future* (New York: Stein and Day, 1986).

US General Accounting Office, *Industrial Policy: Case Studies in the Japanese Experience* (Washington, DC, 1982).

US International Trade Administration, *Japanese Industrial Policies and the Development of High-Technology Industries: Computers and Aircraft* (Washington, DC, February 1983).

URUI, Robert M., *Troubled Industrial Sectors in Japan: The Political Economy of Adjustment*, AAS Paper, January 1990.

VOGEL, Ezra, *Comeback* (New York: Simon and Schuster, 1985).

Background

ABEGGLEN, James C., *The Strategy of Japanese Business* (Cambridge: Ballinger, 1984).

BIEDA, K., *The Structure and Operation of the Japanese Economy* (Sydney: John Wiley, 1970).

BURKS, Ardath W. (ed.), *The Modernizers, Overseas Students, Foreign Employees, and Meiji Japan* (Boulder: Westview, 1985).

CZINKOTA, Michael R., and Jon Woronoff, *Unlocking Japan's Market* (Chicago: Probus, and London: Pitman, 1991).

Dodwell Marketing Consultants, *Industrial Groupings in Japan* (Tokyo, 1988).

——, *Key Players in the Japanese Electronics Industry* (Tokyo, 1985).

HENDERSON, Dan Fenno, *Foreign Enterprise in Japan* (Tokyo: Tuttle, 1973).

HOLLERMAN, Leon, *Japan, Disincorporated* (Stanford: Hoover Institution, 1988).

KOSAI, Yutaka, *The Era of High-Speed Growth* (Tokyo: University of Tokyo Press, 1986).

LOCKWOOD, William W., *The Economic Development of Japan* (Princeton: Princeton University Press, 1954).

——, ed., *The State and Enterprise in Japan* (Princeton: Princeton University Press, 1965).

OKITA, Saburo, *The Developing Countries and Japan* (Tokyo: University of Tokyo Press, 1980).

PATRICK, Hugh, and Henry Rosovsky (eds), *Asia's New Giant, How The Japanese Economy Works* (Washington, DC: Brookings Institution, 1976).

PRESTOWITZ, Clyde, *Trading Places: How We Allowed Japan To Take The Lead* (New York: Basic Books, 1988).

Program on US–Japan Relations, *US–Japan Relations: Learning from Competition* (New Brunswick: Transaction Books, 1986).

SAXONHOUSE, Gary R., and Kozo Yamamura (eds), *Law and Trade Issues of the Japanese Economy* (Seattle: University of Washington Press, 1987).

——, *Policy and Trade Issues of the Japanese Economy* (Seattle: University of Washington Press, 1982).

SCHLOSSSTEIN, Steven, *The End of the American Century* (New York: Congdon & Weed, 1989).

——, *Trade War, Greed, Power, and Industrial Policy on Opposite Sides of the Pacific* (New York: Congdon & Weed, 1984).

SHINOHARA, Myohei, *Industrial Growth, Trade and Dynamic Patterns in the Japanese Economy* (Tokyo: Tokyo University Press, 1982).

TATSUNO, Sheridan, *The Technopolis Strategy: Japan, High Technology, and the Control of the Twenty-First Century* (New York: Prentice-Hall, 1986).

UPHAM, Frank K., *Law and Social Change in Postwar Japan* (Cambridge: Harvard University Press, 1987).

VAN WOLFEREN, Karel, *The Enigma of Japanese Power* (New York: Vintage Books, 1989).

VOGEL, Ezra, *Japan as Number One* (Cambridge: Harvard University Press, 1979).

WORONOFF, Jon, *Asia's 'Miracle' Economies* (Tokyo: Yohan, and Armonk: M. E. Sharpe, 1987).

——, *Japan As – Anything But – Number One* (London: Macmillan, and Armonk: M. E. Sharpe, 1991).

——, *Japan's Commercial Empire* (London: Macmillan, and Armonk: M. E. Sharpe, 1984).

——, *The Japanese Management Mystique* (Chicago: Probus, 1992).

——, *Politics, The Japanese Way* (London: Macmillan, and New York: St Martin's Press, 1988).

——, *The Japan Syndrome* (New Brunswick: Transaction Books, 1985).

——, *World Trade War* (New York: Praeger, 1984).

WRAY, William D. (ed.), *Managing Industrial Enterprise, Cases from Japan's Prewar Experience* (Cambridge: Harvard University Press, 1989).

YAMAMURA, Kozo, *Economic Policy in Postwar Japan: Growth versus Economic Democracy* (Seattle: University of Washington Press, 1967).

——, *Japan's Economic Structure: Should It Change?* (Seattle: Society for Japanese Studies, 1990).

——, and Yasukichi Yasuba (eds), *The Political Economy of Japan, The Domestic Transformation* (Stanford: Stanford University Press, 1987).

ZIELINSKI, Robert, and Nigel Holloway, *Unequal Equities* (Tokyo: Kodansha, 1990).

Index

Abbeglen, James 19, 38, 53–4, 229
administrative guidance 36, 42, 51, 200, 238, 258
aerospace 146, 185–91, 217
Agency for Industrial Science and Technology 32, 40, 119, 125, 134, 136, 143, 169, 174, 181
agriculture 70, 87, 109–11, 216
Airbus Industries 183
aircraft 13, 107, 179–85
airlines 38–9, 70, 106–7
Ajinomoto 171
All Nippon Airways 106–7, 183
aluminum 205–7, 223–4
amakudari 44, 51, 53, 55–6, 238
amenities 67, 84, 236, 238
American Semiconductor Industry Association 127
Ampex 151
antitrust 33, 42, 56, 85–6, 160, 222–3, 228
armaments 12–13, 40, 179–80, 185
automobiles 13, 86, 142–8

Bank of Japan 30, 37–8, 100, 112–13, 143, 259
banks, commercial 13, 37–8, 40–1, 46–7, 67–9, 89, 101, 111–15, 153
Bartlett, Bruce 212
Beckett, Sir Terence 9
Bell Laboratories 130, 151, 167
Bioindustry Development Center 171–3
biotechnology 39, 170–3, 220, 231–2
Boeing 183
British Aerospace 184
Brookings Institution 20
Brother 160, 163
Bucyrus-Erie 157–8
bureaucrats 12, 27–42, 48–57, 66–7, 78–81, 220, 223–5, 226–9, 230–3, 235, 237–8, 253, 259–61
businessmen 12, 33, 42–57, 79–82, 83–93, 220, 227, 230–3, 237–8, 253, 259–61

Canada 176, 265
Canon 160
cartels 33–4, 42, 47, 70, 81, 85, 102–3, 193, 206–7, 228, 256–8
Casio 159–60, 163
Caterpillar 157–8
China 194, 196, 246
Chrysler 145
Citizen 163
coal 98–100, 174, 198–9, 235
Collaborative Research 173
companies
  large 45–7, 64, 91–2, 105, 112, 222–3, 236–7
  small 45, 79, 81, 91, 236–7
company targeting 5, 52, 87–93, 141–64, 171, 226, 231, 233, 254
comparative advantage 16–17, 21, 34, 100, 141, 143, 161–2, 193–6, 213, 218, 225, 229, 247
competition 61–3, 77–82, 90–1, 103, 127, 147–8, 149–51, 154–6, 159–60, 195, 201, 203, 227, 229, 240–50, 252–3
computers 39, 41, 117–23, 125, 216
conspiracy theory 8, 20, 53–6, 250–4
construction equipment 156–8
consumers 39, 58–9, 62–3, 69, 107, 110–11, 114, 131, 140, 145, 149, 154, 176, 187, 190, 199, 202, 207, 226, 234–8, 262
Control Data 121
Corning Glass 167
Cray 121
cross-subsidisation 58, 132, 145–6, 153–4, 160, 163–4, 172
Cusumano, Michael A. 144

Daihatsu 144, 146
Dai-Ichi Kangyo 46, 112
declining industries 19, 33, 42, 52,
    79–82, 98, 103, 192–208, 217,
    223–4, 227, 255–6, 264
defence 66–7, 73, 87, 246–7
Defence Agency 40, 179–80, 185,
    203
definitions 3–6
deliberative councils 44, 57, 83,
    232
Designated Industries Promotion
    Law 33, 52
Diet 35, 87, 98, 112, 176
distribution 46, 63, 89, 124–5,
    139, 145, 159, 163, 219–20,
    236, 257
Dodwell Marketing
    Consultants 47
dumping 8, 102, 105, 115, 127,
    137, 154, 160, 242–5, 262

Economic Planning Agency 21,
    25–6, 41
Economist 19
electricity 98–9, 173–5, 205
electronics 117, 151–6
energy 98–9, 173–9
environment 84–6
Environment Agency 85
Europe 10–11, 29–30, 69, 77,
    110–11, 127, 147–8, 154, 189,
    191, 194–5, 240–7, 258–9,
    263–6
European Community 263, 265
exchange rate 38, 62, 64, 70–1,
    84, 114, 235, 258
Export-Import Bank 30, 37, 41,
    67, 101, 105, 134, 257
exporting 8, 18, 33, 41, 56, 64–5,
    77, 92, 102, 106, 108–9, 123,
    126–8, 132, 137–8, 145–6,
    147–8, 150–1, 154–5, 241–50
export promotion 64, 70, 105,
    133, 137, 153–4

failures 215–18, 221–9, 231–4, 262
Fair Trade Commission 33, 42,
    85, 103, 158, 160, 200, 222, 258

Far Eastern Economic Review
    19–20
Feigenbaum, Edward A. 121–2
fifth-generation computer 121,
    221, 256
financial services 111–15
financial support 15, 30, 33, 37–8,
    40–1, 65–71, 89, 91, 99, 101,
    104, 109–11, 118, 122, 133–4,
    139–40, 143, 153, 169, 176,
    181–2, 187–8, 202, 204, 220
Fiscal and Investment Loan
    Programme 30, 37, 58, 69,
    122, 230
Ford 13, 142, 145
France 10–11, 75, 119, 176, 185,
    245, 265
Fransman, Martin 221
Friedman, David 48–50, 223, 232
Fuji 46, 144, 160, 181, 183,
    189–90
Fujitec 158
Fujitsu 120, 123–6, 129, 132
Furukawa 158

Genentech 173
General Agreement on Tariffs and
    Trade 29, 256–7, 259
General Electric 176
General Motors 13, 142, 145, 147,
    248
Genex 173
Germany 10–11, 15, 66, 75, 138,
    151, 185, 213, 240, 245, 265
Great Britain 66–7, 75, 176, 185,
    194, 245
Green Cross 171
Gregory, Gene 19–20
Groenenboom, Peter 156
growth rates 240

Harley-Davidson 151
Hashimoto, Masahiro 156
Hattori, K. 161–2
Hayashibara 171
Henderson, Dan Fenno 38, 253
Heritage Foundation 20
high-definition television 153,
    155–6

high tech sectors 22–3, 73, 116–40, 165–91, 214, 256
Hino 144, 146
Hitachi 46–7, 105, 120, 123–6, 129, 155, 157–8, 176, 190
Honda 144, 147–51
Honeywell 118
Hong Kong 162, 196, 264
Holland 245
Hollerman, Leon 259
Hout, Thomas H. 4
Hughes 187

IBM 117–20, 123, 125, 160, 248
Idemitsu 99
Ikeda, Hayato 26, 198
import substitution 10, 15, 64–5, 71, 76, 133, 240, 262–3
Industrial Bank of Japan 30, 41, 46, 101, 134, 169
Industrial Policy Bureau 34, 81
Industrial Structure Council 17, 34, 102, 201, 206
infant industry 15–16, 62, 70
insurance 111
Intel 123
International Harvester 157–8
investment
    inward 29–31, 62, 124, 144–5, 219
    outward 148, 260
Ishikawajima-Harima 105, 181, 183, 190
Isuzu 145, 147
Italy 67, 151, 245

Janome 163
Japan Airlines 38–9, 106–7
Japan Atomic Energy Commission 175–6
Japan Automobile Manufacturers Association 146
Japan Broadcasting Corporation 153, 156
Japan Chamber of Commerce and Industry 47
Japan Committee for Economic Development 47–8
Japan Development Bank 30, 37,

40–1, 67, 101, 104, 108, 118, 122, 134, 136, 143, 153, 169, 203, 230
Japan Electronic Computer Corporation 41, 119, 122
Japanese-style targeting 6–9
Japan External Trade Organisation 31, 214
Japan Federation of Economic Organisations 48, 52, 187, 189, 231
Japan, Inc. 8, 20, 53–6, 80–1, 259–60
Japan Industrial Standards 31
Japan Key Technology Centre 39, 167
Japan Line 205
Japan National Railways 38–9, 143
Japan Research Development Corporation 40
Japan Robot Leasing Corporation 41, 169
Japan Shipbuilding Industry Foundation 41, 104
Japan Society for the Promotion of the Machinery Industry 41, 134, 136
Johnson, Chalmers 18, 48–9, 51–2, 54, 212, 230–1, 262
joint ventures 31, 62, 90, 99, 118, 133, 139, 143–5, 153, 157–8, 159–60, 173, 179–80, 182–5

Kahn, Herman 53
Kawasaki 101, 105, 149, 168, 181, 183–4, 189–90
keiretsu 42, 45–7, 87–90, 105, 112, 114, 125, 155, 157, 159, 198, 205, 222, 257
Kishi, Nobusuke 14
Kobe Steel 101
Kokusai Denshin Denwa 129–31
Komatsu 157–8
Konoshiroku 160
Korea 194, 196, 212, 228, 245, 264
Kurashiki 108
Kyocera 166

laissez-faire 8–10, 12–14, 61, 77, 81, 228–9, 260–3
leisure 84–5
Liberal Democratic Party 27, 42, 44, 55, 87, 109, 187
liberalisation 29–30, 113–14, 131, 241
linkages 16–17, 97–8, 202, 243
Lion's Oil 200
List, Frederich 10, 15
Lockwood, William W. 49
Long-Term Credit Bank 30, 40, 67, 101, 134, 169

machine tools 41, 132–8
Macrae, Norman 19, 21, 49
Magaziner, Ira C. 4
Malaysia 264
managed trade 255–6, 259
market manipulation 29–31, 60–5, 72, 88–9, 138–9, 153, 219–20, 225–9, 235
market share 90–2, 127, 147, 149–50, 222, 228, 236, 253
Maruzen 99
Matsushita 46–7, 123, 131, 155–6, 157
Mazda 145, 147
Meiji era 11–12
Meija Seika 171
mergers 81, 102, 105, 119, 144, 200–1, 222
militarism 12–13, 142
Ministry of Agriculture, Forestry and Fisheries 39, 56, 99, 109–11, 171–2, 231
Ministry of Commerce and Industry 12–14, 28, 142, 232
Ministry of Construction 39
Ministry of Education 39–40, 171–2, 186, 231
Ministry of Finance 31, 37–8, 42, 56, 66, 100–1, 103, 114–14, 182, 231, 259
Ministry of Health and Welfare 39, 138–40, 171, 230
Ministry of International Trade and Industry 14, 17–18, 21–3, 25,

28–42, 47, 54, 56, 73, 81–5, 98–103, 108, 117–40, 143–9, 152–3, 156, 160, 162, 166–87, 194–208, 212, 214, 220–4, 228, 230–2, 238, 250–3, 256–9, 262
Ministry of Justice 86
Ministry of Munitions 13–14, 28
Ministry of Post and Telecommunications 25, 39, 56, 69, 113, 129–30, 167, 187, 231
Ministry of Transport 25, 38, 42, 103–7, 143–4, 203–4, 230
Mitsubishi 46, 99, 105, 120, 123–4, 131–2, 142, 145, 155, 157–8, 171, 176, 181, 183–4, 189–90, 205
Mitsui 46, 99, 105, 142, 205
Mochida 171
monopolisation 91–2, 127, 129, 131, 151, 155, 160, 163, 222–3, 228, 251
Moonlight Project 32, 174
Morozumi, Yoshihiko 81
motorcycles 148–51
Motorola 124, 132
McCorduck, Pamela 121–2
McDonnell-Douglas 183, 187

NASA 22, 188–9
National Semiconductor 123
National Space Development Agency 40, 186–9
NCR 159
NEC 120, 123–6, 129, 132, 155, 189–90
new materials 166–8
Nippon Kokan 101, 105
Nippon Steel 46–7, 101–2
Nippon Telegraph & Telephone 39, 56, 70, 122–3, 125–6, 128–32, 159, 166–7, 187–9
Nissan 13, 46–7, 142, 144–8, 190
Nissho Iwai 205
nontariff barriers 61–2, 113, 129, 138, 144–5, 219, 257
nuclear energy 69, 85, 173–9, 217

Occupation 13–14, 100, 104, 107, 148, 179, 186
office automation 158–61
oil 68–9, 174, 178, 198–200, 204
Ojimi, Yoshihisa 21
Oki 120, 123, 129
Okimoto, Daniel I. 48, 51, 75, 121, 201, 220–1
Okita, Saburo 21–2
Omron Tateisi 159
Ono, Eiichi 184
OPEC 174
optical fibre 166–7
Organisation for Economic Cooperation and Development 21, 29, 67, 69, 90, 219
Otis 157–8
overcapacity 103, 106, 127, 150, 163, 178, 195–6, 201, 203–4, 206, 226–8, 236, 253

Pakistan 196
Patrick, Hughes 14–15
people 156–9, 82–7, 178
Pepper, Thomas 4
petrochemicals 98–9, 195, 201–2
pharmaceuticals 39, 138–40
Philips 151, 156, 248
'picking winners' 16–17, 22, 215–18
planning 25–6
politicians 12–14, 25–8, 44, 53–7, 83–7, 175–6, 232, 235, 237–8, 241, 250, 260
Power Reactor and Nuclear Fuel Development Corporation 40, 175
productivity 79
profits 70, 90–2, 127, 147, 153, 204, 227, 229, 233, 236, 248
protectionism
  domestic 8, 11, 13, 15, 29–30, 52, 61–3, 70–1, 77, 101, 108, 110–11, 113, 118, 124, 129, 132, 133, 138–9, 144–5, 148–9, 153, 206, 235, 257–9
  foreign 102, 127–8, 148, 194–5,

219–20, 241–50, 256, 262–5
public corporations 63, 68, 76, 128
  see also JAL, JNR, NTT

rationalisation 32–3, 78–80, 98, 100–2, 105, 135, 144, 162, 222–3
RCA 118, 151
Reconstruction Finance Bank 30, 98, 100, 104, 143
research and development 32, 39–40, 66–7, 72–6, 90, 119–23, 125–7, 130, 134–6, 143, 153, 167, 169, 171–2, 176–8, 206, 220–1, 230, 256–7, 264
rice 70, 109–11
Richardson, Bradley 23
Ricoh 160
robots 41, 137, 168–70
Rolls Royce 183
Rosovsky, Henry 81

Sakoh, Katsuro 20–1
Samuels, Richard J. 48–9, 177, 199, 206–7, 224, 235
Sanko Steamship 204–5
Sanwa 46
savings 68–9, 114
Saxonhouse, Gary 23
scale economies 64, 78–9, 106, 226–7
Schlosstein, Steven 212
Science and Technology Agency 25, 40, 73, 75, 171–2, 175–6, 181–3, 186–7, 231
securities companies 111–14
Seiko 162–3
semiconductors 123–8, 221, 245
sewing machines 161–3
Sharp 123–4, 155, 160
Shinohara, Myohei 17–18
shipbuilding 12–13, 18, 38, 41, 103–6, 202–4
shipping 22, 38, 41, 104–6, 204–5
Silver Seiko 160
socialism 10
software 31, 120–1
Sony 123–4, 151–2, 155–6, 215

Sord 123
Soviet Union 10, 189, 191
space shuttle 188–9
space technology *see* aerospace
Sperry-Rand 118
steel 12–13, 17, 98, 100–3, 105,
    199, 207–8
structure 34–5, 80–1, 102
successes 211–29
Sumitomo 46, 99, 101, 103, 105,
    142, 167, 171, 205
Sunshine Project 32, 174
Suntory 171
supercomputers 121, 123
Suzuki 145, 149
Switzerland 162–3, 245

Takeda 171
Taiwan 162, 194, 196, 264
Tashiro, Yasuhisa 238
taxes 58, 66, 104, 111, 118, 133,
    235–6
technology transfer 15, 31, 71–6,
    90, 101, 108, 143–4, 149,
    172–3, 176, 182, 187, 220
Teijin 171
telecommunications 39, 69, 126,
    128–32, 187
Texas Instruments 123–4, 159
textiles 12, 18, 107–9, 193–8
Toa Domestic Airways 106–7, 183
Tokai 46
Tokyo Electric 159
Tokyo University 50–1, 186
Toshiba 46, 120, 123–5, 131, 155,
    157–8, 176, 189–90
Toyota 46–7, 142, 144–8
trade associations 47–8, 81, 102,
    117, 135, 137, 146, 166, 169,
    171, 175, 181, 196, 203
trade imbalances 242–3, 246
trade unions 13, 22, 59, 142, 204

trading companies 46, 89, 106,
    206, 219, 264
TRW 187
Trezise, Philip 20

Unimation 168
United States 18, 22, 29–30, 66–7,
    69, 72, 75, 77, 99, 107–9, 114,
    123, 126–8, 132, 138, 147–8,
    154, 158, 173, 176, 185,
    187–90, 194–5, 213–14, 240–7,
    258–9, 262–6
United States International Trade
    Commission 4, 23

van Wolferen, Karel 253
Victor Company of Japan 152,
    155
'visions' 35, 82–3, 170, 185, 186,
    218, 223–4, 231, 243, 256
Vogel, Ezra 48

watches 161–2
welfare 84–6, 238
Westinghouse 176
Wolf, Marvin J. 20, 54, 251
workers 79–81, 85, 92–3, 98, 170,
    198–9, 234, 236

Xerox 159–60

Yamaha 149–51, 169
Yamamura, Kozo 42, 223, 228
Yamanaka, Sadanori 212
YKK 161–3
Yoshida, Tadao 161

zaibatsu 12–13, 42, 45–6, 54, 112,
    142
zaikai 45, 48, 55, 238
zippers 161–3